Women Practicing Buddhism
American Experiences

WOMEN PRACTICING BUDDHISM

AMERICAN EXPERIENCES

Edited by Peter N. Gregory
and Susanne Mrozik

WISDOM PUBLICATIONS • BOSTON

Wisdom Publications, Inc.
199 Elm Street
Somerville MA 02144 USA
www.wisdompubs.org

"Just Power" by Helen Tworkov first published in *Tricycle: The Buddhist Review*, vol. 15, no. 2 (winter 2005), pp. 58–61, 116–17.

Library of Congress Cataloging-in-Publication Data
Women practicing Buddhism : American experiences / edited by Peter N. Gregory and Susanne Mrozik.
   p. cm.
   Based on presentations at a conference held at Smith College in Northampton, Mass., Ap. 7-10, 2005.
   What does Buddhist practice mean to American women? / Susanne Mrozik—North American Buddhist women in the international context / Karma Lekshe Tsomo—Moving beyond gender / Bell Hooks—Buddhism and Creativity / Jane Hirshfield, Meredith Monk, Pat Enkyo O'Hara (moderator)—Women changing Buddhism : feminist perspectives / Bell Hooks, Sharon Suh, Karma Lekshe Tsomo, Susanne Mrozik (moderator)—Just power / Helen Tworkov—Engaged Buddhism / Virginia Straus Benson, Diana Lion, Eve Marko, Hilda Ryumon Gutiérrez Baldoquín (moderator)—A Jewish woman and Buddhism / Sheila Peltz Weinberg—Race, ethnicity, and class / Hilda Ryumon Gutiérrez Baldoquín, Sharon Suh, Arinna Weisman, Carolyn Jacobs (moderator)—Fashioning new selves : the experiences of Taiwanese Buddhist women / Carolyn Chen—Growing up Buddhist / Alice Unno—Women dharma teachers' forum / Thubten Chodron, Pat Enkyo O'Hara, Yifa, Carol Wilson.
   ISBN 0-86171-539-X (pbk. : alk. paper)
   1. Buddhist women—Religious life—United States—Congresses. I. Gregory, Peter N., 1945- II. Mrozik, Susanne.
   BQ5450.W63 2007
   294.3082′0973—dc22
                                    2007036420

12 11 10 09 08   5 4 3 2 1

Cover and interior design by Gopa & Ted2, Inc. Set in Palatino 10.25/15.4.

Printed in the United States of America

This book was produced with environmental mindfulness. We have elected to print this title on 50% PCW recycled paper. As a result, we have saved the following resources: 27 trees, 19 million BTUs of energy, 2,398 lbs. of greenhouse gases, 9,953 gallons of water, and 1,278 lbs. of solid waste. For more information, please visit our website, www.wisdompubs.org.

Since 1987 Buddhist women from around the world have begun to unite on a grassroots level and assume leadership in working for the welfare of human society. Now, two decades after the founding of Sakyadhita ("Daughters of the Buddha"): International Association of Buddhist Women, the Buddhist women's movement is recognized as a highly dynamic forum representing some 300 million women worldwide. This movement, emerging from the margins into the international spotlight as a force for social change, is an example of how women can unite their resources and talents, work in harmony, and make significant contributions to global understanding. This innovative movement, while focusing on Buddhist women's issues and perspectives, embraces all living beings. It is innovative in incorporating scholarly perspectives, spiritual practice, grassroots activism, and cultural performance as equally valid dimensions of women's experience. Creating a forum that unites women from such a rich variety of backgrounds, disciplines, and perspectives with respect and appreciation is an expression of women's enormous potential for global transformation.

—Karma Lekshe Tsomo 2005

This book is dedicated to Karma Lekshe Tsomo in gratitude for her work on behalf of the Buddhist women of the world.

Contents

Preface

Peter N. Gregory

T HE FATE OF BUDDHISM in the twenty-first century will be shaped in profound ways by how it addresses issues having to do with the role and status of women. However these issues are resolved, they will unfold in an arena that increasingly brings different Buddhist traditions into interaction with one another. For example, South and Southeast Asian women from Theravāda traditions have recently been ordained in a Chinese Buddhist monastery in Los Angeles. The effort to reestablish ordination lineages for all Buddhist women is helping to forge transnational networks bringing Buddhist women together around the world. Significantly, Western Buddhist nuns are playing a prominent role in this process.

On many other fronts as well, the questions surrounding the role of women in Buddhism comprise one of the most dynamic axes around which Buddhism is being transformed. Even though these issues play out in different ways on either side of the Pacific, as well as among different Buddhist communities within the United States, they provide an especially fertile field in which to explore the tensions and possibilities of a tradition in transition, especially in regard to the complex currents and crosscurrents of influence between various forms of Asian and Western Buddhism.

What's happening in the United States at this juncture is particularly exciting, given how these issues are affecting Western engagements with Buddhism and given the incredible range of different forms of Buddhist practice, thought, and community coexisting and interacting here all at once. The significance of this last point is brought home when we consider that there are more different forms of Buddhism existing together in a single American city such as Los Angeles today than there have ever been at any one time in any one place within the entire history of the tradition.

Women Practicing Buddhism is an attempt to plumb the rich and diverse experiences of individuals who are negotiating this terrain, highlighting via first-person accounts the spectrum of possible approaches. It adds to the growing literature on women in Buddhism and Buddhism in America by drawing attention to traditions not always included in the evolving conversation, such as those of Asians and Asian Americans, who comprise the vast majority of Buddhists in North America. The volume thus attempts, in part, to redress the "tacit unconscious ethnocentrism" (see the essay by Karma Lekshe Tsomo) of books and essays on Buddhism in America that focus primarily on so-called convert communities.

This book grew out of the conference, "Women Practicing Buddhism: American Experiences," held at Smith College in Northampton, Massachusetts April 7–10, 2005. The conference brought together students, scholars, Buddhist teachers, practitioners, artists, activists, and healers to explore the diverse experiences of women practicing Buddhism in contemporary America. The richness and diversity of Buddhism in the Pioneer Valley of Western Massachusetts as well as the vibrancy of the academic study of Buddhism in the area made Smith College an ideal setting for hosting this timely event. Overall, somewhere between 1500 and 2000 people from at least twenty-two states, Canada, and Jamaica attended at least one conference-related event.

The theme of the conference centered on issues of practice, bringing to bear women's particular experiences of Buddhism as it spreads to North America and takes root in new contexts. The conference celebrated the ways in which women are changing Buddhism and explored the array of issues that Buddhist women face today. Talks, panels, and workshops discussed Buddhism in relation to race, ethnicity, class, social activism, creativity, sexuality, feminism, other religious traditions, healing, meditation practice, the law, the workplace, family, and daily life. In planning the conference, we wanted to include women engaged in different types of Buddhist practice, whether monastic or lay, public or private, activist or contemplative. We also wanted to provide a forum for women who were making creative contributions to Buddhism in America but were not widely known, together with some of their better-known colleagues. The focus on practice encouraged women to share their personal experiences. Everyone worked hard to create a space in which people could talk with one another across their differences, enabling us to come away from the conference with a greater understanding of, and respect for, our extraordinary diversity.

From the beginning, those of us involved in planning the conference determined to make it more than an academic event. We decided to include artists as performers and discussants, and to make performance a central element in the conference events, including a poetry reading by Jane Hirshfield and a concert performance by Meredith Monk. Along with talks, panel discussions, and performances, the conference also offered many different kinds of workshops. We put out an open call to women in the area to plan and lead these workshops. The response that we got is a testament to the vibrancy and variety of Buddhism in the area. The workshops were well attended and on all counts made an enormous contribution to the overall success of the conference.

All of us involved in the planning and organization of the conference were quite simply blown away by the number of people who attended (which far exceeded our most audacious expectations), the uniformly high quality of the different events, the tremendous enthusiasm that they generated, and the general spirit of exuberance that pervaded the conference. Susanne Mrozik and I thus decided to move ahead and compile a book out of the conference. We edited the transcripts of the conference tapes and sent them to panelists for their revision. In preparing the final versions for publication, we tried to preserve as much of the oral character that gave life to the panels as we could. The book also afforded a welcome opportunity to broaden and deepen our conversations about women's Buddhist practice in America. We accordingly solicited contributions from Carolyn Chen, Alice Unno, and Sheila Weinberg. We were also delighted to be able to include Ven. Yifa in the "Women Dharma Teachers Forum."

For more details about the conference and all those who helped make it possible, please see the acknowledgments at the end of this book.

What Does Buddhist Practice
Mean to American Women?

Susanne Mrozik

IT DEPENDS on who you are. Buddhist practice can mean everything from meditation, to studying Buddhist scriptures, to performing prostrations before a Buddha image, to caring for monks and nuns, to running a temple Sunday school for children, to engaging in social justice work, to participating in a stress-reduction program, to writing a poem. And that's probably just the tip of the iceberg. Of course, these different forms of Buddhist practice are not mutually exclusive. American women, like Buddhists everywhere, incorporate a variety of practices into their lives. Nevertheless, few of us are aware of just how diverse American Buddhist women's practice is. This volume offers a glimpse into that diversity.

The primary reason for the broad range of women's practice in America is that the women are themselves incredibly diverse. The vast majority of all American Buddhist women are Asian and Asian American women. Their families came from various countries, some as immigrants and others as refugees. Most families have come since 1965 when the U.S. changed its immigration laws, but others came as early as the late nineteenth century. Thus many Asian American women have far deeper roots in the U.S. than I do as the daughter of first-generation

German immigrants. Over the past fifty years growing numbers of non-Asian Americans such as myself have been drawn to Buddhism. These non-Asian Buddhists come from various racial, ethnic, and class backgrounds, although at present they are still predominantly white and middle or upper-middle class.

Along with differences of race, ethnicity, and class, American women practice within many different Buddhist traditions, from the Theravāda traditions rooted in South and Southeast Asia, to the Zen, Pure Land, and Nichiren traditions rooted in East Asia, to the Vajrayāna traditions rooted in Tibet and the Himalayan region. These Buddhist traditions are so diverse that the first generation of European colonial officials and Christian missionaries in Asia did not always recognize that they comprised a single religion. To this day, some scholars ask whether we should speak of "Buddhism" in the singular or "Buddhisms" in the plural. Some American women practice exclusively within one of these traditions, but others maintain ties to more than one Buddhist tradition. There are also deeply committed Jews and Christians, among others, who now combine Buddhist practices like meditation with more traditional forms of Jewish and Christian worship. You do not have to be a Buddhist to engage in Buddhist practice. In fact, you do not even have to be religious. Buddhist forms of meditation are being taught in America today in a variety of secular settings such as medical clinics and prisons. As the essays and conversations in this volume demonstrate, Buddhist practice means many different things to American women.

❖ Moving Out of Our Comfort Zone

Karma Lekshe Tsomo, an American-born Buddhist scholar and fully ordained nun in the Tibetan Buddhist tradition, urges us to "move out of our comfort zone and learn more about 'the other,' in this case, other Buddhists." She directs her comments especially to non-Asian Buddhists, who in spite of their progressive social and political views, "still tend to hang out with people just like themselves and have very little knowledge of or interest in the lives of Asian or Asian American Buddhists." Tsomo attributes this lack of interest to a "tacit, unconscious ethnocentrism." Sharon Suh, a scholar of Korean American Buddhism, adds that Asian American Buddhist women can face numerous barriers to interaction with their non-Asian counterparts, including barriers of language, culture, and financial status. The upshot is that so-called "ethnic" and "convert" Buddhists sometimes know little about each other, including their respective religious practices.

Although we should not exaggerate the gap between ethnic and convert Buddhists since there are significant examples of integrated communities, ethnic and convert Buddhists often have quite different concerns. Asian and Asian American Buddhist centers do double duty as religious and cultural centers. They play a critical role in preserving and transmitting particular cultural, as well as Buddhist, values. This is probably one reason that a surprising number of Asian immigrants claim a Buddhist identity only *after* settling in the U.S. The degree to which non-Asian Buddhists link their practice to a particular Asian culture varies. For instance, a Tibetan Buddhist center, even if comprised largely of non-Asian Buddhists, might still celebrate the Tibetan New Year or otherwise participate in Tibetan cultural events. But an Insight Meditation center, which is rooted in the Theravāda traditions of South and Southeast Asia, might choose to downplay the cultural dimensions of their tradition.

Such differences between and within ethnic and convert communities often result in very different practice priorities. As its name suggests, Insight Meditation centers focus primarily on meditation, as is the case for many convert Buddhist centers. Ethnic Buddhist centers and some convert centers strongly affiliated with a particular Buddhist culture are more likely to engage in the broader range of Buddhist practices traditionally found throughout Asia. Along with meditation, these include participation in the yearly calendar of Buddhist festivals, devotional practices centered on various Buddhist deities, and caring for resident monks and nuns. These differences lead Suh to remind us that whenever we talk about "American Buddhism," we need to ask:

Whose America are we talking about, whose Buddhism do we mean, and which Buddhists are we referring to?

Of course, the labels "ethnic" and "convert" don't really fit all Buddhists anymore. What do we call the children or grandchildren of Asian immigrants who choose to practice in convert Buddhist centers rather than in ethnic Buddhist centers? What do we call the non-Asian Buddhist children of convert Buddhists? With each new generation of Buddhist practitioners in the U.S., the dichotomy between "ethnic" and "convert" Buddhists continues to break down. Rather than assume these two types of Buddhists, we need to recognize that there is a broad spectrum of Buddhists who in varying degrees reflect the concerns of the stereotypic ethnic and convert Buddhist. Getting out of our comfort zone requires more than learning about the Buddhist "other"; it requires learning that there are many, many Buddhist "others," each with potentially different concerns and practices.

Throughout history, Buddhists have repeatedly revisioned their tradition as they adapted their beliefs and practices to new cultures. This is one of the reasons why there are so many different Buddhist traditions in the world today. American Buddhists are now in the process of revisioning Buddhism all over again. The earliest American Buddhists to begin this process were the Japanese and Chinese immigrants who came to the West Coast and Hawaii in the late nineteenth century seeking new economic opportunities. Richard Seager observes in his book *Buddhism in America* that Japanese Pure Land Buddhists, in particular, were the real "trail-blazers of the American dharma" because they were the first to translate Buddhism into American cultural and linguistic terms.[1] These early Buddhist trailblazers also remind us that Buddhism has not always been "hip." Far from it. During World War II Buddhist priests were among the very first Japanese Americans to be placed in internment camps, losing homes and businesses in the process. The U.S. government believed that Buddhist priests were especially likely to be spies for Japan, although, in the end, even a Christian identity afforded Japanese Americans little protection from imprisonment. As the feminist thinker and cultural critic bell hooks notes, Buddhism still isn't acceptable in some communities, including the African American Christian fundamentalist communities in which she was raised. Additionally, Asian and Asian American communities sometimes find it difficult to get legal clearance for building Buddhist temples. Buddhism is so much in the public eye today—whether through Hollywood movies, popular magazines, marketing campaigns, or the charismatic presence of world-famous spiritual and political leaders such as His Holiness the Dalai Lama—that it is easy to forget that many Buddhists have struggled to gain the privilege of practicing Buddhism in America.

❖ Fashioning New Selves

Carolyn Chen describes the Buddhist practice of Taiwanese American women as "fashioning new selves." Similarly Suh describes the practice of Korean American women as "reworking the self." This flies in the face of conventional ways of speaking about Buddhist practice. As anyone who has ever taken a basic high-school or college course on world religions knows, the Buddha denied that there was such a thing as a "self." So why would Taiwanese American and Korean American women speak of the self in such terms?

In order to answer this question, we need to figure out what the Buddha actually meant when he said there was no such thing as a self. His religious rivals, who firmly believed in a self, argued that the self was the eternal and unchanging essence of living beings that linked each and every one of us to the divine. When the Buddha went looking for that self in meditation, he couldn't find it. He couldn't find any part of himself that wasn't constantly changing. Self, as his religious rivals knew it, simply did not exist. But this does not mean that Buddhists can't talk about a self; they just talk about it differently. Charles Johnson, a well-known writer of fiction and nonfiction, best expresses it when he says that for Buddhists "self is not product but process; not a noun but a verb."[2] From a Buddhist perspective, self is fluid because we are always changing in response to our ever-changing environment.

That's good news because it means that we all possess the capacity for radical personal transformation.

The Buddhist doctrine of *no-self* has often troubled American women. On the surface, it sounds too much like an exhortation to be even more self-effacing and more self-sacrificing than we already are. It's important to realize that when Buddhists talk about "letting go of the self" they are actually talking about letting go of the limited and limiting ways in which we define ourselves. For example, Chen speaks of letting go of the self "attached to meeting the expectations of others." When we let go of the self, we let go of whatever prevents us from realizing our full potential as human beings. Ultimately that means we let go of whatever prevents us from experiencing our own buddha nature. The doctrine of no-self isn't about self-effacement; it's about self-actualization.

Self-actualization takes many different forms. Chen and Suh both describe some of the ways in which Buddhist practice enables Taiwanese American and Korean American women to "carve spaces of independence and authority for themselves" (Chen) within the traditional Confucian family. Buddhist practice helps these women cultivate a sense of identity and purpose beyond their roles as wife, mother, and/or daughter. Chen and Suh are careful to point out that most of these women do not overtly reject their traditional family roles. Most wouldn't even call themselves feminists. Nevertheless, as Chen informs us, they use their religious commitments "to negotiate or 'bargain' for more autonomy *within* the constraints of the family." Suh challenges monolithic definitions of feminism that don't acknowledge the extraordinary work Korean American women, in particular, are doing to create further opportunities for self-actualization within their communities.

Radical personal transformation is never easy no matter what one's background. It takes a great deal of courage to let go of the habitual ways in which we have learned to see ourselves. Who would we be if, for instance, we let go of the self "attached to meeting the expectations of others?" In a conversation on "Buddhism and Creativity," the performance artist Meredith Monk and poet Jane Hirshfield speak eloquently about the challenges of opening ourselves up to the unknown. They affirm the difficulty as well as necessity of creating a space in our lives for silence, questions, doubts, mystery, wonder, and discovery. Their art is a vehicle for, and expression of, the Buddhist journey toward self-actualization. Like so many of the women in this volume, they describe that journey as one that leads both inward and outward. When we discover our own buddha nature, we also discover our connection to "the whole fabric of existence," since none of us exists independently of our larger environment. Quoting the thirteenth-century Japanese Zen teacher Dōgen, Hirshfield reminds us that enlightenment is intimacy with all things. This means that the process of fashioning new selves is also a process of fashioning new relationships with other living beings and the world around us.

❖ Restoring This World We Share to Its Wholeness

The Buddha once summarized his teachings by saying: "Both formerly and now, it is only suffering and the stopping of suffering that I describe" (*Majjhima Nikāya* I.140). Many women turn to Buddhist practice to heal themselves of their suffering. When bell hooks was first attracted to Buddhism, she tells us, she was looking for a way to deal with her own spiritual anguish. Alice Unno, who together with her husband leads a Pure Land Buddhist community in Massachusetts, describes how her practice helped her to overcome the self-hatred she developed as a Japanese American growing up in the U.S. during World War II. Rabbi Sheila Peltz Weinberg says that she turned to both Judaism and Buddhism in order to find meaning in the wake of the "twin shadows of Auschwitz and Hiroshima."

Given the Buddhist emphasis on "intimacy with all things," it is not surprising that many women are as dedicated to healing others as they are to healing themselves. Often these women call themselves "Engaged Buddhists," a term first coined by the Vietnamese Buddhist monk and peace activist Thich Nhat Hanh during the Vietnam War.

Diana Lion defines engaged Buddhism as a commitment to "restoring this world we share to its wholeness." A key aspect of her own Buddhist practice is working on behalf of those incarcerated in U.S. prisons. Other women in this volume such as Eve Myōnen Marko and Virginia Straus Benson focus their practice on conflict resolution and world peace, while Pat Enkyō O'Hara is an HIV/AIDS activist. Engaged Buddhists define their practice in a variety of ways including human rights, peace, and environmental activism.

Engaged Buddhism takes many different forms, but across the board, the women in this volume are dedicated to fighting various kinds of discrimination, such as that due to sex, race, ethnicity, class, and sexual orientation. For example, the Zen teacher Hilda Ryūmon Gutiérrez Baldoquín asks the predominantly white, middle- and upper-middle-class convert communities to take an honest look at how race and privilege affect women's experiences in these communities. She is especially concerned with racial discrimination and warns us that "If anyone of us here—and not just folks of color—walks into a dharma community that is predominantly white and doesn't say, 'How come?' we're not awake." Baldoquín's concerns are echoed by Carolyn Jacobs, Sharon Suh, and Arinna Weisman in a conversation among the four of them on "Race, Ethnicity, and Class."

Restoring this world we share to its wholeness isn't going to be easy, but that doesn't stop the women in this volume from trying. In fact, the overall impression we get from their essays and conversations is a sense of confidence in their capacity to use their Buddhist practice to heal themselves, other living beings, and our planet. Tsomo urges Buddhist women to "create a sense of community...that extends beyond identifications and allegiances to particular traditions, ethnicities, lifestyles, teachers, or whatever." She offers the model of Sakyadhita: International Association of Buddhist Women (www.sakyadhita.org), which was founded in 1987. Sakyadhita is a cross-cultural grassroots movement that brings together women from around the world to work toward gender equity and world peace.

❖ When Women Show Up

This volume and the conference that inspired it showcase women's Buddhist practice in America. But are there in fact any differences in the ways women and men practice? Aren't the issues discussed so far— "moving out of our comfort zone," "fashioning new selves," and "restoring this world we share to its wholeness"—equally relevant for American men? I think most Buddhist practitioners would say they are. So what is different about American Buddhist women? Do they practice differently? Do they bring different concerns to their practice? Does their presence affect their communities in different ways from that of men? What actually happens when women show up at Buddhist temples and dharma centers?

This volume offers no single answer to any of these questions. American women are extraordinarily diverse and so are their experiences with Buddhist practice. We learn from Suh that Buddhist practice in Korean American communities *is* highly gendered. Both Korean American women and men describe women's practice as far more devotional than that of men. For example, women are more likely than men to perform devotional practices such as chanting and bowing. But this isn't the case in all Buddhist communities. Studies of Chinese American communities reveal that socio-economic class and level of education account for different practice preferences rather than gender. There are also many communities in America where the practice of all members is fairly uniform.

Still, even when women's and men's practices are not markedly different, women frequently have different concerns about their practice than men do. Institutional androcentrism is a major concern for a number of women in this volume. The Buddhist nuns, Thubten Chodron, Karma Lekshe Tsomo, and Yifa, remind us that most Buddhist women do not have access to full ordination and its educational, economic, and professional privileges. Until recently, full ordination was available for women only in Chinese, Korean, and some Vietnamese lineages. Since the late 1990s, full ordination is also available in Sri Lankan lineages.

Nuns from other countries can seek ordination through these lineages, but their formal ordination status may or may not be recognized by their own religious communities and countries. Buddhist nuns in the U.S. face additional problems because the tradition of lay support for monastics is far less developed in the U.S. than in Asia. Thubten Chodron tells us that what little support is available to monastics in the U.S. is more likely to go to monks than nuns. Ironically, even in Taiwan where nuns are held in high regard, the laity—including laywomen!—still seem to give greater offerings to monks than nuns and prefer monks to preside over ceremonies. Thus Yifa, a nun of high standing in Taiwan, comments that in her experience "it's the women, rather than the men, who need to be educated about women's rights."

Unfortunately both lay and ordained Buddhist women can face gender inequity in American Buddhist communities. Karma Lekshe Tsomo points out that although women are "very visible participants" in Buddhist temples and dharma centers in the U.S., "their roles are often largely supportive to men." They take on a "disproportionate share of responsibility for organization, translation, communications, food preparation, public relations, and other support functions" and consequently do not get enough time to practice. Tsomo argues that we need to make a greater effort to give women the opportunity to train as future dharma teachers. Thubten Chodron and Pat Enkyō O'Hara both raise the issue of female role models in their respective communities. Chodron expresses concern that the lineage lamas and merit field, visualized by her community in their daily practice, consist almost exclusively of male figures. O'Hara's community regularly chants the names of its lineage of teachers; traditionally the list of names is entirely male, but O'Hara has introduced the practice of chanting the names of female teachers as well.

Along with general concerns over gender inequity, the women in this volume also raise other issues that are of special concern to women, including sexual exploitation by male teachers. There was a great deal of discussion during the conversation on "Women Changing Buddhism: Feminist Perspectives" of the need to educate our communities about sexual misconduct. More broadly, some, such as bell hooks, felt we need to find constructive ways to rechannel, rather than suppress or deny, the erotic energy that can arise in teacher-student relationships. The same conversation also brought to the fore women's concerns over how to teach dharma to their children. Both Karma Lekshe Tsomo and Sharon Suh emphasized the need to create programs for children and young adults.

In order to better understand how being a woman affects one's Buddhist practice, Peter Gregory and I turned to four prominent female dharma teachers: Thubten Chodron, Pat Enkyō O'Hara, Yifa, and Carol Wilson. We asked each to discuss their experiences as practitioners and teachers in our "Women Dharma Teachers' Forum." Not surprisingly, we got a range of responses. As a practitioner, Thubten Chodron has had to contend with various forms of discrimination against nuns but doesn't feel that her teaching style is significantly different because she is a woman. Still, she makes a point of including women's perspectives in her teachings and notes that men as well as women are sometimes more comfortable discussing personal problems with a female teacher. Unlike Chodron, Carol Wilson has rarely experienced any sexual discrimination in dharma centers. Although she believes that being a woman informs everything she does, including her teaching, she hesitates to generalize in any way about women's experiences as practitioners or teachers. Pat Enkyō O'Hara feels strongly that her teaching style is deeply informed by the fact that she is a woman, citing qualities such as openness, flexible authority, and a relational, interactive approach to teaching. Yifa expresses great admiration for the will and persistence she sees in women practitioners but concludes that women and men are equally capable of cultivating the love and discipline needed for effective teaching.

Across the board these teachers reject essentialistic representations of women. If Buddhists are right that "self is not product but process," then how can we say that all women at all times possess certain intrinsically female qualities? Buddhists would argue that the association of such qualities with women is largely a matter of historical, cultural, and social convention. Ultimately, our heartminds are neither male nor female. Thus O'Hara and Wilson both remark that they have known male teachers who fully embody stereotypically female qualities such as gentleness and empathy. Helen Tworkov argues in her essay "Just Power" that many of the qualities traditionally associated in the modern West with women—gentleness, modesty, humility, obedience, and selflessness—are more broadly construed in Buddhist literature as desirable virtues for both men and women.

Does this mean that there are no real differences between men's and women's practice? Of course not. Men and women are still socialized differently. Additionally, women still have to contend with various forms of sexism. Thus when women show up at Buddhist temples and dharma centers they often bring different concerns to their communities. The fact that most of these communities are relatively new to the U.S. means that women have an opportunity to shape them from the ground up. More broadly, the transplantation of Buddhism to America gives all Buddhists a chance to think carefully about the kinds of institutions we want to create in this country. This is as much the case for so-called "convert" communities as it is for "ethnic" communities. As one scholar observes, "members of ethnic Buddhist groups often take advantage of their transitional status to reform certain aspects of their Buddhist heritage."[3] Thus the latest turning of the dharma wheel in the West gives all Buddhists, including women, a chance to create communities that enable the self-actualization of diverse practitioners.

❖ Moving Beyond Gender

In her essay "Moving Beyond Gender," bell hooks reminds us that visionary Buddhist teachers "urge us to move beyond gender...so that our attention can be concentrated on what truly matters," namely, spiritual practice. She argues that we can't enter the door of enlightenment without letting go of our attachment to all labels and identities, including the label "woman." When I first saw the title of hooks' essay, I was puzzled. Why would a feminist scholar and teacher suggest we need to move beyond gender? I was also concerned that the call to move beyond gender could silence much-needed conversations about gender inequity. But it soon became apparent that hooks isn't trying to silence conversations about gender inequity or any other form of discrimination. Instead she tackles discrimination head-on by showing us just how limited the identities are that we construct for ourselves or that others project onto us. Similarly, Hilda Ryūmon Gutiérrez Baldoquín demonstrates how attachment to labels and identities perpetuates oppression: "In my experience, systems of oppression necessitate notions of identity, and consequently, our habitual attachment to this notion perpetuates oppression. It is the nature of oppression to obscure the limitless essence, the vastness of who we are—that the nature of our mind is luminous, like a clear pool reflecting a cloudless sky."[4] From a Buddhist perspective all labels and identities are problematic because they define self as product rather than process. They obscure the dynamic complexity of individuals by reducing them to a single label or set of labels like "woman" or "African American woman." Such labels obscure "the vastness of who we are." They prevent us from realizing our innate and unbounded capacity for wisdom and love—a capacity that many Buddhists call buddha nature. Consequently, labels also obscure our connections with others. Baldoquín points out that one of the effects of systems of oppression is to divide all of us into two separate camps: victims and perpetrators.

According to hooks, when we move beyond attachment to labels and identities, we learn how to "hold one another accountable for the positions we occupy in dominator culture without evoking a politics of blame or victimhood." All of us occupy multiple and interrelated positions in dominator culture. Thus hooks asks us to drop our "either/or" approach to identity and embrace a "both/and" approach. This is the Buddhist middle way, a space of "radical openness...that invites true communication." Those familiar with hooks' other writings on Buddhism know that she also defines this space of radical openness as one of love. Moving beyond attachment to labels and identities makes love possible. The challenge for those of us committed to social justice is to combine accountability with love. In Buddhist terms, this entails holding together conventional and ultimate perspectives on reality. A conventional perspective acknowledges the fact that living beings are enormously diverse; an ultimate perspective insists that we are all the same since we share a common buddha nature. Baldoquín suggests in the conversation on "Race, Ethnicity, and Class" that whenever we privilege one perspective over the other, we do violence to ourselves. When we privilege a conventional perspective, we buy into the limited and limiting labels that obscure "the vastness of who we are." When we privilege an ultimate perspective, we pretend that our differences don't matter, which can make us complacent about addressing the inequities in our communities. Combining accountability with love means being mindful of our differences without ever losing sight of the fact that we each share the same precious buddha nature. In Diana Lion's words, it means "holding ourselves and each other accountable, while remembering our wholeness with a tender heart."

The women in this volume reflect on their practice from both conventional and ultimate perspectives. They describe their tremendously diverse experiences as practitioners and celebrate the capacity all of us have to live with wisdom and love.

NOTES

1 Richard Hughes Seager, *Buddhism in America* (New York: Columbia University Press, 1999), p. 69.

2 Charles Johnson, Introduction to *Oxherding Tale* (New York: Plume, 1995), p. xvii.

3 Stuart Chandler, "Chinese Buddhism in America," in *The Faces of Buddhism in America*, eds. Charles S. Prebish and Kenneth K. Tanaka (Berkeley: University of California Press, 1998), p. 24.

4 Rev. Hilda Gutiérrez Baldoquín, "Don't Waste Time," in *Dharma, Color, and Culture: New Voices in Western Buddhism*, ed. Baldoquín (Berkeley: Parallax Press, 2004), pp. 181–82.

North American Buddhist Women
in the International Context

Karma Lekshe Tsomo

UNDERSTANDING North American Buddhist Women from a global perspective is a daunting task because of the enormous diversity of both North American and Asian Buddhist women. The first question is, What does it mean to be a Buddhist? For some, to be a Buddhist means formally going for refuge in the Buddha, dharma, sangha. In other cases, a person is born Buddhist and lives her whole life as a Buddhist, without any special ceremony. Differences like these make it impossible to generalize about Buddhist women's experiences.

When we talk about American Buddhist women, for example, are we talking about the thirty-year-old white Harvard graduate who sits once a week at her local dharma center? Are we talking about the Laotian Buddhist woman who is an engineer at the naval base in San Diego and offers *dāna* to the monks at her local temple on new moon and full moon days? When we talk about international Buddhist women, are we talking about the Korean bhikṣuṇī professor who has a Ph.D., teaches Buddhist studies, and is a national advocate for organ donations among Buddhists? Are we talking about the Tibetan nun who is serving a fifteen-year sentence in Drapchi prison for harboring a photo of the Dalai Lama? Or are we talking about the Thai office clerk who spends her vacations sitting *vipassanā* retreats? Clearly, Buddhist women's experiences are vastly different, both in North America and internationally.

To compound the complexity, there are no statistics even on the numbers of Buddhist women in the world, much less about their educational backgrounds, economic circumstances, Buddhist affiliations, or spiritual practice. I estimate that there are 300 million Buddhist women worldwide. In some places it's very difficult to get even a rough idea of the numbers. In China, for example, many people are Buddhists at heart but may hesitate to publicly identify themselves as Buddhists. It is even more difficult to calculate the exact number of Buddhist nuns in the world. We know that there are more than ten thousand nuns in Korea, more than ten thousand in Taiwan, more than seven thousand in Vietnam, and roughly one hundred thousand Buddhist nuns in Burma, but it is difficult to precisely document these numbers. After living and traveling in Asia for forty years, I conclude that women hold up roughly half of the Buddhist sky.

I became a Buddhist as a child, because my family name was Zenn, a German name apparently misspelled at Immigration. Little kids used to tease my brother and me about being Zen Buddhists, so I went to the public library and found two books on Buddhism, D.T. Suzuki's *Zen Buddhism* and Alan Watts' *The Way of Zen*. I read them from cover to cover and announced to my Southern Baptist Fundamentalist mother, "Mommy, I'm a Buddhist." She was horrified, of course, because according to her belief system that doomed me to eternal hellfire. That was the beginning of my own personal experience of interfaith dialogue.

During the past twenty-eight years as a Buddhist nun, I've been fortunate to stay in many different monasteries in India, Japan, Taiwan, and other parts of Asia. That has been a marvelous opportunity to experience traditional monastic practice, day by day. Over the past thirty years, I've also been very fortunate to be involved in the early stages of establishing Buddhist temples and dharma centers in the

United States, mostly in Hawaii and California, and to experience the ways in which women practice and support these centers. Here we can distinguish between the experiences of Asian Buddhists, Asian American Buddhists, and non-Asian American Buddhists. Not only that, but we can also distinguish between the experiences of lay Buddhists, ordained Buddhists, and a new category in the United States, known as neither lay nor ordained, as Suzuki Rōshi characterized the lifestyle of his American Zen students. Then we can distinguish between rich and poor Buddhists, scholars and meditators, and among the adherents of many different Buddhist traditions.

North American Buddhist women also have different levels of commitment to Buddhism. For some, Buddhism is one interest among many. Some people have a dharma book by their bed, which they read before dropping off to sleep at night. The term "night-stand Buddhists" has been used derogatorily, but to read ten pages of a dharma book every evening is a wonderful way to increase understanding of the Buddhist teachings. There are some people who don't belong to any center but would put "Buddhist" if forced to designate a religious affiliation or if they had to choose someone to officiate at their funeral. In addition, there are serious meditators, serious scholars, and others who simply try to live their lives according to Buddhist principles. These categories are not mutually exclusive. There is considerable crossover among them, and some people find themselves in several different categories. There are Buddhists who have a regular daily practice and those who don't. There are Buddhists who go for intensive retreats for specific lengths of time every year and those who don't. There are those who put Buddhism somewhere on a long list of interests in life, and there are those who value dharma above everything else in life. These differences contribute to the rich variety of Buddhist experience in North America.

We can also distinguish between the experiences of Buddhist laywomen and nuns. Buddhist laypeople can be quite invisible in American society, but it's quite another thing to be very obviously a Buddhist, by wearing traditional robes, for example. A couple of weeks ago as I just walked into the bank, a woman holding a child looked at me and gasped, "Oh, my God!" So, I just gave her a big smile. Another time a woman at the post office asked, "What are you?" And I thought, Well, let's see, a human…, but I said, "I'm a Buddhist." And she said, "Oh, no. We had those in China." Of course, this can play both ways. Some people smile and put their palms together with respect. Others treat us as if we were the Antichrist. Some people think we are absolutely mad. Others immediately gravitate to us and pour out their spiritual life. Some view monastics as a welcome alternative to the consumerism and violence of contemporary society, while others view us as a threat to their values and their chosen lifestyle. Some regard us as a blessing, representing peace and compassion, while others see us quite literally as a curse. In Hong Kong, among gamblers, it's considered inauspicious to see a monk or a nun before the race begins. Once I was living in a monastery in Happy Valley in Hong Kong, right near the racetrack, and in the morning the gamblers would cover their eyes because if they saw me it would bring them bad luck.

⁘ Expanding Our Worldviews

The issue of American Buddhist women in the international context also immediately raises gender issues that are sensitive and potentially explosive. Here I assume we can speak freely, without surveillance from Homeland Security or the Bhikkhu Sangha police, but we need to acknowledge that raising questions of gender inequality immediately stirs the waters and makes some people feel very uncomfortable. Lest we assume that this applies only to Asia, let me assure you that sexism is alive and well in American Buddhism not only among men but also among women. Admittedly, gender issues are important for Western women, but many American women assume that gender equity is something that has already been achieved. They still begin conversations by saying, "Well, I'm not a feminist, but…" The point of Buddhism is to be mindful, and if our eyes are open, we cannot help but see the sexism that's all around us. The leading example of a Buddhist feminist activist is not American but Taiwanese. Ven. Chao Hui, a Taiwanese bhikṣuṇī teacher, scholar, and writer, is little known outside of Taiwan, but she should be. She is not only the leading animal rights activist in Taiwan, but she is also a leading activist for women's rights. She very publicly protested the eight special rules that subordinate nuns to monks in traditional Buddhist cultures and influence attitudes toward women throughout the Buddhist world. In 2002, in anticipation of His Holiness the Dalai Lama's visit, the Venerable Chao Hui and eight Buddhist nuns, monks, and laypersons held a nationally televised press conference in Taipei where they ripped posters inscribed with the eight special rules off the wall. The fact that His Holiness the Dalai Lama was scheduled to arrive at Chiang Kai Shek International Airport for his second-only visit to Taiwan did not go unnoticed. The Tibetans have yet to approve the full ordination of women. It's now been twenty-five years since the Tibetan sangha first began researching the complex legal issues involved in establishing a Tibetan bhikṣuṇī lineage.

I may disagree with Ven. Chao Hui's methods, but I certainly admire her work. And I mention it to alert us to the comfortable assumptions we may make about our own level of awareness and the level of feminist awareness among Asian Buddhist women. We need to recognize the misconception that gender discrimination is a problem that exists in Asia and other parts of the world but has already been solved in the egalitarian haven of North America. The technical term is "failing to recognize one's own oppression." We need to be aware of projecting backward in time, too, and realize that advances for women in North America have been made only very recently and remain quite uncertain. We still have a lot of work to do and, in certain respects, we seem to be regressing. For example, 190 nations have signed the U.N. Declaration on the Rights of Women; the United States is the only country that has not yet signed. So far 172 nations have signed the U.N. Declaration on the Rights of the Child, but the United States is not among them, which is shameful and shocking. We need only look at the halls of government to see that women are by no means fairly represented in those bastions of power. We need to be aware that the stereotypes and preconceptions we may harbor about the lives and attitudes of Western and Asian Buddhist women may be unfounded.

We need only look to Burma, where a 4' 10" Buddhist laywoman, Aung San Suu Kyi, continues to risk her life to challenge one of the world's most brutal military dictatorships, protesting its illegitimacy by remaining under house arrest for nearly twenty years now. She is the democratically elected head of state, but she has not been allowed to take her rightful position. And Ven. Saccawati, a young Burmese bhikkhunī (a Theravada nun) ordained in Sri Lanka, has the entire Bhikkhu Sangha with their robes in knots because she dared to challenge the Burmese Buddhist establishment on the issue of full ordination for women. The monks cannot cope with this tiny nun's assertion of her right to be fully a nun, which they somehow regard as threatening to their authority. They claim that the bhikkhunī lineage has died out and seem oblivious to the fact that there are tens of thousands of bhikṣuṇīs (Mahayana nuns) in Taiwan, Korea, and Vietnam. Most monks are unaware that the bhikkhunī/ bhikṣuṇī ordination has nothing to do with Mahāyāna Buddhism, which they imagine will engulf their country as soon as nuns become ordained. They fail to recognize that, at the time of the Buddha himself, the decision to ordain women was considered a fairly radical move; it threatened the prevailing patriarchal society, which was preventing women from realizing their full spiritual potential. At the present time, Ven. Saccawati has been detained by the government, her passport has been confiscated, and it is unclear what her fate will be. She is the first fully ordained nun who has dared to go back to Burma. The international community needs to be alert to such dramas unfolding on the other side of the globe. After the first group of ten bhikkhunīs from Sri Lanka received full ordination in Sarnath in 1996, they stayed for a year in India because they were afraid of what might happen upon their return to Sri Lanka. But when they eventually arrived at Colombo Airport a year later, instead of a hostile reception, there were thousands of people gathered to welcome them. The astonished nuns were greeted with a golden parasol and led in procession. This was a truly auspicious gathering—welcoming the bhikkhunī lineage back to Sri Lanka after almost a thousand years.

❖ Understanding North American Buddhist Women

To understand women's experiences of Buddhism in North America, I would like to introduce the three communities of North American Buddhists I mentioned earlier—Asian, Asian American, and non-Asian American Buddhists—and the issues that each of these groups are primarily concerned with, as I understand them. The first group, Asian Buddhists, consists of immigrants from Burma, Cambodia, China, Hong Kong, India, Korea, Laos, Mongolia, Nepal, Singapore, Taiwan, Thailand, Tibet, and Vietnam. This is an immensely rich and diverse group of Buddhists, most of whom have immigrated to the United States since the 1970s. In addition to survival, Asian Buddhists in the United States are primarily concerned with cultural preservation, cultural identity, cultural continuity, and service to the community of immigrants from their homeland. They celebrate Buddhist festivals, invite monks to teach and support them, create a supportive community, and help resolve problems that arise in their communities. The temples serve a social as well as a religious function in the lives of the people. The laypeople create merit by supporting the temple, and the monastics serve the lay community by teaching, chanting sūtras and prayers, counseling, presiding at ceremonies, and serving as a focal point for community life. The major challenges facing Asian Buddhist communities are raising funds to build temples, getting permits to build temples, and issues of cultural adaptation, particularly racism, poverty, dealing with government agencies, and raising their children to understand and respect the Buddhist values they cherish.

The second group, Asian American Buddhists, dates back to the late 1800s, with the establishment of traditional Chinese and Japanese temples in California and Hawaii. These Buddhist temples served the same functions and struggled with more or less the same issues that more recent Buddhist immigrant communities face. Issues of racism, poverty, and cultural alienation were even more acute in those early years. The Jōdo Shinshū tradition is a prime example of cultural survival and adaptation: pews replaced *tatami,* hymnals replaced sūtra scrolls, and married ministers replaced monks. When I first visited a Buddhist temple in Los Angeles in 1962, I found the children singing "Buddha loves me, this I know, for the sūtras tell me so." At the Buddha Day celebration in Honolulu in 1995, the Hawaii Buddhist Council, which is entirely Japanese American, passed out rulers to the participants inscribed with "Buddha ♥ Me." Although these examples of cultural adaptation may strike us as slightly amusing today, I think it is extremely important to appreciate the hardships and discrimination that Buddhists endured in the early years, and still do, if we are to understand the experiences of North American Buddhist women as a whole; after all, these were some of the early pioneers of Buddhism in North America.

The third group, non-Asian American Buddhists, has grown especially in the last fifty years. This is a catch-all category that includes Buddhists who do not identify themselves as part of either of the first two groups. They are concerned with accessing Buddhist teachings, translating and interpreting them, and reinterpreting them in light of their own experience. These Buddhists come from a wide variety of ethnic, cultural, educational, social, and economic backgrounds. They may be Euro-American, African American, Latina American, Samoan American, or multicultural; rich or poor; with different family histories, and different sexual orientations. Primarily, however, they are white, middle class, and university educated. They belong to a variety of Buddhist traditions—Zen, Tibetan, Vipassanā, Pure Land, Soka Gakkai, and so forth—and are involved in a variety of practices, especially meditation, chanting, social service, and social activism.

❖ Creating a Sense of Solidarity

The question is how we can create a sense of community among Buddhist women that extends beyond identifications and allegiances to particular traditions, ethnicities, lifestyles, teachers, or whatever. Solidarity is typically reached in the face of a common threat or enemy—invaders, terrorists, other communities, infidels, foreigners, and so on. Buddhist men are certainly not the enemy. They, too, are victims of gender inequalities, though usually not in the same ways or to the same extent as women. Buddhist women need to create an alternative way of fashioning a sense of solidarity, a way that does not alienate others or create enemies. To my mind, this will come from recognizing that Buddhist women have common goals and also experience similar difficulties. Understanding this commonality of experiences and difficulties will help us generate a stronger sense of social justice that will spur us to action.

Despite our common goals and experiences, until recently Buddhist women have been divided by differences of language, social class, economics, culture, Buddhist tradition, and styles of practice. For some women, Buddhism is about meditation, or merit-making, or Buddhist studies. For some, Buddhism is social activism, whereas for others social activism is the very antithesis of Buddhist practice. Some Buddhist women live lives of destitution or sexual servitude, while others live lives of luxury and freedom. But we all have a common ancestor—Mahāprajāpatī, the Buddha's stepmother and auntie, who was the first Buddhist nun and a real pioneer. She showed tremendous courage in transgressing social boundaries to become a nun, and we owe her our gratitude. And we all have a common ally in Ānanda, arguably the first male Buddhist feminist, who pleaded women's case for inclusion in the early sangha; we are also indebted to him. These pioneers started a social movement that opened the way for women to gain full inclusion and equal access to the Buddha's teachings, but progress on the path has not always been easy. If we care about human suffering, we must be aware of the contradictions that exist between theory and practice in the Buddhist world. Although the Buddha's teachings tell us that enlightenment has no gender, glaring gender inequalities still exist in all Buddhist societies. This is just one of the issues in the Buddhist closet that requires openness and honesty.

❖ Recognizing Buddhist Ethnocentrism

To get a sense of the inequalities that exist, we need to move out of our comfort zone and learn more about "the other," in this case, other Buddhists. The three categories of Buddhists in North America distinguished earlier—Asian, Asian American, and non-Asian American—are an imperfect taxonomy, but they give us some insight into the rich diversity and complexity of North American Buddhism. Within each category, there are many groups and subgroups. These different Buddhist groups have much in common, but they are also different in some very fundamental ways, in terms of history, sociology, doctrine, language, food preferences, rituals, and other practices. I remember one time I was invited to speak at a Sōtō Zen temple on Oahu, and afterward they invited me for a lunch of teriyaki beef and beer. This is just one example of cultural differences. Although the majority of the estimated three million Buddhists in the United States are Asian, in attending a conference on American Buddhist women, it is doubtful that many people anticipated associating with Burmese, Thai, Cambodian, or Korean Buddhist women. Oddly, despite the fact that most American Buddhists are very liberal in their attitudes toward race, class, and gender, they still tend to hang out with people just like themselves and have very little knowledge of or interest in the lives of Asian or Asian American Buddhists.

The best way to overcome this tacit, unconscious ethnocentrism is to acquaint ourselves with other Buddhists—other types of Buddhists. Not everyone is fortunate enough to travel to Asia and live in a Buddhist monastery, but anyone can visit Asian Buddhist centers right here in North America. Every semester, my students at the University of San Diego visit Buddhist temples of two different traditions, and they always find these experiences enriching. Often they find the ethnically Asian Buddhist temples especially interesting and welcoming. In some ways these temples may be more traditional than their counterparts in Asia. For example, walking into Wat Boubpharam in San Diego is like stepping into a Buddhist temple in Vientiane, Laos, only more so. The people in San Diego may offer Fritos and Coca-Cola as *dāna* to the monks, but they wear traditional dress, practice ancient Buddhist traditions, and preserve Laotian customs that are being eclipsed by the tentacles of globalization in much of Asia. As it happens, the people in Laos may also offer Fritos and Coca-Cola as *dāna* to the monks.

❖ How Can I Help?

Discrimination against Buddhist women is often simply a matter of ignorance. As a nun, I am often ignored and seated behind monks and laypeople or shooed off to serve myself lunch in the kitchen of an Anglo-American dharma center, while the monks are served in royal style with crystal and silver. This is not an act of intentional cruelty. It simply displays ignorance of the fact that women have equal potential for enlightenment and that nuns have the same practice, the same discipline, the same precepts—often more—than the monks. When Buddhist conferences and publications give primary attention to the activities and ideas of men, this is also simply a lack of awareness, something that needs to be corrected.

Addressing gender discrimination is a matter of education that requires attention and activism on the part of Buddhist women and men. Many women in North American Buddhism are still playing supportive roles to men's activities—mostly very worthwhile activities, to be sure—but without recognizing their own lack of empowerment, still under the illusion that they are already fully liberated and that, therefore, gender equality is a non-issue. Many North American women are also blissfully unaware of the needs of Buddhist women in other countries. For this reason, since its inception the international Buddhist women's movement, under the umbrella of Sakyadhita: International

Association of Buddhist Women, focuses especially on calling attention to the potential of Buddhist women. In particular, Sakyadhita is concerned with bringing about changes for the 99 percent of the world's Buddhist women who live in Asia—most without adequate nutrition, education, or health care.

Sakyadhita's work in bringing to light the glaring inequalities that exist in Buddhist societies, in direct contradiction to the Buddha's own socially liberating teachings, has been highly successful in raising uncomfortable questions about the gender imbalance that exists in Buddhist societies. Remarkably, we've been able to do this without arousing the ire of the monks, at least overtly. In many cases, we intentionally create allies among men, both monks and laymen, which has been a very effective way of strategizing. The first step toward correcting the gender imbalance in Buddhism is recognizing it—considering derogatory references to women in the Buddhist texts and looking at the discriminatory attitudes toward Buddhist women in Buddhist temples and dharma centers. The international Buddhist women's movement that was ignited by the Sakyadhita conference in Bodhgaya in 1987 has brought together thousands of Buddhist women from all around the world and spawned an international network for research, publications, retreat facilities, and a variety of social action projects. This movement has drawn attention to the embarrassing fact that until recently women have had virtually no voice in Buddhist institutions, and that the lives of many Buddhist women are filled with poverty, inequality, and many kinds of suffering.

Despite its meager resources, the international Buddhist women's movement is a pioneering effort in cross-cultural understanding and one of the most far-reaching grassroots movements in the world. Today there is a group of Buddhist women superstars, and each one of them is bringing something very special to this movement—some in quiet ways, some more publicly. This international movement is a genuinely participatory alliance that can help create a vibrant future for Buddhist women. To benefit from this exchange, we need to be openhearted, sincere, and keen to learn. We need to be sensitive to the fact that Buddhist women in Asia and the West are often coming from very different places with different interests and priorities. Even though Buddhist women in traditional Asian cultures have rarely played roles of religious leadership, they have great respect for the dharma. It is the center of their lives. Their primary concerns are survival, education, health care, and caring for others. Buddhist women in Western cultures, especially non-Asian women, are generally new to Buddhism; they are busy learning, interpreting, and figuring out how to adapt the teachings in new cultural settings. They are concerned with meditation, psychology, sexuality, and personal development. By joining together, women in Asia and the West can learn from each other and enhance the tremendous potential for good that Buddhist women embody.

The international Buddhist women's movement deserves support especially for the work it has done to inspire change and improve conditions for the world's disadvantaged Buddhist women. And we need to do more. Sakyadhita gets invitations to attend international conferences, prayer breakfasts, interfaith dialogues, contemplative gatherings, panel discussions, and peace marches, and we need to make time to participate in these events. The world is in such a mess; Buddhist women need to become more active as a force for change both nationally and internationally. There is no time to carve out one's own private domain, whether in the monastery, the studio, or the university. The American mantra of taking care of oneself contradicts the Buddhist mantra of caring for others. If we hope to rescue humanity from the collision course we are on, we desperately need to work together. We need to reach beyond our individual affiliations to speak with united voices on issues of Buddhist practice and social justice. We need to ask: Where are the Buddhist Mother Teresas? Where are the American Aung San Suu Kyis?

Buddhist women need to create solidarity not only to benefit Buddhist women but because Buddhist women have so much to share with the world. We need to create solidarity to be able to speak out effectively against social injustices and to advocate on behalf of the millions of Buddhist women who have no voice, many of whom live under oppressive family or political structures. By educating ourselves, we gain a greater understanding of each other and find common ground to stand up for our values, in a spirit of peace and loving-kindness. In a sense, every Buddhist center is a peace center—or should be.

❖ Together on Common Ground

In some ways Buddhists in Asia and the West are coming from very different places on far more than gender issues. As the anthropologist Melford Spiro observed, Buddhists in Asia generally approach Buddhism either as a means of merit-making toward a better rebirth, as a source of protection and blessing, or as a means to achieve liberation. By contrast, Buddhists in the West tend to approach Buddhism either as philosophy, psychotherapy, or as a spur to activism toward building a more enlightened society. These distinctive foci are merely tendencies, but the varied approaches reflect the different cultural backgrounds of Buddhists in Asia and the West.

The Western therapeutic approach is nothing to be trivialized, of course. The Buddha's teachings can legitimately be called psychology. Lama Thubten Yeshe used to say, "We are all in Lord Buddha's mental hospital." This may explain why hundreds of psychologists, psychiatrists, and psychotherapists in North America are borrowing from the Buddhist teachings in their writings and practices, though often without acknowledging their sources. Nor is a focus on merit-making something to be trivialized, since in the Buddha's own words the achievement of liberation, whether in this lifetime or in the future, depends on the accumulation of merit. From a traditional perspective, as valuable as Buddhism is for coping with the difficulties of life, this focus does not, technically speaking, qualify as dharma, since true dharma practice is not concerned with the things of this life. To truly be dharma, our practice must be concerned with issues of the highest concern: loving-kindness, compassion, and the development of wisdom. So how do we justify a concern with gender issues? By understanding that gender discrimination is a problem for Buddhist women and an impediment to dharma practice for both women and men. It is a source of great suffering. Since loving-kindness, compassion, and wisdom are the issues of highest concern, we must practice these virtues to resolve the sufferings that result from gender discrimination.

Buddhist women in Asia and the West share much in common and also have much to learn from each other. At first glance our situations appear vastly different, but when we look more closely, we find that things are not as different as they may seem. Buddhist women everywhere share common values and are concerned about the welfare of society. There are many exemplary women in Asia, such as Ven. Zhengyan in Taiwan, who have made great contributions to disaster relief, elder care, hospice care, medical care, and relieving the miseries of the poor; they are also renowned for their contributions to monastic life, contemplation, publishing, teaching, Buddhist studies programs, and children's programs. In this connection, we cannot ignore the value of having a dedicated group of monastic women whose time and energies are 100 percent committed to working full-time for the dharma. In the twentieth century in Western countries, social welfare was the responsibility of government, but that is rapidly changing under uncompassionate neoconservatism, so Buddhist women cannot afford to be complacent. We need to be aware that many aspects of liberal democracy are threatened today in the United States and that this could spell trouble for Buddhists and pacifists.

Buddhist women have demonstrated their compassion for the needy, their organizational abilities, and their dedication to social activism in a wide range of areas. In Asia, those in Taiwan and Korea are especially active. Buddhist women in North America have been active in establishing and maintaining Buddhist centers and in social welfare activities, though generally under the leadership of men. Their unique contributions have been in the areas of nonprofit organization, peace activism, antinuclear demonstrations, prison ministry, hospice programs, and environmental activism. In the field of education, Western women currently enjoy educational opportunities roughly equal to men, including higher education, whereas the fortunes of women in Buddhist societies vary widely. For example, many Buddhist women in Cambodia, India, Laos, Mongolia, Nepal, and Tibet lack access to Buddhist education or even to general education, sometimes even to basic literacy. Buddhist women in Taiwan, Korea, and Malaysia, by contrast, are leaders of Buddhist education programs for adults, children, and college students, all generously funded by Buddhist laypeople.

Buddhist women's experiences in Asia and the West are remarkably diverse, but there are common threads: Buddhist institutions are still largely patriarchal, with women generally in supportive roles. Financial and sexual exploitation occur, and there is little transparency and few channels for redress, so sexual predators may continue unchecked, some in the role of dharma teachers. Many Buddhist women still deny that they are feminists, and so there is a critical need for greater awareness. As awareness increases, women are quietly challenging patriarchy, unequal power structures, and the assumption that women should play subordinate roles in Buddhism. As women begin to work for change, they will significantly influence the way Buddhism is understood and practiced in North America and internationally.

At this point, I would like to issue a call to action on the part of North American Buddhists to work for social justice, beginning with support for Buddhist women's aspirations to achieve equal opportunities for secular and religious education, ordination, health care, and economic self-sufficiency. We still need to confront some uncomfortable issues. What are Buddhist women doing to combat sex trafficking? Even one woman or child trafficked is too many. Sexual slavery afflicts Buddhist women far out of proportion to our numbers, as we see in Nepal, a Hindu kingdom, where 75 percent of the women trafficked are Buddhists. What are Buddhists doing to contest the Patriot Act, which threatens all minorities, including religious minorities? How are our local dharma centers helping young people prepare their cases for conscientious objector status? Unfortunately, the young people in our lives may need these files sooner than we imagine. To those of you who are already working to address these significant issues, I would like to offer my heartfelt admiration and gratitude.

Moving Beyond Gender

bell hooks

S UFFERING LED ME to Buddhism. I was searching for a way to
end the anguish of spirit engulfing me since childhood. Like
many of us, I had the outer trappings of success (a bright
young scholarship student academically excelling at Stanford University) while inwardly I was in a constant state of emotional crisis. My
inner life was full of turmoil. Growing up in a fundamentalist Christian home, I had been taught to believe in salvation, to trust in the
redemptive power of divine grace to heal all suffering. Yet even though
I prayed and prayed to be released from the emotional pain that caused
me to despair, often leading me to contemplate suicide, my prayers
were not answered. I was falling into an abyss of sorrow—a dark night
of the soul so overwhelming it was impossible to find a source of light,
a way out.

Ironically, my prayers for salvation were answered as I, clinging to
the hope that there was a way out of suffering, found my way to Buddhism. Just as poetry had been the imaginative process, both through
reading and writing, that sustained my hope that there was reason to
live, it was poetry that turned me toward Buddhism. Reading the
works of the Beat poets—Jack Kerouac, Diane di Prima, Gary Snyder—
I was inspired. Here were poets connecting creative process and spiritual practice. Explaining the significance of the Beat poets in his

essay, "Notes on the Beat Generation and the New Wind," Snyder recalls:

> In a way one can see the beat generation as another aspect of the perpetual "third force" that has been moving through history with its own values of community, love, and freedom.... The beat generation can be seen as an aspect of the worldwide trend for intellectuals to reconsider the nature of the human individual, existence, personal motives, the qualities of love and hatred, and the means of achieving wisdom. Existentialism, the modern pacifist-anarchist movement, the current interest of Occidentals in Zen Buddhism, are all a part of that trend. The beat generation is particularly interesting because it is not an intellectual movement, but a creative one: people who have cut their ties with respectable society in order to live an independent way of life writing poems and painting pictures, making mistakes and taking chances—but finding no reason for apathy or discouragement.[1]

At age eighteen, I was a convert to Buddhist thinking.

At first Buddhism for me was all about reading texts. Meditation was not as vital to me as studying and learning about Buddhism. A serendipitous meeting with Gary Snyder changed all that. One of a few students chosen to have dinner with the poet before a Stanford reading, I declined attending since it meant that I would need to leave my work at the day-care center and rush to the dinner, with no time to wash or change my clothes. Tending two-year-olds, running around all day, I was both funky and exhausted at the end of the day. But the soul force within me stirred my longing to meet the poet, to talk to him, to be in his presence, and rightly pushed me past the inner parental voice from childhood that would only have allowed me to attend this meeting if I was clean and well dressed. I arrived wearing a dirty pink dress over a pair of blue jeans and Snyder welcomed me, this country girl smelling of hard work who longed to be a poet, who longed to find a spiritual

path. By the end of the evening of talk about poetry and poetry reading, intense discussions of farming and our right relation to the earth,
I was invited to come to "kitkitdizzie," Snyder's home in the
foothills of the Sierra Nevada Mountains, to participate in a spring celebration where Buddhist women were going to be present, women
who had taken their vows, women walking the path—*bodhisattvas*.
This was also a place where poetry would be taken seriously.

At Snyder's home in the mountains I sat in his study and pored over
Buddhist texts, taking my journey to Buddhism a step further. Significantly, when that journey began I was also embarking on another journey; I was participating in the feminist movement, taking women's
studies classes, learning feminist theory and practice, writing my first
feminist book. One journey was leading me in the direction of self-
actualization, the other journey was leading me away from all notions
of self. Needless to say, initially choosing these parallel paths did not
lead to an end to suffering. I felt all the more torn as I struggled to balance seemingly disparate and conflicting journeys. My suffering inten-
sified. Yet both paths promised an end to suffering.

High in the California mountains surrounded by manzanita, sleeping under a big open sky, I dreamed that I would find a path of peace,
an end to suffering. What most impressed and inspired my then
young and innocent mind, far more than the beautiful texts I read,
the quiet sitting, the seductive flirtations of male teachers, was the
calm, peaceful presence of Buddhist nuns. The young nun I talked
with most listened to my story of suffering and shared with me that
the path of mindfulness was not for everyone—one had to be ready,
simply longing was not enough. Above all, this transformative
encounter compelled me to maintain hope in the face of suffering.
Afterward, whenever I found myself falling into the abyss of despair,
contemplating death as the easy out, I would find myself holding on,
clinging to the belief that there could and would be a way out of suffering. Buddhist teacher Sharon Salzberg captures this nuance of
falling in her book, *Faith*, describing the powerful sensation of being
held by the dharma:

Being held doesn't halt the falling, doesn't abruptly, according to our desires, change how things actually are. We're not able to stop the unknown from crashing into our expectations, or get the whirlwind of circumstances under our command. What we can do is let go of the encrustations of the past and the fearful projections of the future to connect with the present moment, to find there the natural flow of life and the myriad possibilities within it. We can recognize the mystery spreading out before us and within us all the time. We can step out of the hope/fear gyration and give our capacity to love a chance to flower. These possibilities are what hold us. This is where we can place our faith. Even as we fall, fall endlessly, with faith we are held as we open to each moment.[2]

As I developed greater critical consciousness through intellectual and academic work, feminist theory and practice enabled me to remain committed to Buddhist practice—in the face of the sexism and patriarchal drama that often depressed my spirit—because it empowered me to work within alternative frameworks. Sexism and patriarchy could be observed and critiqued, yet I did not have to become attached to acts of resistance. I could engage in Buddhist practice without subordinating my self to male domination, following in a tradition of women who have opened their hearts to Buddhism without subjugating mind and spirit.

Enlightened women found their way to being Buddha long before patriarchal Buddhists in organized structures gave their endorsement, their permission. We are ever grateful to the many scholars who work to uncover, document, and highlight the presence of women in the history of Buddhism, a presence often buried as a consequence of patriarchal exploitation and oppression globally. In her 1986 essay, "The Balancing of American Buddhism," Joanna Macy affirmed: "As American women opening up to the Dharma, we are participating in something beyond our own little scenarios. We find ourselves reclaiming the equality of the sexes in the Buddha-Dharma. We are participating in a balancing of Buddhism that has great historic significance."[3]

Years later in her work, *Buddhism After Patriarchy*, Rita Gross called for a revalorization of Buddhism that would allow for a critique of patriarchy but not diminish the vitality of Buddhist thought informed by patriarchal thinking. She reminds us: "The assessment that historical Buddhism is androcentric in its thought form and patriarchal in its institutions is an *analysis*, an *accurate description* but not an *accusation*."[4] Gross identifies Western Buddhists as standing at the confluence of "two of the world's most powerful movements toward liberation—Buddhism and feminism." As part of mindful practice, she was among the first to proclaim ten years ago that "Western Buddhists have the opportunity and the responsibility to manifest Buddhism after patriarchy."[5]

When we look at the last ten years of Buddhist thought and practice in the United States, it is most evident that women and men have not only critiqued the patriarchal thinking that informs classical texts and contemporary work, they have created a body of work that embraces a vision of gender equality while simultaneously illuminating the way in which working on behalf of that equality is fundamental to the practice of mindfulness. With this spirit of radical openness they have also created the cultural context for individual Buddhist women teachers to come to power and be fully recognized. There is certainly greater representation of gender equality among circles of Buddhist teachers in the West, more so than in other religious groups. Paradoxically, some individual Buddhist women teachers embrace patriarchal thinking. Others work to teach from a perspective that is consistently antipatriarchal. Visionary teachers urge us to move beyond gender, whether we are in a patriarchal framework or a liberatory feminist context, so that our attention can be concentrated on what truly matters. Spiritual practice is what truly matters. While the critique of patriarchy and the revisioning of Buddhist thought and practice, so that it is no longer informed by patriarchal bias, is a political, ethical, and spiritual struggle that is essential and ongoing, it must never overshadow commitment to Buddhist practice.

No doubt every woman engaged with Buddhism is asked at some point how she can support such a patriarchal religion. Usually sophisticated critics enjoy pointing to the classical legacy of patriarchal thinking and practice as well as its contemporary manifestations to bash Buddhism, especially critiquing the participation of liberated women. Sharon Salzberg shares the insight that we may never really know what the Buddha said about women practitioners—even though he appears to have been revolutionary for his times because of his willingness to share the teaching, irrespective of caste or gender. Her point is that what truly matters is the value of Buddhist practice. She contends: "What we can know is whether the path of practice leads to the end of suffering…"[6] Describing the gratitude her teacher Dipa-Ma felt toward the Buddha for the techniques that helped her even as she questioned elements of the historical beliefs, Salzberg writes: "She saw that the beliefs were extraneous to what she could have faith in—her ability to reach the liberation the Buddha was talking about. Her experience of transformation was the still center of her faith." With profound clarity Salzberg reminds us that: "This is the essential questioning we must bring to any belief system. Can it transform our minds? Can it help reshape our pain into wisdom and love?"[7]

Significantly, in *World as Lover, World as Self*, Joanna Macy emphasizes the importance of the teachings on codependent coarising and the scriptures honoring the Perfection of Wisdom, Mother of All Buddhas. Macy explains: "Her scriptures have a strong corrective. Readjusting the lens through which we see reality, she offers a vision of interdependence so radical that, as we realize anew, no factor or no constituent element can be understood in isolation, in its own separate self-existence…. Knowing…interexistence with all beings, the bodhisattva seeks not perfection but wholeness and healing."[8]

Just as this corrective has altered the nature of Buddhist practice globally, visionary feminist thought and practice that is informed by the awareness of the interrelatedness of systems of domination was the radical breakthrough pushing us past binary thinking, past Western metaphysical dualism, allowing us then to think beyond gender. But always to be thinking, being, living in a way that transforms culture, so that gender equality is recognized and consistently affirmed. Seeing reality in this way, we are able to hold one another accountable for the positions we occupy in dominator culture without evoking a politics of blame or victimhood. An authentic middle way allows us to recognize multiple intentionalities. We can easily move past either/or notions to both/and. To me, the middle way is the space of radical openness, the space that invites true communication. In her chapter, "Widening the Circle of Compassion" (from *When Things Fall Apart*), Pema Chödrön teaches, "Whether it's ourselves, our lovers, bosses, children, local Scrooge, or the political situation, it's more daring and real not to shut anyone out of our hearts and not to make the other into an enemy. If we begin to live like this, we'll find that we can't actually make things completely right or wrong anymore.... Everything is ambiguous, everything is always shifting and changing."[9]

In her introduction to *Buddhist Women on the Edge*, Marianne Dresser states that what she finds most compelling is the Buddhist teaching about the middle way; she interprets it to mean that we do not "deny the real consequences to living beings of the suffering, characteristic of the relative world, even as we practice to see through and beyond it— to recognize our interrelationship with all aspects of reality."[10] In my work I am constantly grappling with ways to end dominator culture. I am constantly face to face with the suffering caused by imperialist white supremacist capitalist patriarchy, describing and critiquing liberatory possibilities. Thinking outside the box of dualism and living a practice of equanimity gives my life balance. But more than that, spiritual practice is the circle surrounding this work, the force empowering me to open my heart, to be Buddha, to have a practice of compassion that joins rather than separates, that takes the broken bits and pieces of our damaged self and world, bringing them together.

My journey to Buddhism has been fundamentally about the practice of mindfulness. It has been about learning awareness, learning to awaken. We all have our Buddha stories that speak to us. One of my favorites tells us that soon after the Buddha's enlightenment, he encountered a stranger on a rural road. The stranger knew nothing about the Buddha but was awestruck by the radiance of Buddha's presence, having never seen anyone who looked so joyful, so serene. When they were close enough for the stranger to speak, the Buddha was asked, "Are you, by chance, a spirit?" The answer was no. "Are you, by chance, an angel?" The answer was no. Then, "Are you perhaps a god?" The answer was no. Frustrated, the stranger wanted to know, "Well, what are you?" The Buddha replied, "I am awake."[11] Being awake, being mindful, is the heart of Buddhist practice; the door to enlightenment that is open to everyone irrespective of race, gender, class, nationality, education. We cannot enter that door without letting go of our attachment to labels, to identity. Living the dharma, we move beyond gender—we move into the community of seekers where spirit truly matters, where the path of compassion leads to peace and an end to suffering.

NOTES

1 Reprinted in *A Place in Space: Ethics, Aesthetics, and Watersheds* (New York: Counterpoint, 1995), pp. 12–13.

2 *Faith: Trusting Your Own Deepest Experience* (New York: Riverhead Books, 2002), pp. 96–97.

3 *Primary Point*, vol. 3, no. 1 (Feb, 1986).

4 *Buddhism After Patriarchy: A Feminist History, Analysis, and Reconstruction of Buddhism* (Albany: State University of New York Press, 1993), p. 23.

5 Ibid., pp. 26–27.

6 *Faith*, p. 61.

7 Ibid., p. 62.

8 *World as Lover, World as Self* (Berkeley: Paralax Press, 1991), p. 239.

9 *When Things Fall Apart* (Boston: Shambhala, 1997), p. 83.

10 *Buddhist Women on the Edge* (Berkeley: North Atlantic Press, 1996), p. xiv.

11 See, for example, *Aṅguttara Nikāya* II.37–39.

Buddhism and Creativity

❖ ❖ ❖ ❖ ❖ ❖ ❖ ❖ ❖ ❖ ❖ ❖ ❖ ❖ ❖ ❖ ❖ ❖ ❖ ❖

A conversation with Jane Hirshfield and Meredith Monk;
moderated by Pat Enkyō O'Hara.

P**AT ENKYŌ O'HARA:** *Welcome to all of you. My name is Enkyō O'Hara, I am a Zen teacher and for twenty years a professor of interactive media at the NYU's Tisch School of the Arts. During that time I worked with students on creative projects, witnessing the ups and downs of creativity and artistic expression. In a piece called "The Way of Expression" (Dōtoku) in his* Shōbōgenzō, *the Zen teacher Dōgen wrote how vital it is that each of us expresses our experience of truth and how the process of expression is, in fact, the Way, the Truth. Even more to the point, we can see our own lives as the medium for us to express the truth. Today we have the opportunity to be in dialogue with two wonderful, creative women—a poet and a performing artist—and to listen to how their lives reveal their creative process and their spiritual practice. We may find through their responses that life, creativity, and spirituality are not different—they're interconnected. I am hoping that this conversation will model for each of us how to express our own truth, how to walk our own spiritual path.*

It would take far too long to recite the accomplishments of these two extraordinary women. Very briefly, Jane Hirshfield is the author of six collections of poetry. She is the editor and cotranslator of two books that are well known to many of us in the Buddhist world: Women in Praise of the Sacred *and* The

Ink Dark Moon. *Jane has also written a book of essays about poetry and the creative process, called* Nine Gates.

Sitting next to her is Meredith Monk, someone about whom it's impossible to find a single word to express what she does! An interdisciplinary performance artist, she is engaged in voice, music, composition, film, and dance; she works with poetic forms, installations, and theater. This year [2005], she's celebrating forty years of her work. She is the recipient of a MacArthur genius grant.

Let us begin with the heart of the matter: Can you describe your engagement with the creative process? How does it work for you?

Meredith Monk: I had said to Jane that I thought it might be really interesting to talk about the similarities and differences of our creative processes. Jane's process as a writer (and I'm sure she'll speak very eloquently about it) is by nature solitary whereas mine has different aspects, depending upon what I am creating. A music project would be different from a film, for example. And even within the practice of composing music, there are works that I make for myself as a soloist and others that I make for my ensemble or for other groups. My process, if I'm working on a solo music piece, is solitary, but if I'm working on a piece for my ensemble, there are different phases. First, I spend a long time alone generating material. My daily discipline is sitting at the piano and working vocally. Then I bring in the shards of material that I have found to rehearsal, and we work on exploring and developing the various possibilities within them. Then I go back alone and complete the final piece. What's very exciting about working this way is that just by offering the musical phrases or fragments to other people, something is going to change, and then I have to let go of a certain kind of control. A sense of mystery has room to enter. My time at the piano is a daily artistic practice that starts with silence. That silence and space allows me to find material in an intuitive way.

When I was working on a series of pieces called "Songs from the Hill" at my sister's house in New Mexico, I would literally go to a particular spot on a hill near her house and sit there every day in the hot, blazing sun until I was inspired by a vocal idea. Then, I would tape it or write it out. Those ideas were just little seeds of something. When I came back East, I developed the seeds into the pieces that they became —complete musical forms. All the songs were inspired by being in that particular environment and landscape, and they retained the quality of the initial impulses. That's an example of my solo process. But basically any process is like that. In a film, which by definition is the most daunting collaborative process, my initial inspiration goes through many people and technologies before it gets to the screen. The challenge there is to keep the integrity of the vision as it goes through all the stages.

To give you a feeling for the process of writing music for the ensemble: as I said before, I spend a lot of time alone preparing material, then I present it to the group. I might say, "Oh, could you try singing this? Or could you try singing that?" I might try turning it upside down or playing with variations. The performers offer their responses, and so it transforms. At first it's a shock because if I tape my voice on four tracks, I'm used to the sound of my own voice. When I go into rehearsal I have to adjust to the fact that other voices are now singing the piece. The piece actually becomes richer and richer because of that opening out to other people. After working so many years with the same performers (I've been very privileged), we now have a kind of shorthand. It's really a particular musical language and way of working, of thinking. A very generous and playful spirit permeates the atmosphere. I would say that over the years, being a Buddhist practitioner has made me more conscious and appreciative of this respect and generosity.

There is a lot of waiting and having to be patient in my process, but then there are moments of discovery. Those moments of discovery are what make life so exciting. Every piece that I work on brings up another set of questions. Beginning a piece can be terrifying, excruciating, but I think that what making art (and living life) is really about is being able to tolerate hanging out in the unknown.

Over the years I have come to believe that performance can be a vehicle for imparting the radiance and richness of human beings. Hopefully when you go to a performance, what is offered to you is a template of possible human behavior. You experience generosity of spirit and the way people share space. There's a figure eight of energy between the people on stage and also between the performers and the audience. The energy and awareness just keeps on flowing, and as performers there's a sensitivity that develops over the years. By a tiny flicker of an eye or a subtle vocal quaver, everyone knows that one person is having a hard time, and everybody pulls for that person. That's the beauty of working with other people and the mystery of it.

Jane Hirshfield: Even though Meredith described something in part quite different from what I do because of its collaborative nature, she used some words that are also central to my own process. One of those words is "mystery." I find it an utter mystery where any word, thought, conception, comes from. You ask me, "What is your process?" and the most honest answer I can give is, "I have no idea."

Also, Meredith spoke of art as emerging from a question, which is something I find is true for me as well. I believe that most art arises out of a question because if you are coursing in perfect fulfillment, you're not likely to be making art. You would probably be quite satisfied with the moment just as it is. I think it is especially in the West that art tends to arise out of a question. In Japan, however, it is sometimes thought that no experience is complete until the poem that comes of it is written. This even includes your own death, though those poems are written before the experience is quite complete, of course. So I do think it's possible for art to be made out of the sense of overflowing perfection. But much more often for me it comes out of a question, a tear in the fabric, something that wants to be looked at more deeply than I'm able to with my everyday mind. In this way, I find that the practice of poetry is deeply parallel to the practice of zazen, or sitting meditation. When I do zazen, I don't write poems. I am entering a condition of concentration, of being with this moment as it is. Things come up in meditation that are, of course, inexpressible. We run out of language very fast when we try to describe the experience of zazen. But in poetry, it's almost as if it is the same request made of my deep self but with the intention pointed toward words rather than toward wordlessness. So I might ask my poetry-concentration, "What would you like to think about today?" I might be trying to find a question that I don't even yet know I have.

Meredith also mentioned silence. I've long believed that silence must be one of a poet's closest friends. If I were not able to enter the silence before words, how could I find any words I don't already know yet? My writing process is a bit like watching paint dry. You don't see anything happen on the outside, you don't hear anything, but something is still changing. I sit at the desk, or in bed, and write, then stop, then write some more, and then think some more…

It doesn't look like much, just like zazen doesn't look like much, and yet from that "not much," a life comes forward into deeper knowledge.

PEO: *Jane, I understand that you took a hiatus from your writing while on a three-year Zen retreat. I wonder, did you write at all during that time?*

JH: I did my monastic training at Tassajara Zen Mountain Center, inland from Big Sur. It was the only Zen monastery in this country at that time. Students practicing there in the 1970s were told that during our time in the monastery, we were to do nothing except Zen. In those years, people were not even allowed to do yoga. Now, of course, everybody's doing yoga because we understand so much more about the toll these practices take on the body. In three years in Tassajara, I wrote one illicit haiku, the summer of my second year. I'd like to claim this was a clandestine thrill, but really, it just came to me, while I was drinking coffee and watching the stars one morning before zazen, so I wrote it down.

It's worth remembering that I was very young when I entered formal Zen training. I was only twenty-one when I arrived for my first year at the city center and twenty-two when I went to Tassajara. I had written from childhood so poetry was my first practice. Poetry also brought me to Zen. Reading Japanese and Chinese poetry introduced me to the concepts of Buddhism. The more I saw, the more I thought, "Oh yes, this is how I understand the world to be. This is what I would like to investigate further." I did realize that if I stopped writing for three years I might never start again. My feeling was very much that if that happened, then I wasn't supposed to write, and I'd do something else with my life. I needed to practice Zen, whatever happened, because I knew a great deal about book learning, I knew a great deal about falling in love and the travails of that, but I didn't know a great deal else about what it meant to be a human being. I knew that I would never write any poems worth reading if I did not pursue a path of deepening my experience and my ability to know and express and discover and sit with my own experience. When I left Tassajara, poetry came back quite organically. And years later, my teacher said that's exactly what was supposed to happen. You stop, and then if it comes back, you let it.

I feel Zen and poetry are complementary to one another in that both are acts of attention. Here is my summary of all Buddhism in seven words: "Everything changes. Everything is connected. Pay attention." After a while, I realized you don't even need the first five words, because, in fact, if you are paying attention, you'll see that everything changes and everything is connected. Anything we human beings do well, with our full energy and our full doubt and our full intention of pressing further, will have its basis in the cultivation of attention. In this way, poetry and Zen practice are the same.

PEO: *I agree. Let's hear from the Vajrayāna perspective. Meredith, you have also been on retreat. Maybe you could talk a little bit about the relationship between retreating and creating.*

MM: I haven't been on a three-year retreat, but I did go to two seven-week winter monastic retreats *(Yarne)* at Gampo Abbey. One of the precepts at the Abbey is no singing and dancing. I wondered about that and came to realize as time went by that the precept is a way of limiting stimulation and distraction. The first time I was there, I thought a lot about how I could give back to the community and came up with the idea of teaching voice as practice since there was extensive chanting every day. Ani Migme, a senior nun at Gampo Abbey, told me that sometimes she would get tired while leading the chanting, especially when the pitch would go down because it was hard to maintain uplifted energy. I asked myself, how could I teach voice for people who didn't want to be performers but wanted to experience voice as practice itself? The second time that I was at the Abbey, I offered a vocal workshop and most of the community came. Teaching there was very inspiring for me. We focused on how the voice is an extension of the breath and how that relates to our sitting practice. Just as our posture is fundamental to our sitting, the commitment with which we produce sound and where it originates in the body is fundamental to how we chant. When the pitch goes down, it's like a vocal slouch. When that happens it becomes harder and harder to keep the energy going in the room. Additionally, when you're in tune with the other voices, the whole space opens up. It's very expansive. The energy fills the room, and the room resonates. Then chanting doesn't take so much effort. Of course, I had to be very careful that everybody knew that what we were chanting was really still the main focus, but there was also a physical awareness of what was going on in the body and what was going on in the breath. How people responded became incredibly touching to me; one of the most fulfilling teaching experiences I've ever had.

As far as creating is concerned, we were sitting eight or nine hours a day, and of course ideas would come up. My discipline was to not really get attached to them, but sometimes when I got back to my room I would write them down. I was trying not to get too involved with this or with thinking about my next piece but to really, really commit to being where I was in the moment. During the second retreat I didn't read anything other than dharma because for me, reading is another way that I habitually escape the moment. So, I really tried to just stay with the practice.

PEO: *And how did that work for you? Students often ask me what to do when a brilliant idea arises during meditation. The classic instruction, of course, is to let it go and continue sitting, but students often want to stop and write it down. I have even heard of those who sit with a pen and notebook!*

MM: You can't write it down. I think the ideas that need to make themselves known come back later. It's really an interesting discipline to let those thoughts go as they come up during sitting practice. When you garden, you plant many seeds in the ground but only certain ones grow.

JH: As for me, well, I hope this isn't disillusioning, but the thoughts that might come into my mind when I sit zazen are not brilliant ideas, they're quite quotidian.

MM: Like "when is lunch?"

JH: I don't think I ever found and lost a great poem on the cushion…. Would it were so easy.

PEO: *A great poem, a great idea—how do we recognize them and take them seriously? I think this is a question for women in particular. Thinking back to your childhood, what was it that allowed you to take yourselves seriously as artists, that drives you to this day to affirm your efforts and work seriously?*

JH: Let me start with a scholarly answer. For any of you interested in this question, there's a wonderful book by the feminist historian, Gerda Lerner, *The Creation of Feminist Consciousness*, in which she talks about how early women artists—women who were historically assigned to roles of silence by their cultures—authorized themselves to speak. She suggests there were several possible forms of self-authorization. For example, some medieval poems were written in the form of mothers giving advice to their sons. Another authorization is passion, love poems. Another is a strong experience in the realm of the spiritual— many of the women mystics included in *Women in Praise of the Sacred* could not be silent, they had such an overpowering experience of the sacred in their lives that they had to bear witness to it. In other cases you could say the poems flowed out of them as naturally and inevitably as song flows out of a nightingale. So that's a bit of conceptual background for this question.

For myself, the reason to write was probably closer to desperation. Mine was not an easy family in which to be vulnerable, in which to be exposed, to find a deep truth. I needed to find a way toward my own self in circumstances in which that was not particularly encouraged. So for me writing—which was something I did secretly, hiding the poems under my mattress—was a way to craft both self and self-knowledge. It was a way to craft a space of development for a young child who was actually quite lost.

MM: I am very moved, Jane, by how you found your way against all odds. I would say that Jane's and my internal experiences were not so dissimilar in that we both had to find personal space within challenging circumstances. My background, though, is very different. I'm the fourth generation singer in my family. My great-grandfather was a cantor in Russia. And my grandfather came to the United States in the late nineteenth century because he received a music conservatory scholarship. Later he opened a conservatory of his own in New York and sang in churches, temples, and concert halls. My mother was the original Chiquita Banana, Muriel Cigar, Schafer Beer, Blue Bonnet Margarine, and Royal Pudding girl.

Part of my childhood was spent in radio control booths at NBC and CBS basically being told to be quiet. I also had a lot of physical problems as a child. I was born unable to fuse two images with my eyes and was quite uncoordinated because of that. I also had eczema. My earliest memories include a sense of physical discomfort and irritation. I think that singing was a very early personal language that gave me a feeling of comfort. If Jane's image is hiding her poems under the mattress, mine would be singing myself to sleep. I sang all the time. But it was really hard to be a singer in a family of singers. And yet I will always be grateful that I was exposed to the joy of music at an early age. Because my mother saw that simple physical activity like skipping was difficult for me, she looked around for a movement class, heard about Dalcroze Eurhythmics, and took me to lessons. In the late nineteenth century, Eugene Dalcroze from Switzerland developed a way of teaching music to children through their bodies. He invented wonderful rhythmic and concentration exercises: lively ways of playing and learning the fundamentals of music with an integrated, holistic approach. It is a very beautiful way of learning music kinesthetically. For me it was the other way around—music was very familiar to me, but my body was very uncoordinated, and so that work was a way of connecting to my body. I adored those classes. In a way they allowed me to focus on something different from singing, something that didn't feel competitive within my own family. I got through my childhood by going more into dance and movement. I still sang, played piano and guitar, and wrote simple piano compositions, but my main focus was dance. Later, I went to Sarah Lawrence and in my senior year designed a Combined Performing Arts program for myself that included voice, music composition, dance and dance composition, and theatre. I always had an instinct that I wanted to create something rather than be an interpreter. I began making pieces combining different elements while I was still in school. When I graduated, I came to New York and began presenting pieces in galleries and other performance spaces. Even though I had been in the voice department in school, I was doing pieces that didn't have much singing in them but instead included visual images, gestures, sound, and cinematic structure. After about six months, I realized that I missed singing very much. And so I went back to the piano and started vocalizing. One day I had a revelation that the voice could be an instrument like the body; that I could find a vocabulary built on my own vocal instrument and that my voice could move like a spine or a foot. I understood in a flash that within the voice are male and female, all ages, different characters, landscapes, colors, textures, and ways of using the breath, limitless possibilities of producing sound. At that moment, I also had an incredible feeling of coming back to my own blood but coming back in my own way. From that point on, I began a deep exploration of the voice as the first human instrument, an exploration that continues to this day and is the center of my work.

PEO: *I am wondering what kinds of influences were operating when you began your creative work. Even little Jane, hiding her poems under the bed, must have had inspiration. Let's hear about the people and things you two may have read or heard or experienced that moved you forward.*

JH: There are so many poets who were models and exemplars of inspiration for me, whose work I absorbed like a sponge. To give only one example, early on, and rather inexplicably given that I grew up on the lower east side of New York City, I fell in love with Japanese poetry. The first book I bought for myself, at age eight, was one of those one-dollar Peter Piper Press books of Japanese haiku. What was an eight-year-old, twentieth-century, urban, American girl finding in these poems? Is it possible that I intuited in any way the deeper movements? Was I just nature starved? But somehow, you know, I must have been like a little plant, turning its leaves toward the light before it can even know what light is. I think I'll just let it rest with that.

MM: At a young age, I already had an intuition about working with and combining different aspects of perception to make a poetry for the senses. Thinking back, it seems like it was a very personal way of integrating my different interests in order to find an authentic self. But I was also aware early on that there were social ramifications as well. This notion of weaving senses together and affirming the perceptual richness of both artist and audience offers an antidote to the fragmented world in which we live. This approach becomes a metaphor for being awake and appreciative of the sensory world of phenomena that graces our lives.

It was instinctive for me to work this way, but I was also influenced by non-Western performance traditions, which differed from the segregated art forms more characteristic of the Western European tradition. In African and Asian cultures, or the accounts that we have of very ancient traditions, performance was often a form of worship and an expression of mystery. The specialization that developed in the

Western tradition had to do with the rationalist concept that humankind was meant to control nature, that a human being had to fit into a finite, logical structure, and that art was for the court. A great example of this is ballet, where the individual related primarily to geometric lines in space. In many Asian dance forms, however, the body relates more to a sphere around itself, and gesture is always within human scale.

At Sarah Lawrence, I was also deeply fortunate to have two wonderful female teachers. One was Bessie Schönberg, who was the head of both Dance and Theatre. She was a woman of the theatre in the largest sense of the word. Bessie perceived that I was a wild, intense little horse that had to be given some rein but not too much. Her mother had been a singer so she understood that I passionately wanted to find out about the voice. And then my music teacher was Ruth Lloyd. She taught Music for Dance as well as Music Composition. She saw me as a musician immediately and always encouraged me to find my own way. Between those two women, I was nurtured and challenged. If I didn't have them guiding me at that point in my life, I'm not sure what would have happened to me. I am so grateful for what they gave me.

PEO: *I hope you were able to tell them that.*

MM: Yes, I'm profoundly happy that I was able to.

PEO: *Virginia Woolf famously said that in order to create, a woman requires time, a room of her own, and five guineas in her pocket. For Woolf, autonomy was crucial. I wonder what you two think are the essential ingredients to be creative.*

JH: For my particular psyche, Woolf named it exactly: undisturbed time and space. But it's important to acknowledge that there isn't only one process or one right way. Wallace Stevens would walk to the insurance company where he worked with a notebook in his pocket, and suddenly he'd just stop on the street and write. Though it would be a nightmare for me, I know a few women poets who similarly find public places fertile ground in which to work. Once in a great while, an idea will come to me in the course of outer events, but then I don't stop and write the poem itself, I just recognize that it will be there, waiting for me when I can meet it. To find my way to deep thought requires courage and fearlessness, and so I need to be in a place where I can be absolutely vulnerable and exposed, free from distraction. And that means a place with the assuredness of privacy and quiet.

MM: I would say very much the same thing. It's having enough time and space to be able to try again. One of my favorite places to work is in an artists' colony, where basically I am alone all day and then at night I have the companionship of others to share what their process has been like that day. I have the luxury of having the time to walk away from my work and come back to it over and over again. It's almost impossible to do this in New York, where time is very fragmented.

JH: I feel the same way. Perhaps because I had been at Tassajara first, the experience of being in an artists' colony feels quite monastic to me. It feels like an opportunity for concentration, a place where the structures of concentration are provided by the schedule and the architecture and the generosity and effort of others' support. I've been very, very grateful for that over the years.

PEO: *On the surface, it looks as if we are all quite unique in the way that we work, but underneath it seems to me that there is a unifying quality of courage and internal trust that allows the time to develop an idea that moves slowly. Often in my own work, and that of my students, there is a question of how to proceed when you run up against a wall. Would each of you talk about the obstacles and fears that arise when you're working on a project?*

MM: First of all I think that one of the things that has kept me going all these years is my curiosity. The beginning of every process is like jumping off a cliff into the unknown. Doing it is very challenging and terrifying, actually. Sometimes, I think: Why do I keep doing this to myself? You're stumbling in the dark, following a tiny glimpse of something, like a detective paying attention to every clue or hunch. I wrote an article for the spring, 2004 issue of *Buddhadharma* that they named "The Art of Being Present," and after I turned it in, I thought, You know, this sounds a little too rosy. I didn't talk about what happens when you don't have any ideas and when you're having a really hard time, when doubt is taking up almost all of your consciousness. There definitely have been times like that in my life when I think, Well, I've explored everything and I'll never find anything new again. At those times my energy is very low and there is a painful sense of emptiness. Like many artists, I was taught to believe that if I don't make something, then I'm worthless. I struggle with that a lot: the delusion that I'm not worthwhile just as a being; that plain old Meredith is not enough.

I had a period like that in the late 90s. During that time I read *Edge of Taos Desert: An Escape to Reality*, a wonderful account by Mabel Dodge Luhan, a rich society woman born in the early twentieth century, who eventually went to live in Taos, New Mexico. She married a Native American man, Tony Luhan, who was brought up in the Taos Pueblo. She noticed that in the winter, everyone in the Pueblo tiptoed around. They wore very soft moccasins and walked with no sound. The whole place was very silent. People didn't talk much. When she asked why that was, Tony Luhan said that we need to be quiet because Mother Nature needs her rest so that in the spring she can come forth again. That thought was so comforting and inspiring to me. We need to honor those times we think of as fallow because what we think of as empty is really full of potential. So it's important to surrender to those periods of time, to let questions come up, because doubt itself is a kind of blessing that leads to change and renewal. It's really just being able to keep your seat and stay with the difficulty. In retrospect I see that those periods have been transforming. That's something that I try to continue to remember.

JH: Beautifully described. For me, I would say two things. One is that affirming the difficult is a central part of my path. While I would never

have sought out the hard patches and difficult times or the truly devastating times, many of my poems are in fact the evidence of how I deal
with hindrances in my life. I would add, on a more mundane level—
because it's always good to remember the quotidian—that the hindrances to art-making are also sleepiness, laziness, distraction, the
ordinary practicalities, getting caught by the superficialities of the culture. And so, as with the practice of Buddhism in any of its forms, the
struggle isn't just with the obvious difficulties, the struggle is also over
the fundamental question: How do I stay awake, how do I remember
that it feels better not to lead a shallow life? The temptation to fall
asleep in life—that's the real hindrance, for me.

PEO: *It seems that even when you're doubting, you both recognize that this,
too, is your practice, your life, and will develop into your creative outflow at
some other point. I think of Dōgen again, who says that doubt itself is the Way.
Often when I've been with discouraged students, it has been helpful to suggest that even the condition of "stuckness" is itself skillful to investigate.*

JH: I like to remember that the first noble truth—life is suffering—is the
start of the path. Life is suffering, life is difficult, and it doesn't give us
what we think we want and need. Suffering is what puts us on the path.
Hindrance isn't a contradiction to the path, it is the path.

PEO: *On the other hand, tell me what delights you. Tell me about those times
when it does seem worth all the effort and the energy.*

MM: I love moments of discovery, and as Jane said earlier, I have no
idea how they come. Someone will say, "How do you start a piece?" I
actually have no idea. Sometimes even at the beginning, there is a kind
of quickening, and then it's so exciting. Maybe I come upon something
that I've never done before or something that I've never heard before.
Those moments are exhilarating. Sometimes in performing there's a
sensation of total focus, pinpoint focus, and at the same time total
expansion and openness. Nothing else exists, and I am one with what

is flowing through me. That is utter delight, and it can happen alone or with other people.

JH: One of Dōgen's fascicles in the *Shōbōgenzō* is titled, "Total Dynamic Action" *(Zenki)*. To feel the world's ongoing unfolding in such a way, uninterrupted by the narrow self, is one of the greatest pleasures of art-making. As for what else delights me, it's very much what Meredith said, the surprise of discovery. I don't practice an art in order to record something I know. I practice it in order to find what I do not yet know. Another source of great pleasure is the way that art connects us to the whole fabric of existence. Dōgen defined enlightenment with wonderful simplicity as intimacy with all things. I think art brings us to that feeling as well. It isn't possible to make art without a realization of both interconnection and intimacy. If I use the image of a fence in a poem, that fence and I become one. There's no separation between us. Another rather surprising thing that art has brought into my life is a different kind of intimacy—my connection with all of you here, today. How did writing bring the introverted child I was, hiding her poems under a mattress, to intimacy with you? You think you're pursuing a path of solitude, and you find out that it counterbalances your basic nature and eventually allows you to be able to talk to strangers.

PEO: *So how do you find balance in this world we live in now? How do you maintain that creative, nourishing energy at a time when there is war, economic and spiritual deprivation, the spoiling of the earth and air, and much of it at the hands of the very nation in which you live and work? It can be very discouraging. I wonder if you can speak from your creative wisdom, and give us some sense of how you're dealing with these realities and how you see your work as being part of the healing of the world.*

MM: On the practical level, the level of survival, it's very hard right now because we're living in such difficult times, but I truly believe that art has the power to heal. Art provides a template of possible human behavior. We need art so badly right now. And we need to pass it on to young people. I've been doing some performing and teaching in different universities. I try to pass on the value of actually trusting the inspiration that comes to you and acting on it, instead of being afraid or not being interested in anything at all. I've always wanted to keep learning my whole life. How do I share that enthusiasm with my students? How do I encourage them to listen to their inner voices and dreams in a world that commodifies everything and only values what can be seen and, even worse, sold? The alternative to the fear and degradation is a life of being awake. I think that it really does start with education. You don't know what you're missing if you haven't been exposed to it. Young people need to feel that they have the right to know this. Everything is telling them not to ask questions. Everything is about diversion and conformity, just accepting social reality as it is. More and more I feel that what I really can give right now as an older person and artist is encouragement and support for young people to live conscious lives, connecting to the truth of their inner vision, and from there learning to be helpful to other people. I try to rouse the students to go with their creativity, go with their questions. I let them know that they can do it, they're allowed to do it. This doesn't sound like a practical solution to the suffering of the world, but it's like throwing a stone into a pond. The ripples move out and out.

JH: For some reason I'm thinking of something that Chekov said in a letter to his brother: "Our task is to eliminate the last traces of slave nature we carry within us." Their grandfather had been a slave, so the sentence was grounded in literal family history, but I think that this impulse toward an ever-deepening freedom, a liberation, is a task for each of us. It can only happen person by person, one at a time, in the lives and hearts of each of us. Liberation has to be continually refound, each moment, because times come when we are each afraid and all too likely to duck. So my first responsibility to the disastrous condition of the world is to question my own condition. I'm thinking now of the end of Voltaire's *Candide,* where Candide says, "Well, better go home and take care of my own garden." It's difficult to do good work in the world until one is coming to that work from a condition of clarity. Clarity first, then out of that clarity, helpfulness toward others comes.

There is also the matter of our simple and mysterious interconnection. Of the almost 300 million Americans, let alone the 6.5 billion people on this planet, there aren't going to be that many who ever see a poem of mine. It's just not that likely. Yet what can I do except try to speak the truth and hope that whatever ripple effect that might have will do its work. Additionally when I have the opportunity to be in public, I do speak explicitly to these issues. Like Meredith I go to many colleges and work with young people. One thing I do is simply to state that perhaps human beings might find a different way to resolve their conflicts than the one we've thus far been pursuing, to suggest that there must be another way. I'm not offering any answer but planting a question. And in the poems themselves, all I can do is try to formulate a few words perhaps worth hearing and remembering, which convey the values of interconnection, reflection, and peace, and then toss them out into the world. It's not then my responsibility whether they're picked up or not. To make art of any kind is an act of faith, part of which is the willingness to fail in having any effect on the world at all. Buddhism rests on a tripod, as one traditional saying goes, of great effort, great faith, and great doubt. All I can do, whether in practice or in my life as a poet, is sit on that tripod.

PEO: *Both of your responses call to mind the ideal of the bodhisattva. For those unfamiliar with the term, a* bodhisattva *is an enlightened being who chooses to be of service in the world. You both described this bodhisattva activity in the world. You pointed out that we don't know the results of our actions. Meredith doesn't know whom she will affect when she stands on a stage. Someone backstage, someone in the audience, or someone told about the performance, they all may be changed by her work. And Jane doesn't know—a poem is assigned in a class, someone picks up a book at a bookstore, and the waves of effect move on and on. This is Buddhism. Rather than hearing from these two women about how Buddhism affects their creativity or their service, what we've been hearing is that their very lives are what we call bodhisattva activ-*

ity. As they find their truth within themselves, they are sharing it as artists. This seems like the perfect time to hear questions and remarks from the attendees of the conference, the other half of the dialogue.

Q: *For a while, I've been wondering about the balance between egotism on the one hand, and self-assertion on the other. How do we balance humility and being self-focused?*

MM: Ultimately I want my art to be useful. I think that we often believe in the West that art comes from neurosis and torture, so if you're a good artist, you're also a terrible person. Somebody might say, "I'm afraid to do meditation practice because maybe then I will never do art again. I'll never be inspired if I get my neuroses all cleaned up and then I can never be an artist again." That has been proven to be totally false. Life and art are really a matter of balance. To navigate the world takes courage and insight. How do you participate in an enlightened way? How do you actually move through the world with some sense of energy, commitment, and confidence but without causing bodies to fall by the wayside? To do this requires coming up with a new model. I rely on my ensemble, my audience, and the office of wonderful people with whom I've worked for many years. Because I work on large performances involving many people, I need to have that support structure. The office is a very warm place with a lot of laughter and an attentiveness to the humane aspects of being in the world. We try to let the spirit of the work color the way it is presented. We conduct business with the recognition that there is an alternative to aggression. Affirmation is quite different from aggression. Working in the world doesn't have to be violent, and it doesn't have to follow the old principle that if one person goes up, somebody else has to go down. There is enough room for everyone. Also sometimes I have the strange sensation that reality is fluid. Going into things more gently, what looks like a wall suddenly starts melting, and reality starts shifting.

Our world is very compressed right now. We see in history that after a period of compression, there is expansion. When I came up as a young artist in the 1960s, it was a time of incredible expansion—an "anything is possible" kind of mind prevailed. Now everything is quite compressed, but it's clear that one thing you can do as an artist is to continue to have faith in that "I don't know" mind and to share that spirit. From the work that you have done on yourself and the compassion that you have for other people comes the wisdom of your art.

JH: Meredith answered the question quite wonderfully, by addressing the myth that art comes from neurosis and torture. I'm going to address a complementary myth, which is that an awakened person does not have a strong self or a strong particularity to their actions. I know this was something that I as a young practitioner of Zen had to reeducate myself about. If you read Dōgen, you see that there's never been a more idiosyncratic, experimental, wild, and vivid writer. To have a starting place that is not centered in ego does not mean that a person might not have a recognizable, unique, particular, and even—dare I say it?—authoritative voice. When the larger self comes through, it's not going to come through as a vague mist. It's going to come through as a great clarity.

Q: *There's a quality of anger that is wisdom—a fierceness that stands on behalf of anyone being harmed. I wonder if you could comment about any particular challenges you might have faced as women Buddhist artists in letting that fierceness into your art? This seems to me to be a problem that affects us doubly since, as women, we are socialized to suppress our anger, and as Buddhists, we take vows not to be angry. How does being a woman and being a Buddhist affect the way you deal with rage as an artist?*

MM: I remember the first time I heard Patti Smith sing, I was really stunned that a woman was actually publicly displaying anger and outrage and was using that anger and outrage as the primary content of her work. She really made me think. What you are talking about is a sense of outrage about what is going on in the world.

Since I rarely use words, it's hard to address this directly. I think what I try to do instead with my music, is to offer the full spectrum of emotion that is inherent in the human voice. The human voice is a language in itself. It can conjure up and delineate feelings and energies for which we don't have words. Anger and the shades of feeling around anger are definitely fundamental energies. The energy of anger, if used properly, is very powerful.

JH: I think good Buddhists do get angry. For a long time I carried within me the question, What is the emotional life of a buddha? Eventually I came to this answer: If the Buddha happens to be walking around in a human body, that Buddha is going to feel the full spectrum of human emotions, only not in the service of narrow ego. We have evidence for the inclusion of a non–self-centered anger in various traditions. In the Mahāyāna tradition, there's Mañjuśrī's sword; in the Tibetan tradition, the wrathful deities.

When a person enters practice, there's often a real confusion around the question of what relationship we should have with our emotions. Many different ideas about this are in the air, usually not very well sorted through. There's everything from the idea that if you practice well enough the emotions will simply wither away, to the presentation in Tibetan Buddhism of many figures embodying the passions as potential strengths and aids in practice. But to return to the core of your question, which concerns how we speak as women: my whole life, from childhood, whether as a poet or as a practitioner, has been an attempt to move from initial timidity into a greater courage and a greater connectedness with what is. I see no separation between these things. I live in a woman's body; I speak with a woman's voice; I've had a woman's experiences—but I don't actually much worry about that. It's a given. So all I have to worry about is, What am I going to do next? What is the next step, and what direction does it move toward? How can I find the courage to take it?

Q: *You have been a lifelong inspiration to me, Meredith, in the way that you have manifested egolessness throughout your artistic career. You have been able to maintain your artistic vision and integrity even in the face of incomprehension on the part of some critics and audiences, especially in your early years. When I was a graduate student at Harvard University you performed* Education of the Girlchild *at the American Repertory Theatre. Your performance was a momentous and transformative experience for me, but I recall that half the audience left before the end of the performance. This was not uncommon in the beginning of your career because you were making work that was radical in its meditative quality and that required a different kind of attentiveness from the audience. Your courage and stamina in those years before you received critical acclaim has been an enduring inspiration to my own work as a performance artist and as a professor teaching performance art. To me it is the core of Buddhist practice that you have remained unwavering in the face of praise and blame.*

MM: Thank you very much. I really appreciate your comments.

PEO: *How do you handle praise and blame? It's something we all have to deal with.*

MM: I have a friend who said, "You know, it would be really funny if we had a gallery show and everyone put their really bad reviews up on the wall." It would be funny because some of them are really awful —some of the ones that I've had would make your hair stand on end! I usually don't think about this, but I have friends who believe that female artists are sometimes treated differently from male artists in reviews. They have told me that they think reviews of female artists are sometimes more disrespectful or personally vicious than reviews of male artists. Perhaps this is because we are stepping over some perceived boundary, since we are basically doing what we want. Some people react angrily to this. My work also deals with emotions or feelings that some people really have a hard time with. So my work might be threatening to them.

One story I can tell you is about ATLAS, an opera that I composed, wrote the scenario for, and directed. It was commissioned by the Houston Grand Opera, and its theme was exploration as a metaphor for spiritual quest. The main character was loosely based on Alexandra David-Neel, the first Western woman to reach Tibet. It wasn't really a narrative but was more like a poem. I heard that there was a terrible review of ATLAS in *The New York Times*; the critic wrote something like, "Who could possibly be interested in an opera about some woman who wants to be a yogi?" I never read the review since I don't read reviews too often. Either way the words affect you. You can get too attached to praise and too hurt by blame. Either poison can be terrible to have in your mind. Grabbing onto praise is one more way of getting carried away, and attaching to negative words just feeds your neuroses and discouragement. It's hard enough to keep on going, as it is, dealing with the harsh voices in your mind. This is not to say that criticism can't be helpful, but we instinctively know the difference between clear-eyed feedback and vicious attack.

JH: We have egos. We all want to be loved. But that isn't actually the point. I don't protect myself. I let the knives go right through. Although poets, of course, don't get reviewed in *The New York Times* terribly often. So my own ego blows in this way are usually less public than Meredith's. Still, we live with egos. It's part of the animal: we're social animals, pack animals. Pack animals have an exquisitely acute sensitivity to hierarchy and status, to their relative standing in the herd. All you can do is try to be graceful about it.

Q: *When you perform or write, you share your present truth with your audience. But art, like life, is a process, so your own experience of truth is constantly unfolding. How do you balance the feeling of attempting to arrive at a final destination without attempting to arrive there?*

MM: One of the things that I love so much about live performing is that it is always in process. Performance is a temporal art so it always has the potential to change or develop. The piece becomes more and more refined but also more free as we perform it and know more about it. The most wonderful thing about a live performance is that it is always evolving but without any particular destination. The journey is the goal. The audience feels this and becomes part of the journey. It's different if I make films or recordings because at a certain point the form is fixed. There's an internalized pressure to create the "definitive version." It's very hard to change anything once a project is finished because of the demands of technology. And so you sort of have to live with what you did. This is quite different from a live performance that only exists in the moment. That's the beauty and sadness of impermanence. Jane can look at a poem ten years from now and say, "That's what I was thinking at that particular time," but a performance just disappears into the universe, and the only way you can actually examine the development of your aesthetic or your growth as an artist, is to remount it. Sometimes we have done that, but then it becomes a very different piece. The beauty and paradox of live performance is that it never ends really. It's always ongoing.

JH: For some reason, the image that came into my mind as Meredith was talking was of the preserved footprints in Tanzania, found by researchers working under the Leakeys. They discovered an eighty-foot-long trail of two people walking side by side, 3.6 million years ago—by far the earliest trace anyone had ever found of erect hominids. There's a moment where you can see, by what the footprints are doing, that the two had stopped, and the smaller one had turned around and looked back. It's just breathtaking. I feel as if art is like those footprints. We leave them behind as we walk. The living interest is in the next poem—what's the next poem going to be? We live in the gaze, not the footprints.

Q: *This question is more for Jane. There's a movement now among writers toward writing circles, toward bouncing ideas off each other and finding creativity in the sharing of ideas and the sharing of inspiration. I wonder if you've thought about or experimented with that direction at all and what your views are on that way of tapping the wellspring of creativity.*

JH: My personal muse is very, very recalcitrant about taking suggestions from others. Always has been. She's just that way. But most poets in America share their poems with other people for comment before they're published. I'm one of the very few who mostly doesn't. I had the great privilege of going to Emily Dickinson's house yesterday and being left alone for a few minutes in her bedroom. I looked at the little dresser where the bound booklets of her poems were found after her death. Even someone as solitary as Emily Dickinson was part of a family and a community. She put her poems into letters. Her work was part of a conversation, and it was received by others, even if it was only in the private realm. Art is something that joins human beings to one another. It may happen as boldly as all of us sitting in this room together as we are now, or it may be as quiet and unobtrusive as a woman putting her poems into a dresser drawer but writing in one of them, "This is my letter to the world." This conversation, this community, this sangha—all exist in so many different forms and ways and are an essential part of what we do.

PEO: *Thank you, Jane. Do you have any last words, Meredith?*

MM: Oh gosh. Have fun.

Women Changing Buddhism: Feminist Perspectives

A conversation with bell hooks, Sharon Suh, and Karma Lekshe Tsomo; moderated by Susanne Mrozik.

S USANNE MROZIK: *Welcome to our conversation on "Women Changing Buddhism: Feminist Perspectives." My name is Susanne Mrozik. I am a member of the Religion Department at Mount Holyoke College, where I teach courses on Buddhism and comparative religion. I am delighted to introduce our panelists. Well-known visionary feminist thinker, cultural critic, and writer bell hooks is Distinguished Professor in Residence at Berea College in Kentucky. Sharon Suh is the director of Asian Studies and an associate professor of world religions at Seattle University. She writes and lectures on Korean American Buddhist experiences. Karma Lekshe Tsomo is an associate professor at San Diego University, the president of Sakyadhita: International Association of Buddhist Women, and the director of Jamyang Foundation, an initiative to provide educational opportunities for women in the Indian Himalayas.*

This panel explores the diverse contributions that diverse kinds of women are making to Buddhism in the U.S. today. Yesterday Karma Lekshe Tsomo observed that it is "impossible to generalize about Buddhist women's experiences" because there is so much diversity. Before we begin I would like to remind all of us that no one person on this panel, as no one person in this room, speaks for all Buddhist women. Our discussion of the many ways in which women are changing Buddhism in the U.S. reflects the particular perspectives and experiences of those of us sitting on this panel. I will leave time at the end of our session for those of you in the audience to share your own experiences in the form of comments and/or questions.

Let me begin by asking each of you the central question of this panel: How are women changing Buddhism in the U.S. today?

Karma Lekshe Tsomo: It is really challenging to look at all the different ways that women are going about this. Right away, we can note that women are very visible participants in the life of many Buddhist centers and temples in the United States, though their roles are often largely supportive to men. Another way that women are changing Buddhism is in the translation and interpretation of texts for their communities. Two processes are involved here. First, we need to translate Buddhist texts into English—a process similar to one that took several hundred years in China and Tibet. Second, we need to translate Buddhist ideas and practices in ways that are meaningful in North American culture. Whenever Buddhism is introduced to a new land, it is read through the lens of that culture. For example, in the United States we have a long history of philosophy and psychology, so we are reading Buddhism through the lens of Descartes, Freud, Jung, Einstein, and so on. My concern is that we read Buddhism authentically and not begin adapting too quickly before we have sufficiently understood the original texts.

Another way that women are changing Buddhism is by taking leadership roles. Here I would like to focus on an example from the Vietnamese community. The Venerable Dam Luu arrived in the United States as a refugee from Vietnam with just twenty-six dollars in her pocket. After spending a year in a refugee camp in the Philippines, she landed in San Jose, where she and two monks pledged they would help each other. She collected garbage on the streets of San Jose and gradually built the magnificent Duc Vien Temple, where she began to educate a generation of young nuns as well as the Vietnamese lay community. Now, on any given Sunday morning, three hundred members of her congregation gather together to study and practice the dharma. When I gave a talk there a few years ago, I was really impressed by how well educated this community of practitioners is about Buddhism. We were able to discuss Madhyamaka philosophy on a very deep level because they are real practitioners who study the teachings as well as meditate on them. So, here is an example of a woman who came to the United States without knowing English, with no resources, and yet she was able to make this huge sea change in American Buddhism. Her work is little known outside the Vietnamese community, but I think that she is a very inspiring example.

Sharon Suh: Let me first simply say thank you for inviting me to this panel. It is not everyday that one gets to sit with bell hooks *and* Karma Lekshe Tsomo, so I wanted to just acknowledge that I am really thrilled to be here. In order to answer your question, I need to raise another question: What do we mean by American Buddhism? There tends to be an assumption that American Buddhism is separate from Asian American Buddhisms or ethnic Buddhisms. I would argue that we need to view Asian American Buddhisms as a distinct but nevertheless integral component of Buddhism in America. There has been a long history of invisibility vis-à-vis Asian American Buddhisms. Some of this invisibility is imposed internally since many immigrants do not wish to venture outside of their own ethnic group. There are also many external forces such as language barriers, cultural barriers, and economic barriers that make it difficult for Asian American Buddhist groups to converse and interact with dominant white European American sanghas.

When looking at Korean American Buddhism, we could argue that women are changing Buddhism through increased lay participation. I do not think increased religious activity is a phenomenon unique to Korean immigrants. Many immigrants to this country have claimed that they are more religious in the United States than they were in their home countries. Korean American Buddhists are no exception to this general trend. So we see an increased lay participation on the part of Korean American Buddhist women. Moreover, we see that these lay-women are taking on more leadership roles in their communities. In this capacity they are called *pogyo sa*, or disseminators of the dharma. This title grants them the authority as leaders of the community to transmit their Buddhist tradition to the younger generations. Lay-women thus play a very important role in Korean American Buddhist communities.

Additionally, there are now a number of new Buddhist colleges asso-ciated with Korean American temples, which, in turn, are affiliated with temples in Korea, especially in Seoul. On Friday nights women attend classes in Buddhist studies from eight to nine o'clock. This is after working six or seven days a week. These women are working toward a certificate in Buddhist Studies. I would argue that one of the primary motives behind this practice is the desire to rework or edify the self. You need to be able to have a self before you can actually be selfless. The women that I have met are most concerned with the cre-ation of a sense of subjectivity and the development of self-esteem. When you come to the United States, your sense of identity is dramat-ically altered. Where do you go when things fall apart? For many women, they go to temple to find a community of fellow ethnic Bud-dhist practitioners and to learn how to cultivate a positive sense of worth and value. For example, a woman estranged from her husband might turn to Buddhist practice in order to learn how to interpret her difficult marital relationship in light of the Buddhist doctrine of karma. Because of my interactions with these laywomen, I have learned that the value of Buddhism comes from its ability to help people come to terms with everyday struggle. These women are less concerned with becoming selfless than they are with reworking the self. If we take the concerns of Korean American Buddhist women seriously, we see American Buddhism in a new way.

bell hooks: I think first about how Buddhism changes women—that comes first. I shared last night my own confusion and how Buddhism has helped me to center. It is after Buddhism has changed women that women Buddhists are able to have a powerful impact in the United States. I recall Thich Nhat Hanh speaking about the significance of the presence of the teacher. I have been enormously affected by the presence of Buddhist women—the centeredness, the calm, and the strength they convey. Many of us have felt that here at this conference. Far from taking one into subordination, the Buddhism chosen by many women brings a centeredness, strength, and power of being.

SM: *The panel is subtitled "Feminist Perspectives." I added that subtitle knowing that it might be controversial because certainly not all Buddhist women—and perhaps not even the majority of Buddhist women—define themselves as feminists. Therefore before we can discuss how feminism is influencing Buddhism in America, we need to begin with a more basic question: Who identifies as a feminist? Do the women you know in the communities in which you participate define themselves as feminist? Why or why not?*

SS: In many ways I am frustrated by what I still perceive to be a very monolithic sense of feminism in America. Last night bell hooks spoke about moving beyond dichotomies and dualisms. I do not think we do that when discussing feminism in the West. I find this frustrating because when I teach "Buddhism and Gender" courses to my students, they have such a tendency to polarize East and West. They often assume that the East is so heavily influenced by Confucian values that women are, by necessity, oppressed. I always urge my students to try to reconceptualize what they mean by power, resistance, and a positive sense of self. If you were to ask the women that I know in Korean American communities whether they consider themselves feminist, they might respond by saying, "Why are you asking me this question?" On the other hand, if you were to sit and really discuss the issue with them, it would be apparent that there are many ways in which women conceive of their practices as being directly aimed at cultivating a positive sense of self.

We need to open up our definition of feminism to include the experiences of people that have ordinarily been considered "other." I do not think that many Korean American women would explicitly call themselves feminists. But they have the same experience of limitations and the same desire for equality as those who call themselves feminists. There is more than one way of being powerful. There is more than one way of resisting power hierarchies. There is more than one way of cultivating a positive sense of self. I have observed that women often tacitly resist power from behind the scenes instead of challenging it directly. My students want to see women fundamentally altering social and institutional structures. That level of change is not helpful for many immigrant women. If you come to the United States and you do not speak English, you do not have a lot of social resources outside of your own community. It does not make sense to try to completely alter certain patriarchal structures. It is more important for these women to learn how to resist power and create change in ways that are meaningful to them without disrupting social structures like family or institutional structures like the temple.

The Korean American Buddhist women that I know don't meditate. Sometimes meditation is a luxury. When you work 24/7 and you have a family, it is very hard to find the time to meditate. Therefore devotional practices such as chanting and prayer become more important. Women go to temple to perform these devotional practices. Coming together in community for devotional practices gives women the support to tacitly resist power from behind the scenes. One of the most interesting things that I experienced was sitting with women in the Diamond Sūtra Recitation Group. This is a completely lay-centered group of women who get together to chant Buddhist scripture. The chanting helps to cleanse and purify the mind. The chanting group, however, also creates a space for resistance by creating an intimate setting in which women feel comfortable, for instance, to poke fun at their husbands. I remember one night sitting and watching women make tortillas to feed everybody after the service. As they rolled their tortillas, one of the laywomen said, "You know the Buddha teaches us that we should look at all beings as if they are the Buddha. Okay, so, incorporating teachings of buddha nature. But, when I look at my husband, I can't imagine that the Buddha would look as bad as that." That was a very funny moment, but it was also a very telling moment. It shows us that our assumptions about the compliance or submissiveness of these women are wrong. These women are part of a community. It is a space that is intimate. It is a space where women can air out grievances and really make certain kinds of changes in the moment. We need to look at these kinds of communities if we are interested in understanding power, resistance, and the cultivation of a positive sense of self.

bh: I prefer the word "agency" to power, precisely because power is such a loaded term. Even in situations of powerlessness, people find ways to assert agency, especially women. All over the world, women are finding ways to assert agency in circumstances that may seem to us to be ones in which they have no power whatsoever. In the United States, Black women in particular often seem to be engaged with critical consciousness and feminist practice prior to coming to Buddhism. Many of us are coming, as I was, from fundamentalist Christianity. The very agency that allows you to move from fundamentalist Christianity to even thinking about Buddhism is in a sense a feminist practice. Although many of you laugh with me when I tell you that my mother says, "Buddhism is satanic," she really believes that. She believes that the devil and the Buddha are one. I teach at a Christian college. I live in a fundamentalist Christian environment, and in that environment, very unlike New York City where I also live sometimes, Buddhism is not cool or chic. It can be dangerous to talk about Buddhism in certain contexts. How do we have a working Buddhism, a lived Buddhism, in a context that is actually very, very hostile to the presence of Buddhism? Almost all the women I know, but particularly the Black women I know in fundamentalist contexts, come to Buddhism in part out of a courageous feminism. This feminism empowers us to stand with a tradition that is perceived to be so far away from what many think of as the more organic or fundamental "Black" experience.

KLT: Someone defined feminism as the radical view that women are fully human. If that is the case, then I think all Buddhist women in North America would support that. Many of them do not use the word "feminism," especially in the Asian and Asian American Buddhist communities. Even in the non-Asian Buddhist communities, I do not find very many women defining themselves as feminist, although I believe most of them are. This raises a number of issues. It is certainly true that there are certain areas of responsibility where women exert their agency, and one of them is the kitchen. The kitchen in most Buddhist temples of all types is completely a woman's realm. Except for some Zen centers, in this realm women are in complete control. In Theravāda communities, the monks are completely dependent on women for life, for food. And the monks respect women's competence and appreciate their support. Tibetan monks can cook, but most monks of other traditions cannot, so they are completely dependent on, and grateful to, the women who support them. The agency that women exert in this role is very, very important and not to be taken lightly.

Another example is women's financial competence. In the Theravāda tradition, the nuns are not fully ordained and are therefore subordinate to monks, but the flipside is that they can handle money. Ironically, in Theravāda temples nuns often handle donations on behalf of the monks, who are not allowed to touch money. In the Theravāda custom, the laypeople pin dollar bills to a money tree and offer them to the monks. Out of hundreds of people, the nuns are trusted by the whole community to handle this huge bag full of cash, which is very empowering. Outsiders might understand this very differently, but in these small ways, women are empowered and deserve respect for the important roles they play in the smooth functioning of the temples.

North American Buddhism is generally very lay oriented, which is a new direction for Buddhism. Except in Japan, the ideal has always been to have a class of celibate religious specialists who dedicate their full time and energy to Buddhist learning and practice. The only model we have for lay Buddhism is Japan, where most male priests are married, and the temples have become hereditary. The eldest son inherits the temple and is expected to become a priest, even if he is not interested. This model of lay Buddhism needs to be scrutinized very carefully. The introduction of Buddhism to North America is still in process and is constantly changing. Whereas in the beginning the orientation was very much toward lay Buddhism, we can already see a change, with many women becoming interested in ordination.

SM: *Do women practice differently from men? If they do, how are these differences evaluated by the women themselves and by their communities?*

bh: When I reflect on that question, what comes to mind is that people often practice according to their circumstance. Let's say that as a young innocent female Buddhist, I was actually being preyed upon by patriarchal Buddhist men. That's a very gendered reality for many, many young women entering into communities where there are older male teachers. We do not talk enough about this particular gendered experience. How do you deal with inappropriate behavior when you adore a teacher? I remember the awe I felt when I first met a highly esteemed male teacher. I just felt that the teacher could ask anything of me. You would want to give anything to the teacher because you are so in awe of him. You are so humbled. So how do you cope? Practicing Buddhism has to focus on a balance between the will to subordinate oneself to a teacher and the will to protect oneself as well. This is especially the case for young women when they first enter into a patriarchal context in which there are male teachers. I remember years ago that I feared going to Naropa and meeting Chögyam Trungpa because I had heard many stories of seduction and power. I was really frightened that in such a context I would not be able to resist someone saying, "Come do this, do that." How do you find balance? Now as I look back at myself when I was seventeen, eighteen, and nineteen years old encountering many, many male predators, I see that I was often uncertain about what to do. What was really useful then was being aware that they were predators and, in many cases, staying away from them. In the future, we will have much more awareness of the need to create varied contexts for practice. How can you fully surrender to the presence of a teacher if you fear exploitation? We may need different kinds of settings for people who are younger because the mixed gender situations carry this possibility of sexual predation and threat.

KLT: For many women of my generation, part of the shaping of our feminist consciousness was resisting seduction attempts. Even nuns sometimes encounter these problems. Unfortunately some women are unable to resist the temptation to become "special" by entering into a sexual liaison with an idealized figure who heads a temple or dharma center. Male teachers who travel are also vulnerable. Some take advantage of their elevated status to seduce women, whereas some are the objects of seduction attempts. At one dharma center, we had to post guards outside the door of a certain teacher all night to protect him from unwanted advances. The Buddhist precepts are very clear about avoiding sexual misconduct, but unfortunately it is quite common, and it is a two-sided equation.

In this connection, another way that women are changing Buddhism is increased transparency. This is a very delicate issue, because right speech is a central Buddhist principle and Buddhists try to avoid revealing others' faults. At the same time, we need systems or structures to alert people if a teacher is not reliable. For example, if an attractive young woman says she plans to do a retreat with a particular teacher who is notorious, how can we alert her to the problem without being accused of gossip or wrong speech? Of course, some might say that speaking out about dangers like this is right speech. Nurturing women as dharma teachers is obviously one solution to the issue of sexual predation, since happily there have been few, if any, scandals involving women teachers. Increased transparency, new leadership styles, and new organizational structures are all ways that American women are helping to change Buddhism.

In my experience, North American women practicing dharma are generally very sincere. In addition to intellectual curiosity, they approach Buddhist practice genuinely, from the heart. But because women take a disproportionate share of responsibility for organization, translation, communications, food preparation, public relations, and other support functions in the temples and dharma centers, they often do not have as much time as men to study. This is a pattern that I see repeated again and again. Women deserve support to develop as teachers. A person does not become a qualified Buddhist teacher overnight. In the Tibetan tradition, becoming a teacher requires at least twenty years of intensive study and practice. Sincerity and meditation alone are not enough. We cannot teach what we do not know—we need to think in terms of nurturing a generation of women, so they can evolve as fully qualified teachers.

SS: I have found that practice is highly gendered in Asian American Buddhist temples, as I report in *Being Buddhist in a Christian World*. There is no question about it. The space itself is always gendered. Women are on one side. Men are on the other side. But there are always so many more women than men. Often it is said that religion is women's work. I have always wondered why this is the case.

Men and women have very different conceptions of practice. Whereas women perform devotional practices at the temple, men rarely come to the temple. I used to ask women at a particular temple in Koreatown, Los Angeles, where I spent two years working, "Where are the men?" They told me, "The men are off playing golf," or "Men are working a lot so they probably do not have very much time off to come to the temple." I would ask, "Why are you here? What does Buddhism mean to you?" The women told me, "Buddhism is about finding and knowing my mind. Knowing my heart." In many Asian traditions, the idea of separating your heart and your mind does not make sense. The terms themselves are literally mind/heart *(maйm)*. Women perform devotional practices at the temple in order to transform their mind/heart. I also asked the men, "Why are the men not at temple? Why are there so many more women?" The men told me:

> Well, you see, men don't believe in praying for help to solve their problems. Life is difficult and exhausting, so in order to comfort their minds, men will go off on their own to get rid of stress by drinking. But a woman cannot let go of stress like a man because it looks bad in our culture. So women look to religion in order to alleviate stress, and they seek out programs for support. Men are not dependent and so don't rely on others. They don't think about going in front of the Buddha and begging for things. Women can do that because they are more sensitive, where men are more intellectually oriented. If you want to have a lot of men come to temple, then you have to have a program that matches men. A more rational program. Then the men will come.

According to one woman, men were too arrogant and too embarrassed or proud to come to the temple for devotional worship. Another woman told me:

> You see, men like my husband tend to practice religion through the intellect by studying the Buddhist teaching. But I don't think that is enough. Men think that they are too good to bow down to the Buddha or look like they are too attached to the Buddha, especially in the company of women. So a lot of times, men may pray at home, but they certainly won't in front of others. As for me, my personality is best suited for prayer and for focusing on finding one's mind.

Clearly the perceptions of male and female practices are very different. Men tend to view women's devotional practices as being associated primarily with the body: Bowing down with the body. Putting the hands together in prayer. They associate these kinds of practices with a less authentic version of Buddhism. They associate authentic Buddhism with the intellect. As one man put it, "Buddhism is about awakening to your buddha nature. I do not have to be in temple for that. Anywhere you go is the seat of enlightenment. I can sit in my car while driving to work. I can be in my office. I do not need the temple." For many men the main form of practice is meditation. They regard meditation as an intellectual practice and value it more than prayer, which they regard as too devotional. Interestingly, the image of the ideal Buddhist self espoused by men seems to parallel Confucian models of maleness. The ideal male in a Confucian culture is a male scholar. How do you cultivate a positive sense of self if you are a man who has come to the United States in search of the American dream and that dream eludes you? One way to do that in a Buddhist context is to equate the ideal Buddhist self with the ideal Confucian male: the male scholar, the head of the household, the independent and powerful figure in the family.

Women acknowledge the fact that their practice is different from men's. In fact, they embrace this difference. For them, devotion is a much more powerful means of reworking the self than meditation. For example, devotion helps women to let go of attachment to a sense of having been wronged by their husbands. Devotion helps them to let go of these negative thoughts, feelings, and self-images. In the end, devotion is really about letting go of ego, that is, letting go of limited and limiting conceptions of the self. For these women, letting go of ego is something that can only be done by bowing in front of the Buddha.

SM: *Everyone on this panel is a college professor. How do your own experiences as Buddhist practitioners and as members of different Buddhist communities affect your teaching and your pedagogical goals? Does your engagement with Buddhism spill over into the classroom?*

KLT: I teach Buddhism and world religions to undergraduates and comparative religious ethics in a graduate program at the University of San Diego, a Catholic institution. In all my classes, I try to incorporate feminist perspectives at every opportunity. I also include special units on religion and gender, Buddhism and gender, and women's human rights. I raise issues of the construction of gender, social justice, and sexual orientation continually. We discuss gendered images of God and human perfection, the story of the Buddha hesitating to ordain women, leadership opportunities for women in religious communities, and similar topics. Every semester, I require the students to visit two places of worship in the community. Whether they visit a temple, mosque, or synagogue, I encourage them to take note of the roles women play and to compare them to those played by men. When students come to discuss possible field research topics, among other suggestions, I recommend a critical analysis of women's roles in religious institutions. These are some of the ways I bring gender issues into the classroom.

bh: I think it is important to consider the impact the presence of powerful Buddhist women teachers will have on males devoting themselves to those teachers. To what extent will this reality change the nature of conventional gendered structures within Buddhism? I do not hear men expressing the same kind of adoration for women teachers that they have expressed for powerful male teachers like Chögyam Trungpa or Thich Nhat Hanh. At the same time, I see tremendous movement right now in terms of the emergence of strong women teachers like Pema Chödrön. To what extent will that begin to alter our perceptions of the teacher?

Last night after my talk, I had a big discussion with a group of women about the whole idea of being transgendered. There was a confusion in our conversation because some people speaking didn't make a distinction between nuns and monks. They saw all robed people as monks. We talked about the whole visage of gender identity being wiped away to some extent by the absence of the demarcations that usually signify gender in the Buddhist context. Many of us have had the experience of being on retreat, or being somewhere where you could not easily tell the gender of the teacher in the same way. I wonder what impact this moving beyond gender will have on Western Buddhism. Here we are talking about the experiential place of learning, which is different from the place of words. It is really exciting to begin to think about a movement beyond gender where women can be powerful teachers and be recognized as women, but the fact that they are women is not the central reason that we go to them. We go to teachers because of the power of their presence and the power of their capacity to transform our understanding, not because they are male or female.

SS: In terms of pedagogy, I teach classes at Seattle University, which is a Jesuit university. I begin all of my classes—Buddhism and Gender, Introduction to Buddhism, World Religions, and Asian Religions—with a chapter on the study of non-Western cultures from Martha Nussbaum's *Cultivating Humanity: A Classical Defense of Reform in Liberal Education*. All students at Seattle University are required to take a theology course. They often want to take my classes because they think we will cover traditions that are the exact opposite of what they have experienced. Therefore I try to de-exoticize Buddhism for them. For example, some of my students come into my classes with an assumption that Buddhism is a world-renouncing religion. They imagine Buddhists seated alone on top of a mountain meditating. I teach my students that Buddhist practice is about everyday life; it's not about transcending everyday life. The challenge is to maintain mindfulness in the midst of the chaos of everyday life. I try to get my students to understand that Buddhism is lived experience. That means that it is full of trouble, it is full of suffering, and it is also full of great joy. I think a lot of my students assume that when Buddhists transcend suffering they also transcend happiness. I tell them that most of the monks and nuns I know are actually very happy people. They are not completely depressed. Students get very caught up in the First Noble Truth, which states that "life is suffering." I tell them, "Life is not suffering, but in life there is suffering. So what are you going to do about it?"

I also incorporate a lot of ethnography. When I teach my students, I always say that if you want to know what Buddhists are thinking, you have to ask them. You cannot read about them. You have to ask them. Then the exoticized Buddhist out there becomes the person right here. I also encourage students to move beyond sole reliance on texts. I think we have highlighted texts to the point where we have completely over-looked material culture. Students become so much more knowledge-able when they understand that the active presence of women does not just have to be in a text. For example, we can look at the material con-tributions *(dāna)* women traditionally make to monastic communities in order to see how vital their role is in the maintenance and transmis-sion of the dharma. I encourage my students to look for women where they are and where they have been historically, not where they have been historically excluded.

bh: I'd like to add this to Sharon's point about Buddhism and transcen-dence. I'm very obsessed this year with equanimity and balance. I believe that what is exciting about Buddhism right now is both its grounding in reality and also its transcending of everyday reality. I want us to acknowledge that we can hold onto both things. There is a very grounded bell hooks engaged in ordinary life, but there is also a bell hooks who spends a tremendous amount of time in contemplation and in silence, which is about transcendence. The practice of moving beyond dualism and either/or models requires that we open up a space where we can sense that we can have both—a practice addressing everyday reality and a focus on transcending this reality. I do not have to choose one over the other. I can embrace the totality of being in which there are moments of groundedness and moments of transcendence.

SS: That is a very helpful insight. When I look at Buddhist practice and the circumstances of a lot of women, I see the desire to have these moments of transcendence, but at the same time I see so many difficul-ties in terms of achieving such moments. Many of us are struggling to find time for mindfulness and contemplation. *I'm* struggling to find that time. Mindfulness and contemplation are the carrots that are constantly held in front of me. I sometimes think, There is no way I could really be a Buddhist because I do not have the time to meditate. My meditation is the two minutes before I go to bed.

I also believe that we need to spend more time examining the role of devotional practices in overcoming suffering. The women I know are not trying to find time to meditate; their focus is on going to temple to pray. What I want to do in my work is to place devotion on an equal footing with meditation. We do not focus enough attention on devotional practices when talking about Buddhism in America. But these practices are the core practices of many—if not most—Buddhist women in this country.

bh: Maybe we have to think differently about those two minutes. Maybe we have to see those two minutes as just as valuable as two hours or ten hours. Those few minutes may be very precious if someone is struggling with overwhelming everyday realities. Those two minutes of meditation or devotion may mean more than when someone is free to give ten hours.

SM: *At this point I would like to open up the conversation to our audience.*

Q: *This is a question for bell hooks. Could you say more about your experience of practicing Buddhism within fundamentalist Christian communities?*

bh: An important text for me has always been *The Raft Is Not the Shore*—the conversation with Thich Nhat Hanh and Daniel Berrigan—because it gave me a framework for talking within Christianity about Buddhism and for drawing from both traditions. If we study the work of Thich Nhat Hanh in the last ten years, we see how he constantly recognizes the power of Christianity within this nation. He shows us that there are parallel teachings within Buddhism and Christianity. It is in these parallel teachings that fundamentalist Christians are more able to hear a Buddhist perspective. Christianity becomes defamiliarized because lots of everyday Christians assume that Christianity is the only religion that has thought of certain things. So simply sharing with people texts, ideas, and stories has been very useful in a fundamentalist Christian context. Often my students really are resistant because of their fundamentalist Christianity to any challenge that they be radically open. As a consequence of being raised in a fundamentalist Christian context, I can set my knowledge of the Bible alongside Buddhist texts and Buddhist ways of thinking. Addressing commonalities is a useful intervention.

Q: *Do you find that the nature of the students in your classroom changes how you teach Buddhism?*

KLT: I definitely think you have to read your audience. Teaching at a Catholic university, most of my students identify themselves as Catholic or unaffiliated, and a few are evangelical Christians. When I introduce Buddhist meditation, to make them feel more comfortable, I always say, "If meditation conflicts with your religious beliefs, please think of it as stress reduction." Also, as bell said, drawing parallels between the traditions in terms of contemplation, ethics, social issues, and compassion is very, very helpful.

Q: *Concerning sexual predation, I wonder if you can comment on how Buddhist monastic regulations (vinaya) can fail so completely in some situations and how in other situations they sometimes succeed in protecting people. Perhaps even a little more broadly, could you comment on what the point of monastic discipline is for American women practicing Buddhism?*

KLT: There is definitely a place for monastic practice in American Buddhism. In this respect, I would like to stick up for the tradition. In any society, there will always be some people who are naturally inclined to a contemplative life and are not interested in family life, so it is good to have monasticism as an option for that kind of person. The monastery is designed to be a safe space—a place where people do not have to think about issues of appearance, sexual attraction, and sexual predation. In the Buddhist teachings, certain passages say that when you see a monk, you can feel safe and at ease because you know that he is not going to hit you—or hit on you.

Of course, to be a celibate monastic is not easy, especially in contemporary society. It is always a bit sad when someone leaves the monastic life, but it is not surprising, considering all the temptations of modern society. Monastic life represents an alternative to hedonistic, consumerist culture, but it is not easy, so we need to support monastics by helping them keep their precepts. In all Buddhist traditions, there is always the option of dropping out, but as long as monastics wear the robes, they are expected to keep the precepts.

Here it is important to clarify the difference between a monk and a lama. The term *lama* means guru, and *guru* means teacher, especially a spiritual teacher. In all Buddhist traditions, there are teachers who are laypeople. Not all teachers are monks or nuns. There are many monks and nuns who are not qualified to teach, but they live a disciplined monastic life. So we need to distinguish between monastic teachers, who are celibate, and lay teachers, who may be married. The confusion comes when a monk teacher succumbs to temptation and gets involved in a sexual relationship but, instead of honestly returning to lay life, continues to wear the robes of a monastic. Admittedly, it is very difficult to maintain a celibate lifestyle in a pleasure-loving society, unless a person is extremely well disciplined. Many former monks are now working in factories. This is quite sad because they have been trained in Buddhism for ten or twenty years, and there is a desperate need for qualified Buddhist teachers here. But once a monk loses his monastic vocation, he usually either gives up teaching to support his family or falsely represents himself as a monk when, in fact, he has broken the precepts. Sometimes I joke that it is unwise to invite a monk to the West unless he is over seventy and extremely ugly.

In a sense, monastics are transgendered. Nuns are often mistaken for monks. In airports and shops, I am often addressed as "sir," which is only slightly annoying. I remember an incident about twenty years ago in Honolulu, when the nuns were finally allowed to participate fully in a fire *pūjā* with Situ Rinpoche. Afterward I heard two Anglo women saying, "Isn't that disgusting? The nuns are just clones of the monks." Finally we had been fully included as monastics in a ceremony, for the first time, and yet we were misinterpreted as trying to become monks. In some communities in the United States, women monastics prefer to be called monks. But I find this odd because you will never find a man wanting to be called a nun. As a young woman, I always wanted to be a monk, and it took me many years to reconcile myself to becoming a nun. Why do the two terms conjure up such different connotations? Since the term *nun* simply means a celibate female monastic, I think the term is appropriate, and we should embrace it.

There are many perks to the monastic lifestyle. We save a lot on hair-styling and shampoo. We do not have to worry about what to wear in the morning, since we wear the same thing everyday. Our time is our own, and we have very few distractions. We have complete freedom to practice dharma morning, noon, and night. Of course, monastic life is not for everyone. It requires discipline, commitment, and hard work. It is important to clarify that monastics do not consider them-selves superior to laypeople. I hope we can dispel this notion once and for all. Monasticism is simply a chosen lifestyle. It is not an attempt to assert power or superiority over anyone. Nuns often face great hardships and also humiliation. It is a great practice in developing humility.

bh: Could we talk a little bit about the eroticization of the teacher? We brought up the issue of predation, but it is also the case that often a good student wants to be special. I would say my students eroticize me way more than I have ever considered them erotic. I feel that in the future, visionary pedagogy, which includes a focus on spiritual prac-tice, will make a place for more evolved discussions about the power of the erotic and what to do with it. I have tried to write about construc-tive uses of erotic energy in my teaching books. Part of what has hap-pened in monastic and other cloistered settings, is that our denial of the erotic leads to negative transgressive sexuality because we are pretending it does not exist. Therefore we cannot address sexuality even when it so clearly exists in the form of predation. We must come up with other forms where we can express the radiance of that attraction because there is a tremendous, tremendous attraction to the teacher that is eroticized. I like to think of that attraction as energy and fuel that can be used to strengthen spiritual practice. We cannot do that if we deny its existence or if we want to define it as bad, rather than thinking of it as a force that can strengthen us, that can be part of devotion. I think that is very, very hard, particularly here in the United States where almost all our ways of thinking about sexuality and desire are patriarchal and spring from dominator culture. Although it is very hard to honor erotic energy and to see it as potentially constructive, this is the task of visionary feminist thinking for the future, both in terms of spiritual practice and the culture as a whole. How can we remap sexuality and the erotic, so that that tension between teacher and student can in fact be seen as a powerful, useful tension and not an occasion for shame, grandiosity, or exploitation?

KLT: What I think you are talking about is the charisma of a teacher. Why is it necessarily sexualized? Why does it have to be eroticized? Why can it not just be a genuine warmth and spiritual power?

bh: That is like the little kids asking me why are we different colors. That is a really hard question because I do not know where that desire to grasp, to touch, to move beyond simple appreciation of the charisma comes from. I don't know why it is eroticized. Does anyone have any ideas?

Q: *I think it is because we're born into this human body and sexuality is part of who we are. Often women and men, but especially women, come to a practice when they are searching to find out who they are. And they do this right when they are at the height of their sexuality, when it's very easy to be seduced by a teacher. I've seen an effort, at least in my lineage, to reeducate the* *senior men and women so that we recognize the importance of transparency. We've recently gone through a case of sexual predation in our sangha. This particular case did not involve a young woman, so it is also important to realize that anyone can be the target of sexual predation. It can happen when we come to a community and are unsure of ourselves and have low self-esteem. I agree with bell hooks that we need to remap erotic sexual energy. Sexual predation is often just about the desire for approval. Men want approval too, but it usually doesn't play itself out in the same sexual way.*

Eroticism necessarily gets expressed in teacher/student relationships because opening up to our conditioning as sexual persons is part of the process of awakening. The challenge for us as teachers is to see this as part of an unfolding process in which there is the potential for shifting from a personal attraction to the teacher to feeling the passion of being alive in the moment. We need to understand that erotic energy is part of the process of awakening, but as a teacher I think it is incredibly challenging not to personalize this energy. It is extraordinarily difficult to keep holding that boundary.

When we point out sexual misconduct we are using right speech, not wrong speech. We must come together as women to support each other and to find ways to create a context for speaking about sexual misconduct. As elders, we should warn younger women in our communities that this can happen. We need to develop the language to speak to each other about sexual misconduct, so that we can educate each other, educate monks, and educate men about this erotic energy. So that leads me to this question: What can we bring back from this conference to the men and women in our communities in order to change these communities?

KLT: In addition to everything that has been said yesterday and today, which I fully support, I would also ask you to think about the children, the younger generation. If we do not create programs for children, we may not have a next generation of American Buddhists, so those are my words of advice.

SS: Thank you for saying that. This is a huge issue. What do we do with the children? How do we incorporate the children into Buddhist communities? I picked up *Buddhist Women on the Edge* before coming to this conference. So much in there is exciting to me. But some of it also worries me. One article in the book suggests that in America we spend far too much time and energy on work and family and not enough time developing the kinds of practice communities that contribute to a sane life. I'm hoping that you take home to your communities an understanding that a Buddhist life can also be worked out within the context of family, and that this life can be sane. There are many Buddhist communities such as Vietnamese, Chinese, and Korean that are losing their children. The children are not coming to temple because they are being increasingly Christianized. Let's face it, Christian organizations often have a monopoly on college campuses in terms of recruitment. This is a particular challenge for Asian American communities. So we have to figure out what to do with the second, third, and fourth generations of children, especially since they may not speak the language of their parents and first-generation monastics. There is a huge group of children that are being lost or that are going to churches. The question is, how do you retain them inside the community or the sangha?

bh: I like the idea that we start where we are. All of you know your communities more intimately than any of us. Only you will be able to decide what will be useful for you to bring back to your community. This is your visionary challenge in the present moment. We cannot say what would be useful for your community. I feel that in my community, which is so deeply a small Christian community, there is at times a competition between Buddhism and Christianity. So I turn to the contemplation and practice of equanimity. I encourage folk in my community to see that we can have Christianity and Buddhism. We can have both. Whenever we ask people to give up something, there is a violence in asking them to do that. Rather than seeing Buddhism and Christianity as opposed, rather than thinking we must choose between one faith or another, let's focus on connections, on codependent arising. This allows for interdependency. As I said last night, I read my Bible, and I pray every day. I meditate. I read Buddhist texts. I feel we're too

Just Power

Helen Tworkov

I MAGINE LEAFING through a pamphlet or perhaps a monthly magazine and coming across a guide to good behavior with advice that included the following:

Put on an ever-smiling countenance.
Do not move furniture and chairs noisily.
Do not open doors with violence.
Take pleasure in the practice of humility.
Always strive to learn from everyone.
Speak with moderation, gently.
Express yourself with modesty.

For many contemporary Westerners the assumption that this advice was intended for women probably runs so deep as to go undetected. Maybe your imagination has already leaped ahead to the idea that this could be a list of idealized feminine virtues of the Victorian era; or a set of guidelines for prim boarding-school girls of the 1940s; or perhaps a compendium of traits that the feminists of the 1970s rejected in favor of male behavioral models. But in fact, these behaviors were extolled in *The Way of the Bodhisattva*, a seminal text by the great Buddhist sage

Shantideva, and delivered to his fellow—all-male—monastics at Nalanda University in eighth-century India.

Throughout Buddhist history the enlightened masters have advocated behavior—such as the quintessential bodhisattva ideal of putting others before oneself—that progressive women today can easily associate with a legacy of oppression. And yet, with the world in such perilous straits, and in light of recent patriarchal and god-sponsored warfare, these behavioral archetypes have ramifications that, like the teachings themselves, expand far beyond gender. Putting down the cultural baggage, however, is easier said than done.

A thirteenth-century Zen teaching points to how the mind variously refracts the same object and offers us a way to approach this issue:

> First mountains are mountains.
> Then mountains are not mountains.
> Then mountains are mountains again.

This saying, first attributed to Chan master Qingyuan, has itself been refracted through many interpretations and differing doctrinal schemes. In the first line, "mountains are mountains" can convey a conventional view of reality based on accepted, collective, perceptual norms. The second line expresses a deliberative remove from convention, in which "mountain" is understood to be a construct of the human imagination, devoid of any independent meaning or existence. In the third line, when once again "mountains are mountains," there remains only the pure, unfiltered view, neither constructed nor deconstructed, beyond acceptance or denial, beyond the duality of relative and absolute.

Using this Zen teaching as a lens through which to view Buddhism's prized attributes—those that many Western women associate with oppression—we first see a mountain of human attributes classically associated in the West with the feminine: gentleness, modesty, speaking softly, humility, equanimity, altruism, consideration, obedience, generosity. With the second line we can deconstruct the cultural reality to uncover the myth of normalcy. Here, we are forced to consider that the cultural ideal has often been a very poor fit with the actual experience of women's lives, that living a life of duty to one's family, husband, and children can be accompanied by tightly harnessed feelings of anger, inadequacy, and humiliation. Here the attributes appear as external masks, so that, say, generosity masks greed, kindness masks anger, obedience masks servility. In this view, not even women embody the so-called female virtues: mountains are not mountains, and women, as defined in the first line, are not women, any more than the traits they exhibit are virtuous. In the third and final line, the mountain appears again to represent the same attributes we see in the first view, but now, generosity is *just* generosity itself; obedience is *just* obedience—with no subtext, no gender, no psychology, and no history. *Just* obedience, *just* modesty, *just* humility—beyond female and male, beyond oppressor and oppressed.

It's important to note that the above traits do not actually lie outside of constructed values and, in this way, do not reflect Zen teachings represented in the third line. Just the same, Shantideva identifies these attributes as those most appropriate for the followers of the Buddha; they are conditioned behaviors allied with taming the ego. By supporting liberation from self-centeredness, they help create possibilities for engaging in the sacred nondual dance of interdependence beyond relative and absolute.

American women have come a long way through hard-won ideological battles and changes in our educational and legal systems. All these efforts have significantly altered the way we live and have increased possibilities for women. There's a lot more work to be done, but I think that we've come far enough to ask ourselves not only how we can increase opportunities but also what we are going to use them for. The commitment to equality without attention to its application threatens to leave us emulating the flawed system we fought so hard to change. The shift that we're seeking is not a lateral gender move from, say, George Bush to Condoleezza Rice, although in some quarters, this is precisely what is happening. Consider, for instance, that the commanding officer at Abu Ghraib was a woman, as were two of the six U.S. soldiers charged with sadistic abuses at the prison. For many of us in the West, the photographs of Abu Ghraib and, in particular, the one of PFC Lynndie England holding an Iraqi prisoner on a leash, reinforce the necessity of rethinking women's strategies for equality; as well, they intensify the need for a whole new experience of what power might look and feel like from an enlightened perspective.

For half a century, in the name of gender and religious equality and values, American women and American Buddhist leaders have beaten a path from the cultural margins toward the center, as if the center itself held the key to the kingdom. At this point in history, to continue in that direction without examination seems foolish, if not dangerously destructive. We're challenged to do no less than formulate another view of power, or to adopt one more consistent with our Buddhist values. Returning to Shantideva, his injunction to remain "like a log" provides an apt image around which we might initiate a discussion about enlightened views of power.

Remaining like a log is not an action the American military would associate with the exercise of power. Yet Shantideva uses the phrase again and again to depict internal strength. For Buddhist practitioners who have struggled mightily to overcome the dominance of ego, "remaining like a log" can suggest new definitions of control, of dominion, and of power.

> When the urge arises in the mind
> To feelings of desire or wrathful hate,
> Do not act! Be silent, do not speak!
> And like a log of wood be sure to stay.
> (5.48)

Shantideva advocates restraint, discipline, and nonreactivity. He speaks of taming, training, and subjugating one's own ego. The invitation in Buddhist practice is to yoke, or leash, one's own mind, not another being.

Considering this nontraditional view of power, it's perhaps not surprising that when Buddhism entered into the margins of American culture, gender played a pronounced role. In the 1950s we see two distinct streams of attraction to dharma: one was almost all male, the other almost all female. We have an intellectual interest catalyzed primarily by the books of D. T. Suzuki and Alan Watts and championed by the Beat poets. But, with few exceptions, this interest did not extend to practice. The Beat scene was pervasively male, and, for all its attraction to Eastern philosophies and its pungent and theatrical critiques of the United States, it enshrined the ethos of rugged cowboy individualism as much as Hollywood Westerns.

At the same time—the late 50s—the first Zen retreats were held in the United States. Photographs reveal that almost all the participants of these first Zen retreats were middle-aged women. Taking the time to sit down, keep quiet, and "do nothing" was apparently a very unmanly activity, despite the fact that of all the Buddhist traditions, Zen strikes many as being archly masculine. But Japanese Zen came packaged with the so-called Zen arts, such as tea ceremony and flower arranging. And in the United States, appreciation for art (not making art—that was male) was considered a woman's domain. The refined aesthetics of Japanese Zen went a long way toward legitimizing Zen in this country and particularly among women. So there was a period when the Beat scene—which definitely popularized Zen—was as solidly male, with its aggressive homoeroticism and its legendary chauvinism, as the Zen retreat scene was female. It would be another few years, and not without the advent of the counterculture, before Zen retreats would have equal numbers of men and women.

The counterculture of the 1960s derived from opposition to the culturally sanctioned Vietnam War. But there was also a division within the counterculture into spiritual and political. The spiritual wing was characterized by, as Timothy Leary famously put it, "turning on, tuning in, and dropping out." A lot of these people, including myself, are those who—if we got lucky—found our way to Buddhism.

Both the political and spiritual wings of the counterculture were characterized in part by defying gender stereotypes. While some feminists experimented with decidedly male forms, the spiritual wing embodied a feminized form. Both men and women who dropped out were wearing long hair, loose, braided, beaded; both genders were wearing jewelry, and the slogan of that time that best encapsulates this feminization was "Make Love, Not War."

From within this sphere of the dropout counterculture, Buddhism began to attract young Americans new to dharma. Rejecting the compromised glory of the Vietnam War, many identified with the Vietnamese (and Buddhist) victims of American aggression. So, in completely monolithic, relative, and reductive terms, the hippie movement, which includes convert Buddhism, looks very feminine compared to the conventions of the mainstream middle class.

Through the 70s, we see the growth of several big Zen centers, and we have the development of the Vipassanā community in Barre, Massachusetts. And by the early 70s, we begin to see an influx of Tibetan teachers. We see equal numbers of men and women students but almost all male teachers and a disproportionate number of men with organizational authority.

I started my own Buddhist studies with Tibetan teachers. Then, in 1981, I moved into the Zen Community of New York, where every morning we chanted the names of our "ancestors," which happened to be eighty generations of Zen patriarchs. What was more subtle and difficult to apprehend was that "the ideal Zen student"—in whatever body, male or female—looked a lot like a classic old-fashioned version of a gentleman's perfect wife.

Particularly in the Tibetan and Zen scenes, you had, more often than not, an authoritative male teacher surrounded by students who were, more often than not,

- Soft-spoken
- Deferential
- Subservient
- Modest

- Respectful
- Receptive
- Smiling
- Willing
- Passive
- Without strong views or opinions

Now, it so happens that we see very similar kinds of behavior in people, and particularly in women, with issues of low self-esteem or with very entrenched neurotic patterns of worthlessness that fit together perfectly with identifying oneself as the servant. And, as it happens, there were a lot of students who, with issues of low self-esteem and/or abuse, were very comfortable with a continuation of certain neurotic behaviors, especially if that meant they were upheld as ideal Buddhist students. This, not surprisingly, became a source of great confusion. After all, we know that the quintessential core of Mahāyāna Buddhism is putting others before oneself. And that historically the quintessential work of womanhood was—and in many parts of the world still is—to put the needs and wants of husband, in-laws, parents, and children first. Thousands of texts present this bodhisattva principle, but to quote Shantideva again:

With perfect and unyielding faith,
With steadfastness, respect, and courtesy,
With modesty and conscientiousness,
Work calmly for the happiness of others.
(5.55)

And so it is that if I want contentment,
I should never seek to please myself.
And likewise, if I wish to save myself,
I'll always be the guardian of others.
(8.173)

We know that to embrace unenlightened female forms may affirm individual and collective patterns of abuse and low self-esteem. If we continue to look at them as expressions of male dominance, then, of course, we will wish to abandon them. Yet to reject these qualities is to reject the teachings of the buddhas. If we trust that they are gender-free Buddhist values, then we may be able to use them to help frame a distinctly different value system.

By the mid-80s, Buddhist women began looking at their own practice centers through the feminist lens, describing women's situations in terms of what we did not have: the absence of authority, the lack of equality. But there was something else going on in the women's movement as it continued a quieter trajectory from the chaos of the 70s through the 80s. Impelled in part by President Reagan's aggressive nuclear arms buildup and Strategic Defense Initiative—dubbed the "Star Wars" defense by the popular press—and by a widespread awareness of environmental devastation, some political voices in the women's movement proposed traditional "female" qualities as critical to pulling the world back from the brink—qualities such as compassion, deep listening, nurturing, serving. They identified the so-called "weaknesses" of women as the very strengths that the planet most needed to survive. Yet while this ideology can infuse a context for change, without an internal shift, and one that goes far beyond the issues of gender, its effect will—and has—remained limited.

Within a decade, young women became openly antagonistic to the feminism of the baby boomer generation. "Feminism" itself became a dirty word, and the feminists of the 60s were faulted for advocating a male value system at the expense of female-identified forms. Rather than engage in literal and symbolic bra burning, young women retained the quest for equal opportunities but dressed up in Victoria's Secret. The quieter feminism of the eighties, which advocated an embrace of female-identified behavior, did not get much play, either. And consequently the very nature of power itself was not questioned. At the same time, the ground for change has been tilled. And the rise of patriarchal fundamentalism and of religious militarism is so untenable that perhaps the time is right to make real shifts in how we understand power.

Perhaps the unmasked politics of fundamentalism, economic domination, and the loathsome consequences of unbridled greed have descended to such horrific lows that, however unwittingly, they can spawn a new story or uncover an unborn dream by which we can navigate the realities of where we are, who we are, and who we wish to be.

Is it possible to imagine that power might be defined by presence of mind; that the more one is no longer controlled by compulsions, addictions, patterns, habits, the more power one has to act in service of wisdom and compassion? What if we said that power is internal freedom, that power is the capacity for choice? Can we—women and men—stand the heat of appearing to be passive, of remaining like a log? Can we imagine, compassionately, that in our society this might be much more difficult for men than for women?

Following 9/11 there was never a possibility of not bombing Afghanistan. It wasn't just the president and the politicians who disallowed nonaction; the mindset of the American people demanded retaliation. I use this example not to suggest that inaction in this particular case would have been a more enlightened strategy but to suggest that "strategy," or any form of intelligent, wise consideration, was made impossible by the blinding thirst for revenge. A primitive, dualistic response—however easy it was to explain—ruled the day. Remaining like a log is not a political position. It is neither passive nor pacifist. Rather, it describes a state of mind capable of making wise decisions, unplugged from the emotional charge of compulsive reactivity. Remaining like a log describes a mind that has options, one that is not merely being jerked around by selfish responses to external circumstances and that can therefore serve a larger reality with clear, cool insight.

In my own experience, Buddhist practice is indescribably difficult. I know of nothing in this world that is more challenging than the Buddha's invitation to an enlightened way of life. I don't think that the actual process of transformation from a selfish, self-oriented, me-first person into a bodhisattva of wisdom and compassion who consistently puts others first is any easier for one sex than it is for another. Yet my hope for all those living on the American sidelines—such as women and Buddhists—is that we use our compromised status to our best advantage; that we capitalize on our experiences and strengths and training to investigate alternatives to conventional views of power. Perhaps it is worthwhile to figure out what it takes—and what kind of power is required—to "remain like a log."

NOTE

All references to Shantideva's *The Way of the Bodhisattva* come from the Padmakara translation (Boston: Shambhala, 2003).

Engaged Buddhism

A conversation with Virginia Straus Benson, Diana Lion, and Eve Marko; moderated by Hilda Ryūmon Gutiérrez Baldoquín.

I AM HILDA GUTIÉRREZ BALDOQUÍN, *my dharma name is Ryūmon, and I have the honor of moderating this panel on "Engaged Buddhism" this afternoon. I would like to introduce the three women who will be speaking with each other for the next hour, after which we'll turn it over to you to join in the conversation with them.*

First, I'd like to introduce Eve Myōnen Marko, who is the cofounder of Peacemaker Circle International with Bernie Glassman. Eve's work in coalition building has taken her to Latin America and the Middle East, working both with project directors and training programs. For ten years, Eve worked with the Greyston Mandala, which is the Buddhist-inspired network of organizations, both for profit and nonprofit, in Yonkers, New York. The work of the Greyston Mandala over the years has provided thousands of children, women, and men with housing, childcare, jobs, job training, and AIDS-related medical services. Anchoring activism in spiritual practice, Eve Marko is a founding teacher of the Zen Peacemaker Order.

Next is Diana Lion. In her roles as both a founding director of the Buddhist Peace Fellowship Prison Program and as associate director for programs for the Buddhist Peace Fellowship, as well as beings a graduate of the Spirit Rock Meditation Center Community Dharma Leaders' Program, Diana brings three decades of experience in the activist arena in the areas of women, human rights, diversity work, farm workers' rights, LGBT issues, and peace work. Born in Canada, Diana's two full paths as a dharma practitioner and a long-term activist meet in her day-to-day work, both as a member of the teaching team of the first Buddhist chaplaincy program in the San Francisco Bay area and also as a certified trainer in Nonviolent Communication.

Next is Virginia Straus Benson, whose work is about cultivating community and taking action at the macro level. She does this in her role as executive director of the Boston Research Center for the 21st Century, which was founded by Daisaku Ikeda, a Buddhist teacher and president of the Soka Gakkai International. BRC is a peace and justice center committed to social change. The programs that the center focuses on involve women's leadership for peace, global citizenship education, and the philosophy and practice of community building. Ginny also brings a depth of knowledge in public policy from working in think tanks, the legislative arena, and the White House.

So, please join me in welcoming these three jewels of the socially engaged Buddhist movement.

I'd like to begin by making a few introductory points on the topic, then each of the panelists will tell you a little about who they are, what they've been doing, and how they got there. Following that, I will engage them in some questions and exchange, and then we'll open it up to questions from the floor.

It's important to name the context within which we are speaking at the present moment. We're speaking here in the United States, and although we've used the word "America" and "American" throughout this conference, we must keep in mind that there's more than one America, and that the subject being addressed today is being addressed from a dominant culture perspective. It's important to call attention to the issue of naming because naming has the power to render some people visible and other people invisible.

The emphasis of Buddhist teachings in guiding and sustaining how we relate to social issues is not a modern phenomenon, exclusively found in this time when we have entered a third millennium of living within systems of oppression and privilege, conflict and injustice, and wealth and poverty. It behooves us to remember that throughout history Buddhist women, our fore-mothers, have contributed to what we now refer to as engaged Buddhism. The contemporary usage of this term was coined by the Reverend Zen Master

Thich Nhat Hanh to fuse Buddhism and activism. So, engaged Buddhism is defined as social action based on Buddhist principles. Thich Nhat Hanh once said, "To speak of engaged Buddhism is to be completely redundant." From his perspective, Buddhism is, by definition, socially engaged. So, let's enter the conversation.

Diana Lion: If I had to encapsulate socially engaged Buddhism in one sentence I'd say that *it's about restoring this world we share to its wholeness*. As women we find ourselves doing this in many different ways. As mothers, stepmothers, grandmothers, aunties, daughters, nuns, activists, healers, artists, academics, poets, farmers, laborers, students, teachers, artists, and visionaries, we heal, we hold, we make whole again. And we're often the ones who make connections. We make connections between each other, between the personal and the political, between ourselves and the greater world, and between ourselves and nature. Izumi Shikibu said it beautifully about a thousand years ago in Jane Hirshfield's felicitous translation: "Watching the moon at dawn, / Solitary, mid sky, / I knew myself completely, / No part left out."

So, what does it mean to know ourselves completely and to leave no part out? I'm thinking about us in this country right now. I always really appreciate it when people remember that there's more than one America (as Ryūmon just mentioned) because I'm Canadian, and whenever I hear the word "America" used to mean solely the United States I wince, because I grew up in Montreal, Quebec.

I'm from a Jewish family, and I'm a practicing Jewish Buddhist. My mother grew up in Quebec City, and she's from the oldest Jewish family in Canada. My dad is a Holocaust survivor. He's from Vienna, Austria. Having a refugee dad meant many things: one was that I was surrounded by people who all spoke foreign (Eastern European) languages when I was growing up, even though I didn't speak any of those languages. To this day I notice how relaxed I feel when I hear Eastern European accents in older people's voices, probably because they sound like my childhood and the background murmur of the other

Holocaust survivors who hung out at our home. I knew from the time before I could speak that you were never supposed to ask a Holocaust survivor what had happened during the war—and that you were always supposed to have a passport ready in case you had to get out in a hurry. I never had to be told that. I just knew.

I grew up in a fractured world. The pieces fell down hard on me personally. Damaged people can damage other people around them, without meaning to, but simply because large parts of themselves are unhealed. It would be many years before people knew about the phenomenon that we now call Post-traumatic Stress Disorder (PTSD). However, that didn't mean it did not exist. It just meant it was not named. That's the naming that Ryūmon was talking about, the naming that makes the invisible visible. So I was surrounded by adult war survivors, and I was affected by that in many different ways. We all know that war is a horrific form of *duḥkha*, and that war does not stop when the bombs stop dropping.

Our house was heavy with secrets, and not just because of the war. My parents were young when they had me; I was their firstborn and only daughter. They had many friends who had survived the Holocaust, and they would spend long amounts of time at our house with us. One of them was my father's closest friend, and he became a favorite among us children. We even called him "uncle." Things became complicated, however, when he started molesting me repeatedly at a young age. He told me not to tell anybody, or it would hurt my parents. This was a secret that I kept throughout my childhood and adolescence. Like any "good girl" with a strong case of internalized oppression, I started acting out instead. By the age of fifteen, I had such an overwhelming sense of shame and loneliness and being trapped that I started fantasizing about throwing myself in front of trains as I crossed the tracks to go to school. I had no one to talk to about the scariest secrets in my life and couldn't see any way out other than ending everything. In school, I was a rebel—basically a really angry young woman.

When I was sixteen, I finally told my mother what was happening, and the good news is that she believed me. But the bad news is that she had no idea what to do. In those days, we didn't even have words to name it. It wasn't until I was in my twenties that I read an article in the newspaper that had the words "molest" and "sexual abuse" in it. I remember feeling an overwhelming sense of relief. I thought, Oh, you mean, someone else has had this happen to them? Then, in 1968, I found the women's movement, which helped me put some of my individual experiences into a broader context and allowed me to feel less isolated, less alone. I also got involved in radical class politics, which laid the foundation for an ongoing progressive political analysis. And then in succession, I found therapy, the dharma, and later, Nonviolent Communication.

In the 1990s, after having gotten years of solid practice under my belt (or tush), I started doing regular prison dharma work with people who had committed murder and rape, among other criminal activities. Sister Helen Prejean, the nun who wrote *Dead Man Walking*, said: "Every human being is worth more than the worst thing they ever did." That single sentiment was powerful and changed me. It spoke to me about myself for one thing, because I've done things I regret. It spoke to me about the people I work with inside prisons, and perhaps most importantly, it spoke to me about the man who had abused me all those years before. Everything in my training was leading me toward holding that value. It was transformative.

Then my younger brother died unexpectedly of cancer. He'd been in remission, but he'd had a recurrence that he hadn't told us about. Our family was stunned and sad. I went back to Canada to be with my family and decided to meet with the man who had molested me. I'd avoided seeing him for many years, but by that time I had done decades of work in therapy and meditation. I went with no agenda, except some curiosity and apprehension. I simply wanted to see him—perhaps to close a circle that remained fragmented within myself. After years of my own work, I no longer needed anything from him, which was a good place to see him from. We spent a couple of hours together, walking around outside on a windy summer day. By this time, he was elderly and much frailer than when I had last seen him so many years before. He seemed much smaller and more stooped. We chatted about a few idle topics, and I remembered our connection from so many years ago. He seemed very tired, and my curiosity was satisfied. It was strange to see this person who had loomed so large in my earlier years: an old stooped frail man.

And then, I don't know why, out of the blue I asked if he had any regrets about his life. I'd come to this meeting with an awareness of the fleetingness of life because my brother had just died, and it was clear that this man's life was going to end soon. He said, "Yes, of course, I have regrets. At my age, we all have regrets." I thought, Yes of course, so true. We kept walking when all of a sudden he stopped and turned to me and said with great intensity, "But you know, I do have one big regret. And that's what I did to you." I stopped, stunned. I really hadn't expected any acknowledgment from him at all. I was too surprised to move, actually. And then he apologized. He poured out how he had seen me as his refuge (and this word choice surprised me), after his terrible war experiences. He hadn't found anyone who could understand what he had gone through. He had molested me out of his need for some place to go for refuge; I guess he thought he could find some comfort and understanding in me. There is no way to know, really. I just listened, like I have done so many times with the prisoners I work with. I started imagining what it would be like to be him: so much loneliness, lostness, shame. I was now able to offer him some compassion for what that must have been like for him.

And in that moment, forgiveness happened. I'm not saying it was in any way okay what he did. Of course it wasn't. Just as murder and rape are never okay anywhere, anytime. Just as war is never okay. But what was obvious to me was that along with the horrible acts he had committed against me, he also had a simple humanity, and that if things had been different, it could have been me in his position, doing what he had done. I don't know. Who's to say what I'd have done after living through the war as he had? The violence that can arise from self-righteousness is not something I want to keep indulging in.

Several hundred wars have been fought on our planet since the end of World War II. When we look closely, we find that on the surface wars are often about land, or oil, or power and control, or financial gain. But wars are *always* at least partly about seeing people as "other." So, by taking a stand against this othering—whether it's about class or race or gender or sexual orientation—we can make peace and continue to reweave the threads of our human connection. And, while we're seeing everyone's buddha nature, we still need to keep our swords of discernment sharp as we decide which policies to support and which to oppose. It's not an either/or situation. Especially now in the midst of a rising tide of fundamentalist policies, I see it as more important than ever to keep seeing each other's potential wholeness. I hope that we will not let any kind of othering get in the way of that.

The women's movement taught us many things. A big one was that the personal is political. The dharma teaches us countless things, including that what we take as personal is not so solid after all. Our experience is very particular and also quite impersonal and therefore universal. Socially engaged Buddhism helps us remember that whatever we do, we all affect each other. It also offers us an exquisitely complex possibility—seeing the beauty of each being's essential nature in all our commonality and diversity, at the same time making wise decisions that support the nourishing of our planet and the freeing of all beings from greed, hatred, and delusion.

On a personal level, a real key to freedom has been given to me by my work with prisoners who have murdered people. They have afforded me many opportunities to remember a person's humanity and at the same time to see their crime without flinching. I'm trying to do that with the current Administration in Washington, D.C. May we all keep holding ourselves and each other accountable, while remembering our wholeness with a tender heart.

Virginia Straus Benson: Diana shared a deeply moving experience about transforming intense personal suffering into healing. As her wholeness emerged through Buddhist practice, she uncovered a mission in life for which her experience uniquely prepared her. Although my background is very different from Diana's, I can relate to the trajectory of her life. In the school of Buddhism I practice, based on the *Lotus Sūtra*, we have a modern term for the beautiful lotus flower as it emerges from a muddy swamp—*human revolution*. Like Diana, I will weave my story of human revolution into my calling in the field of socially engaged Buddhism.

As a child, probably since I was the youngest, I hated the pecking order in my family and was always trying to escape it. I emerged from the rough and tumble of kid life with a nasty case of low self-esteem but big dreams of changing the world—a stressful combination. Too timid for direct confrontation, I loved to lie on my bed and read inspiring novels in which underdogs triumphed.

Rightly or wrongly, I held my father responsible for the survival-of-the-fittest ethic among the kids because in the 1950s we all just assumed the buck stopped with the dad. My father was emotionally distant and had a wry wit. Mother was more outgoing and warm-hearted, a highly educated stay-at-home mom. Why is this woman doing all the housework? I wondered. As the least powerful kid, I was naturally expected to help her the most. I worried, was I walking into a trap—becoming an understudy to a very bright underdog? Not for me! I resolved to make a difference in the wider world. But what would it be? Thirty-six years ago, I dropped out of Smith College in my junior year in an attempt to answer that question. Today, after many career ups and downs, I am finally answering it in a way uniquely suited to heal my middle-class childhood angst.

My early career was spent in government in Washington, D.C. during the 1970s, when I worked as a public policy analyst in the Congress, the Treasury, and then finally at the White House. Inevitably, no matter how good the job sounded at the outset, I always ended up as a gal Friday. All around me I saw men in charge of the big picture—a picture that was not at all rosy or promising—and women saddled with the details. There were more women in the workplace than ever before, yes, but at what level?

Worse, the game was always the same. Republicans vs. Democrats, debate within a closed box, and ineffectual compromise, usually designed to shore up egos. One of my troubling dreams at the time was that I was sitting in the back seat of a car careening out of control, a drunken man at the wheel. I grew tired of helping men at their own game. I wanted to fundamentally change the game. Finally, I gave up on Washington. The necessary change, I concluded, would have to come from the grassroots.

When I left D.C. for New York City in the early 1980s, I began practicing Nichiren Buddhism. One of the books that convinced me to practice was *Choose Life,* a dialogue between Daisaku Ikeda and the renowned British historian, Arnold Toynbee. In reading this book, I felt I was walking into an open space beyond nationalism and Western philosophy, where Eastern and Western wisdom could be pooled to solve global problems. By reading *Choose Life,* I became interested in the potential of applied Buddhist philosophy as a "third way"—or an integrating and balancing force—that could help break through the social dilemmas created by the somewhat arbitrary either/or choices of conventional politics. I dimly perceived the outlines of socially engaged Buddhism, although I was unfamiliar with the term at the time.

At any rate, my interest was piqued by *Choose Life,* and I was ready to consider the daily practice of Nichiren Buddhism. With some hesitation over the time commitment involved, I gradually adopted a daily routine of morning and evening *gongyō.* Meaning "assiduous practice," *gongyō* is the recitation of two key portions of the *Lotus Sūtra* followed by abundant chanting of the sūtra's title, *Nam-myōhō-renge-kyō.* This mantra, called *daimoku,* loosely translates as, "I fuse my life with the mystic law of simultaneous cause and effect through sound."

I was assured by my new friends, the Soka Gakkai members who helped me practice, that world peace could be accomplished through individual change, or what SGI calls human revolution. A bold claim! In contrast to social revolution, they explained, human revolution is a one-by-one inner-directed process of changing negative karma. This shift in one person's destiny then radiates outward benefiting family, community, and workmates. Hmmm, I thought, have I stumbled on the "grassroots change" I was seeking when I left Washington?

During my first few weeks of practice, this deceptively simple chant—*Nam-myōhō-renge-kyō*—worked powerful effects in the depths of my unconscious. An inner drama unfolded. A recurring nightmare, beginning in my youth, featured a violent man who lurked in the shadows waiting to murder me. In the postchanting dreamscape, I didn't run away this time. I faced him, and suddenly out of nowhere a weapon appeared in my hand. I fought him off and won—twice. He never returned.

As I continued to practice during the next ten years, I witnessed many other profound inner changes. I also gradually transformed my relationships with family and friends. This happened largely because I began to master the art of conversation—something I had always wished for. I found that if I could bring my whole heart into a conversation, especially when I was feeling alienated or disempowered, as I had felt growing up in my family, then I could open a path of growth and happiness not just for myself but also for the very people I was shrinking away from.

Still, my career path was riddled with obstacles. By the early 1990s, I was working at Pioneer Institute, a state and local public policy think tank in Boston, where we were commissioning academic studies to help solve local problems. At least the academic approach was less partisan than politics-as-usual and state government closer to the grassroots than federal, but the backers of the think tank still had too much faith in market forces and too little faith in humanity. I wanted to do peace research and explore the directions that Ikeda and Toynbee had laid out in *Choose Life*. At this point, though, peace research was just a dream and a prayer.

Then I was invited to take part in a seminar of leading SGI-USA academics with Mr. Ikeda in Japan. There, I confided in him my wish to help with the East-West dialogues that he had been conducting for many years. Ironically, his answer, though it was "no thank you," led directly to a career change that enabled me to play a key role in the international dialogue effort of the SGI. In essence, he urged me to be successful in my own right. He told me that every person has a unique mission in the world that only she can fulfill. Rather than imitating anyone else, he urged, become a brilliant shining sun in your own field of action.

His encouragement spurred me on to challenge my job situation and take responsibility for my own happiness. As a result, I broke through a glass ceiling I was imposing on myself due to my painful feelings of inferiority in relation to the men around me. I, the woman with the low self-esteem at the crucial moment, stood up with new confidence in myself, engaged assertively with the male hierarchy controlling the institute, and became executive director. This hard-won victory strengthened my backbone and gave me important training and experience for the Boston Research Center when Mr. Ikeda established it a year later and hired me as the director.

One of the first assignments I took on when the BRC was quite new was to write about the so-called "peace, culture, and education movement" of the SGI. This was a good exercise because, from it, I realized how this fledgling institute fit into the larger picture of engaged Buddhism. Of course, I knew that the SGI under President Ikeda's leadership conducts extensive programs promoting peace awareness, humanistic education, and cultural exchange and has done so since 1975 when SGI was established. Affiliated institutions, such as schools, universities, museums, and institutes, carry out various aspects of these programs in the Americas, Europe, and Asia. BRC was a new player added to the mix, the only peace institute in the United States at the time, and we were encouraged to find our own niche in the global movement.

In the midst of this writing assignment, I arrived at some personal insights into SGI's dialogical and educational approach to engaged Buddhism. In short, I believe that SGI is doing what it can to weave together the strands of a worldwide human web. This is SGI's way to speed up the attainment of world peace. President Ikeda must have concluded long ago that in order to fundamentally "change the game"—before we blow each other up—the world needs more than just a whole lot of peaceful Buddhists! People of good will everywhere, whatever their culture or religion, need to connect with one another through heart-to-heart dialogue. This way, the peaceful undercurrents in people's lives have a chance to grow into a collective force capable of shifting the trend of history at the deepest level.

What does the center do to contribute to this process? I want to touch on two of the latest programs of the BRC that I think may interest you. First is the Ikeda Forum for Intercultural Dialogue. We initiated this program last year with the help of two scholars of American Transcendentalism, Ron Bosco and Joel Myerson, who are engaged in a soon-to-be-published dialogue with Mr. Ikeda. The forum series explores points of connection between the American renaissance and Eastern wisdom. The era of Emerson, Thoreau, and Whitman coincides with the first introduction in the United States of English translations of Eastern philosophical texts. Inspired in part by this exchange with the East, the Transcendentalists pioneered a universal religiosity and language of Nature that broke the bounds of narrow religious dogma. By returning to the Transcendentalists and standing in their shoes, we have tried to imagine how we can restore a sense of the sacred to public life today. Can awe and wonder become an antidote to religious fundamentalism?

We've coupled this educational initiative aimed at knitting Eastern and Western thinking together on a global basis with a local counterpart exploring praxis, the BRC Learning Circle on Community Building. This practical experiment brings together seventeen leading community builders from the Boston area to pool the wisdom they have gained from their work among women, Buddhists, and diverse cultural groupings of Asian Americans, African Americans, and Latin Americans to see if they can arrive at a common core of insights into the art of community building. What kinds of dialogue and interactions among people create the best conditions for our underlying interconnectedness to emerge and for trust and cocreativity to grow? Through this hands-on experience, involving a series of circle gatherings over a two-year period, we hope to develop insights that can be shared with a wider public. The overarching goal of the learning circle is to contribute to a shift in U.S. culture from isolation, violence, and war to connectedness, nonviolence, and peace.

In closing my tale of human revolution—turning karma into mission—I'd like to share a brief passage from the poem "Beginners" by Denise Levertov (from her 1982 collection, *Candles in Babylon*). Her words have encouraged me in my work. They evoke the promise of dialogue for interconnectedness, the form of Buddhist social engagement I've discussed today:

> *We have only begun to know*
> *The power that is in us if we would join*
> *Our solitudes in the communion of struggle.*

> *So much is unfolding that must complete its gesture,*

> *So much is in bud.*

Eve Marko: Twenty years ago I came from New York City up to Riverdale, to a place that was owned by the Zen Community of New York. They weren't sitting in meditation that evening. Instead, they were sitting around this big dining room talking about their plans to do something called social action. They were going to work with a shelter in Yonkers, which was three miles north. And cook. But they were also going to start a project to build homes for homeless families. This was 1985. I think by now we pretty much take for granted that Buddhist sanghas do social action. I don't think I know any sangha that isn't engaged in some form of community involvement or action. But at that time, it was really a no-no to do that. Subsequently when I joined and got involved, I can't tell you how many people used to come to our community and tell us we were not Zen. We were not Buddhist because if we were, we wouldn't be wasting our time doing what we were doing on the streets of Yonkers, we'd be sitting in meditation all day. So that's what happened twenty years ago.

As I sat in that dining room and listened, I had a sense that there was something really important happening, and I thought, I want to be part of this. So I jumped in, and six months later I jumped even more and left my work and my home and went to live and work there. I spent pretty much the next ten or eleven years helping to create this whole mandala of for-profits and not-for-profits: building housing for home-less families, an AIDS center, housing for people with AIDS, and child-care centers. I also helped to develop study programs for the Zen Community of New York, which continue to do very well today. The Greyston Mandala still flourishes and helps some twelve-hundred people every year. But in 1996 we left to create the Zen Peacemaker Order, a home for Zen practitioners who wanted to do peacemaking and social action in the world. A few years later, we formed something called Peacemaker Circle International, dedicated to creating networks of spiritually based social activists. Not just networks, but coalitions. And not just coalitions, but circles. This really relates to Ginny's point that we need to learn how to change the game. We had done a lot of direct service—building homes, taking care of kids, taking care of the sick, creating jobs for people. What we noticed is that if we just did this one thing, each of us could only do so much. Even if each of us did a wonderful job, it was still just that one job. Now, how do you take care of the poor? How do you take care of people who have AIDS in Africa when all you can do is just one job? So you need to change the game. Instead of always competing with everybody for money and recogni-tion and all of the politics that NGOs and not-for-profits engage in, why don't we spend some of that energy to start linking—linking and cre-ating a real force for social action that's made up of all of us working together. I believe that this is the new game Ginny is referring to.

If somebody says, "What is Buddhist about this?" I would ask, "How do you define Buddhism?" If it's about awakening to the oneness of life, then this is a real way to do it. Working together is a wonderful way to wake up to this oneness. So we started bringing this work to different countries. We started in Europe. Then we went to the Middle East. And then we started in Latin America.

In the last few years I've focused my energies on the Middle East; we worked in Jordan, Israel, and Palestine—mostly the West Bank because it was almost impossible to get into Gaza. When we started in Israel, there were a hundred and fifty organizations that did work on coexistence between Arabs and Jews. But they never worked together. So we introduced this model of organizing interlocking circles and began planning how these different groups could work together to help each other, instead of working separately.

Key to creating these circles and learning how to work together were the three tenets of our Zen Peacemaker Order. The first was *not knowing*, which meant letting go of fixed ideas. The second was *bearing witness*, which involved really listening to the other person in the circle who's saying something that you think is absolutely crazy. Can you really put yourself in their shoes for a few minutes and just listen and try to see life in their way? This is exactly what Zen kōan study is about. If you can do that, then some real action will emerge, action that's integrated, that comes from all of the voices, not just from one voice or two voices—and that's the third tenet, *loving action*. This is the work that I was supervising in the Middle East.

It was a lot more difficult in the West Bank just because people could not physically come together. It's only a thirty-minute car ride between Ramallah and Bethlehem, but with all the checkpoints, you were lucky if you made it in a day. When we had training sessions people would take back roads, get stopped by soldiers and be turned back, then try again. They would walk, take another car, get out of that car and take another car. And that's what it takes to attend circle meetings over there. In Palestine we also got involved in nonviolence training. There's a very strong nonviolent consciousness in the West Bank—one of the better-kept secrets about the conflict in the Middle East, unfortunately.

Because my friends here spoke personally about their lives, I just want to add that I was born in Israel though I grew up here. My mother is a Holocaust survivor from the camps. Some of you may even know that our order has sponsored annual retreats at Auschwitz Berkenau every November. I've been at Auschwitz about eight times. So I have a very good sense of the karma of this family. My mother is extremely right wing. She lives in Israel. She has gone to jail to protest giving up land. So when I worked there I would go to Bethlehem and Ramallah—

which she has never visited and has no intention of ever visiting—and she would go to Gush Katif, the Gaza settlements that the Israeli government wanted to withdraw from [the withdrawal took place in August 2005]. One person in my family demonstrates with the settlers and says that we shouldn't give up an inch, and her daughter works with Palestinians. And then we come together in a lot of silence because for all my training in speaking and listening from the heart, I have not been able to open this up with her in a deep way. The few times my work has come up, my mother lets me know with absolute certainty that I betray her family, I betray the people from her family who died in the concentration camps, I betray the Jewish nation, and I betray the country I was born to.

I realize that a big reason why I do this work is that when I looked at my family's karma—concentration camps, fighting in wars, going to Israel, raising a big army, being soldiers, and all that—it was clear to me that I wanted to make a little shift in that karma, to loosen up the rigid action/reaction that I could see going on there. As Diana alluded, it's not just personal karma that causes us to do what we do, it's also bigger family and social karmas that interact to create this moment.

HRGB: *Several things struck me as I was listening to each of you tell your stories and talk about your previous work and how you got here. Diana, I heard you say at one point—the phrase jumped out at me—"witnessing a world that was fractured and in pieces." Ginny, I heard you say—and Eve commented on it—that you wanted to change the game. And Eve, I heard you talk about the building of circles of spiritually anchored activists or individuals. In the work that you each do, issues of power seem to be embedded at the core— whether it's the Middle East, prison work, or community building on a local or global scale. My question is: How do you see the trifold dimensions of the social, the political, and the spiritual interlocking to address these issues of power?*

Hmmm, as each person went around saying essentially the same thing. At the end, they asked us whether we accepted Jesus Christ as our personal Lord and savior, and we said, "Well…umm…we accept his values." But they told us that wasn't good enough. Anyway, there was a big uproar, and they wanted to send us home. But the chaplain intervened and quoted some Bible verses and got them to accept that we had come there for free, so they put up with us. But we were on probation. I was on crutches at that time because I have a disability and my foot was not doing well. The correctional officer who was assigned to our group was really short—and short COs [correctional officers] are usually bad news in prison because they have more to prove. I spent some time talking with him after class, asking about his wife and kids, because he looked tired to me, and I was curious about who he was. This was clearly not an easy job for him. When I went back the next day, my foot was feeling better, and I didn't need my crutches. Meanwhile, the men inside saw our team's sincerity and that we had something to offer, and they started enjoying the workshop. They started using the skills we were teaching with their COs and got results they enjoyed, so the whole workshop turned a corner. One morning, the short CO came into the room to check on things. When he didn't see my crutches, he inquired with some concern about them, much to the amazement of the men. They'd never seen his human side before. By the end of the four days, we had all shed many tears, and the warmth in the room was palpable. One of the men told me that if he had known these skills years before that he would still have his children with him. As I was leading the final exercise, this same (short) CO came in and told us that it was time to end. Our team was aware that Texas prisons are not known for their flexible attitude toward time and scheduling! So I gulped and said to him, "Office Proctor, we need about ten more minutes, and I'm wondering if you'd be willing to let us have it." Now, that's just not done in a Texas prison. He hesitated and then said, "All right." The guys looked at me, and their jaws dropped. After he left the room, they said with great reverence, "Jesus was in the room!" While our team didn't literally agree that Jesus had been in the room, we could see that the qualities he had preached of love, mercy, compassion, kindness—had certainly been there. We didn't feel any need to quibble about the particular.

I realized that we all had fundamentally similar values. What those men taught me during that workshop really stayed with me. I was then able to put it into an amicus brief for the Simmons case, which was won on March 1, 2005, ending the death penalty for juvenile offenders in this country. Socially engaged Buddhism is about seeing our interconnectedness and allowing each circle to take us on to the next one.

VSB: Your question about power, Ryūmon, gets to the heart of what we're all talking about here. I think that community building needs to be done globally and locally. Globally I see it as bringing together through dialogue a core of values across cultures and religions—this is a kind of dialogue effort that we carry out at the center. The heart of these shared values is respect for human dignity, the absolute spiritual equality of all people. Locally, I'm struck by how much our practices for living together in dignity owe to indigenous people. When we started the BRC Learning Circle, a group of community builders working in diverse constituencies in the Boston area, we brought in a member of the Tlingit tribe from the Yukon called Harold Gatensby. He led us through the experience of the Tlingit peacemaking circle as a way of making heart connections among us, because our goal was to create a lived community. Through our lived community we wanted to provide something that would help with a cultural shift we needed from isolated individualism to cooperative living. It was really important for Harold to establish a common spiritual basis for the circle before it began. We had a long discussion because he had never heard about Buddhism, and I was explaining the mystic law, or the dharma, and he said, "Don't you believe in God?" And I said, "No, I believe in the mystic law." Finally, after intense brainstorming, he arrived at a phrase we could all accept—it was the *ever-flowing river of life.* I thought it was brilliant, to bring us together in spirit through an image of nature. He and an African American woman, Gwen Chandler-Rhivers, representing the most wounded parts of our culture with no academic credentials, forged a heart connection among these seventeen highly trained professionals in just four days. This group is now working together to come up with a philosophy and practice of interdependence. They are continuing the struggle to deepen their connections based on heart and spirit, rather than on relative skill levels and schooling, the unspoken hierarchy that usually prevails among academics and professionals.

HRGB: *Thank you. Now I'd like to open it up to the floor. Who'd like to begin with a question?*

Q: *I belong to a local sangha that has an outreach program at a local prison, where we go twice a week to teach meditation. The way you've been talking about engaged Buddhism makes it seem different from outreach. To me, outreach involves missionary work, trying to reach out to bring people into Buddhism, whereas what I'm hearing you saying is that engaged Buddhism is not about having people become Buddhists. So, I was wondering if you could say something to clarify the difference between engaged Buddhism and outreach.*

VSB: Some commentators have described the Soka Gakkai International as a form of "evangelical" Buddhism. In the faith organization, we do proselytize. There is active outreach to friends and family to bring them in, and sometimes we have annoyed people. We make our meetings very open. People come, and we try to share the dharma.

But we don't proselytize in our social engagement activities within the SGI's peace, culture, and education movement. For example, we're not trying to teach people to chant at the Boston Research Center. Instead, we want to set up a level playing field in which various religious and cultural ideas and sensibilities can be expressed openly and evaluated according to how beneficial they are to the future of humanity and all life. We're sharing our Buddhist-inspired humanism, in other words, and inviting non-Buddhists to share their humanistic visions, whatever their inspiration, so that we can find common ground to come together in our interconnectedness. When we harmonize the best of our wisdom in this way through dialogue, we hope that everyone can strengthen and broaden their own philosophy of life, so that we can draw closer as human beings.

Q: *A lot of the discussion was about yourselves, your personal story, and how that inspires people to action. I wonder if you could say more about how you balance a focus on self and a focus on activism.*

HRGB: *Let me quote John Daidō Loori Rōshi, abbot of Zen Mountain Monastery in Mt. Tremper, New York, who said in a dharma talk published in* Shambhala Sun, *"I've been reading and hearing a great deal about engaged Buddhism, and I've been thinking about the dangers inherent in doing engaged Buddhism without basing our actions in the practice heart of the dharma in wisdom and compassion. It is not wrong to engage in social activism. Doing good is always valuable. But we should understand that doing good is different from realizing compassion. It is only doing good. We should examine what is being served when we do good. Doing good almost always arises from a sense of self. In compassion, there's no sense of self. No sense of the doer. No sense of the thing the doer is doing. The only true compassion of Buddhism is realized Buddhism." [July 2001, p. 40]*

DL: I know that at different times in my own practice there are varying degrees of identification with self. I was really clear that I wanted, especially in an academic institution, to tell a personal story—to tell a story about myself. To be really honest about what led to much of my motivation for activism. Having said that, part of my own practice around activism is progressively shedding layers of self that get in the way. It's a real process for me, and can be tricky for us as women, and also for us as members of other disenfranchised groups in our society: if we're women of color, or queer, or disabled, or Jewish, or working class, and so on. On the one hand, we're reclaiming our wholeness, and on the other hand, we're shedding whatever notions we have of an inherently separate self. Sometimes I notice that my "self" is front and center. When I heard your question, I noticed the thought, Oh, my God,

I did something wrong. The "self" that wants to be doing the right thing and be liked, etc., was right there! Then I had a moment of mindfulness and thought, Okay. I see that. That's just the process that I go through over and over. It's a continuous process of dismantling through clear seeing, recognizing (with tenderness), and letting go. And I certainly need to have a sense of humor to be able to deal with what I see at times!

VSB: I would like to add something about personal story. As I pointed out in my presentation, the educators who founded the Soka Gakkai have a term for how social change takes place. It's called human revolution. There's a saying to the effect that a great personal transformation or great human revolution in just a single individual can change the destiny of a family, a community, a nation, and even the entire world. These stories of personal transformation invariably involve a victory over the ego, a hard-won victory in which a larger self interconnected with the whole cosmos emerges and prevails—the buddha nature. As this profound inner change occurs, the added buddha presence in just one person radiates outward to work transformations at a deep level in her relationships and circumstances. Therefore, I do believe personal experiences, when they involve breaking the shackles of the ego and finding something larger within, which is then mirrored on the outside, do advance social change. They provide a stronger foothold at a new milepost in the spiritual journey of the teller, and they inspire others to forge ahead with renewed energy in their own inner revolutionary struggles.

Q: *I was very moved by your personal stories and how they led you to social activism. I know I often carry around a certain level of guilt that I'm not doing enough in terms of social action. Do you have any advice about how to handle that sense of guilt?*

VSB: I think you reach out and mend the small piece of the world that you can touch. Everyone has a unique mission to do that. Dialogue is critical, together with ethical behavior coming from the heart. Women are key because I think their voices reach the most heavily barricaded heart. I believe that whenever you manifest your buddhahood, in any circumstance and at any moment through your thoughts, words, and deeds, you create a small shift in the world. These small changes in the direction of more buddha presence accumulate one by one. Gradually the accumulation of small shifts sets the stage for the larger shift that we all yearn for but can't yet see.

References

The Ink Dark Moon: Love Poems by Ono no Komachi and Izumi Shikibu, Women of the Ancient Court of Japan, trans. Jane Hirshfield with Mariko Aratani (New York: Vintage Classics, 1986), p. 89.

Arnold Toynbee and Daisaku Ikeda, Choose Life: A Dialogue (New York: Oxford University Press, 1989).

"Beginners" can be found in Denise Levertov's collection *Candles in Babylon* (New York: New Directions, 1982).

A Jewish Woman
and Buddhism

Rabbi Sheila Peltz Weinberg

I WAS BORN in the Bronx in 1946 and grew up there. I lived in a totally Jewish neighborhood as a child. My entire life has been spent absorbed with Jews and Judaism. I have worked with Jews, studied and taught Judaism, celebrated our festivals and life cycles. I have worried about the future of the Jewish people and their traditions for as long as I can remember. I have been a rabbi for the last twenty years. Yet, here I am contributing to a volume on women and Buddhism.

The bookshelves in my home office tell the story. To my right are several large bookcases filled with commentaries on the Hebrew Bible, rabbinic literature, Jewish history, philosophy, literature, and culture. To my left, on my desk, is a copy of *The Middle Length Discourses of the Buddha: A Translation of the Majjhima Nikāya*—a hefty hardback volume in a brown and gold jacket. I am a practicing Jew with an abiding interest in the dharma and in the teachings of the Buddha. That is the simple and not so simple truth.

Every few months, without fail, someone in my life, somewhere on the planet, sends me an email with the subject Zen Judaism. Usually my correspondent writes a short apologetic note saying: "you've probably seen these before...but I couldn't resist..." Then comes the litany:

- If there is no self, whose arthritis is this?
- Be here now. Be someplace else later. Is that so complicated?
- Drink tea and nourish life. With the first cup sip…enjoy. With the second…satisfaction, with the third…peace. With the fourth, a Danish.
- Wherever you go, there you are. Your luggage is another story.
- Accept misfortune as a blessing. Do not wish for perfect health or a life without problems. What would you talk about?
- The Tao does not speak. The Tao does not blame. The Tao does not take sides. The Tao has no expectations. The Tao demands nothing of others. The Tao is not Jewish.
- Let your mind be as a floating cloud. Let your stillness be as a wooded glen. And sit up straight. You'll never meet the Buddha with such rounded shoulders.
- Be patient and achieve all things. Be impatient and achieve all things faster.
- To find the Buddha, look within. Deep inside you are ten thousand flowers. Each flower blossoms ten thousand times. Each blossom has ten thousand petals. You might want to see a specialist.

My usual impulse is to delete these jokes immediately. I find them offensive to two of the things in the world that I love most. In one fell swoop these jokes dismiss the dharma and demean the Jews. They do express a certain dichotomy that is fairly prevalent. What do the jokes say about the Jews? We are impatient, hypochondriacal, anxious, demanding, blaming, food-oriented, complainers. We have embodied the irreverence, aggressivity, and materialism of secular culture and would be the least likely to open to the poetic sensibilities of Zen. These poems do not identify Jews as spiritual seekers or Judaism as a source of wisdom or compassion.

The Zen jokes reflect cultural stereotypes of an immigrant nation. Jews who came to America were by and large looking for economic and political security rather than spiritual fulfillment. They were quite willing to leave behind the centers of Jewish learning and devotion in Europe for these golden shores. Life here was tough, and, like other immigrants, Jews worked hard to give the next generation the advantages their parents did not have. They wanted Jewish identity and tradition to survive, but they also embraced the individualism and secularism of their new home. I am reminded of the words of Karma Lekshe Tsomo speaking in this volume about Asian Buddhists in America, who since the 1970s have been "primarily concerned with cultural preservation, cultural identity, cultural continuity, and service to the community of immigrants from their homeland."

My parents were children of immigrants. The Jewish cultural identity that they lived was very powerful, but it had shallow roots. Life was more about "making it" in America than living a life of connection to spirit. I knew I was supposed to be a good person, and I grew up hearing Yiddish spoken, but concepts like spiritual practice, self-reflection, or sacred community were as foreign to me as Latin or Greek. I was well fed and clothed enough to be able to dismiss "things" as the source of meaning. I needed something else. I yearned for something. That very yearning has been at the core of my love affair with both Judaism and the dharma. I was also a child of my times, born in the twin shadows of Auschwitz and Hiroshima. I was one of that generation who needed to seek the light of meaning through these shadows.

What were the primary motivations operating in my search and struggle? There are two that may be really one. First is the aspiration to be part of sacred community, to find relationships that celebrate and embrace the infinitely mysterious life force within all creation. The second is the urgency to face and heal the broken, frightening, and wounded aspects of the soul encountered in myself and others.

❖ The Search for Sacred Community

My interest in sacred community was sparked, I believe, by attending Camp Ramah between the ages of nine and sixteen. I was introduced to a new language, Hebrew, to the Torah, to daily prayer, and to the Sabbath. These were not tools to master, like English and mathematics.

They were special, different. They were meant to connect us as a Jewish community, to our ancestors and to the sacred—something deep, lasting, and precious. I remember feeling that the text and the language and the other practices that I learned in those summers were pure and purifying, were dedicated to a higher goal than the usual affairs of the day in my regular, non-camp life.

I have never stopped being passionately interested in sacred community. I have worked professionally as a rabbi and Jewish leader to realize that passion. I have been part of a sacred community of Jewish feminists, women's support groups, and interfaith clergy groups. I have also sought out teachers from many paths and practices to hear their wisdom—psychotherapists, Sufis, Buddhists, Christian mystics. I have been a member of a twelve-step group for two decades.

In 1990 I was introduced to mindfulness or insight meditation. I was curious about the possibility of sitting in silence for a long period of time. I was exhausted in my job as a rabbi. There was always more to read and study. There was always more to do and prepare and write. In particular I felt weighed down by the words—the many wonderful but also burdensome words of our tradition. I craved some space that might surround the words and illuminate them anew for myself and those I served. I was intrigued and also frightened by what would emerge in the silence.

The first ten-day silent retreat I attended at Insight Meditation Society in Barre, Massachusetts, was a powerful and difficult experience. I was asked to be with the contents of my own mind-body without distraction and just to notice what arose. What I noticed was a microcosm of the world in which I live. There was great judgment and fear, a desire to do well and compete, a desire to attain and obtain, to know for sure that I was safe because I had that elusive "something." I saw that I was always planning the next moment. I saw that I was frightened of the sacred, frightened of the present, frightened of stillness. What a dilemma. Here I was, a spiritual teacher, and my mind was pandemonium. It was racing around without a home, afloat in a sea of chaos and desire. This was not the totality of that experience, however. I was given a glimmer of how to be with what I saw. It was enough of an opening to cause me to return for another retreat, and another, and to begin to sit myself.

At first I was terribly confused because as a rabbi, the last thing I was looking for was a new religion. I did not want to become a Buddhist, not that there was any pressure from the retreat leaders for me to do so. However, fairly soon I realized that the teachings, called dharma, at these retreats, were nothing other than the teachings of Torah, teachings leading me toward sacred community and healing. I realized that as my mind settled in silence, the wisdom that arose was none other than the inner teachings of Judaism. Since then, as I have come to understand the nature of my mind more deeply, I see how these teachings could be practiced and integrated into sacred Jewish community. I meet, in the stillness, again and again, pain, fear, and confusion, and learn that awareness itself is the key to ongoing healing.

In *Deuteronomy* 30:11–14, it is written: "For this commandment which I command you this day, is not concealed from you, nor is it far away. It is not in heaven, that you should say, 'Who will go up to heaven for us and fetch it for us, to tell [it] to us, so that we can fulfill it?' Nor is it beyond the sea, that you should say, 'Who will cross to the other side of the sea for us and fetch it for us, to tell [it] to us, so that we can fulfill it?' Rather, [this] thing is very close to you; it is in your mouth and in your heart, so that you can fulfill it." This summarizes the approach of mindfulness practice. We learn the reality that our capacities to live a spiritual life do not reside in some faraway place. They reside within our own experience. We are each endowed with an essence that is sacred and pure. The qualities that we seek to expand and express are already part of our nature. This is the meaning of being created in the Divine image, as I understand this core teaching in the *Book of Genesis*. If we want to access compassion, it is within our capacity to be present in the midst of pain. We simply need to do it. We need to practice, again and again. We need to train or retrain our mind and heart in the way that is wholesome, life affirming, nonviolent, and loving. We need to see how deeply connected we are to life and to each other and practice acting on the basis of that reality. This also teaches us that we cannot work to reform something external when we are not in internal alignment. If we are angry and spiteful, that will be the result of our actions even if we speak about generosity and goodwill.

What really hooked me? What was it at Camp Ramah in my teens that I found again in Barre in my forties? It comes down to three things: the teachings, the teachers, and the practices. But mostly it is the non-separation between these three.

❖ Teachers and Teachings Are One

Reading or hearing sacred teachings does not have the impact of experiencing a teacher who embodies the practice and who can, herself, speak about her experience of transformation through practice. This is an integrated transmission. We are inspired by this living model to accept that there is something we can do for ourselves. We do not depend upon the teacher to "do" for us. The practices will become the teacher and teaching for each person in her unique way. At the same time, the universality of the human mind and heart is revealed as the teacher points to how similar we are in our wounds, our conditioning, in our longing for wholeness, and in our desire to be seen, known, and loved.

In some ways the nearly seventeen years since that first retreat have been for me a working out of the relationship between the Torah and the dharma. It has been a bumpy and beautiful journey. The public part of the process began with small gatherings at the Barre Center for Buddhist Studies. It was made up of Buddhist teachers who had Jewish origins and Jewish teachers who were interested in mysticism and meditation. Through these events I met Sylvia Boorstein, who became a mentor and beloved friend. As we began teaching together, at first she was the dharma teacher, and I was the rabbi. As time went on those boundaries dissipated. I started giving instructions for meditation, and Sylvia started chanting Torah. Eventually, joined by Rabbi Jeff Roth, we offered retreats to rabbis and other Jewish leaders where we taught mindfulness in a Jewish idiom. We understood mindfulness as a non-denominational way to practice Judaism in thought, speech, and action. We realized that Jewish stories, rituals, songs, and teachings were accessible vehicles to impart the dharma. We also discovered that fostering conditions where people could practice paying attention to their own experience moment to moment helped expand their understanding of prayer, learning, and action in the world immensely. Eventually this work culminated in the creation of the Institute for Jewish Spirituality, which brings rabbis, cantors, Jewish educators, and laypeople together to learn mindfulness and its relationship to Jewish learning and practice, to renew their spiritual lives and the lives of their sacred communities (see http://www.ijs-online.org).

I do not have any trouble translating fundamental Jewish ideas and images into the language of dharma. I think we are all talking about the same thing. A well-known scholar of Jewish mysticism, Arthur Green, puts it this way: "The job of each human being is to teach every other human being that we are all One, and to find ways in our behavior as well as our thought to include all other creatures within that vision of Oneness as well."[1] Similarly, Sharon Salzberg writes: "This is the essential questioning we must bring to any belief system. Can it transform our minds? Can it help reshape our pain into wisdom and love?"[2] It seems to me that if we really could see that we are all One, then we could not help but function with greater wisdom and compassion toward each other and the earth.

❖ Musings on Torah and Dharma

Over the years I have written some poems that reflect my love of dharma and Torah. They emerge from intensive retreat practice when I come face to face with my own stumbling blocks to clear seeing, wisdom, and kindness. In the quiet I have a chance to see how full the ego is of itself and how false ideas of being separate and different, less than or better than, obscure the truth of oneness and connection. What happens to me frequently on retreat is that a word or phrase from Jewish liturgy or narrative will pop into my head. That language speaks through my experience and gives it contours in a miraculous way. I thought I would share a few of those musings (could I call them poems?) to illustrate the way an integration of experience and tradition occurs for me.

This is the practice,
This is how the heart gets purified,
This is how we get to know God.
Again and again and again—
Ill at ease
Distant
Separate
Uncomfortable
Critical thoughts of self and other
Race in the mind,
Inadequate, not quite okay, just off-center
Like mice in a maze.
The mind is the
Mice and the maze.
Again and again,
Until a moment of—oh, yes—
This is suffering, non-dramatic,
Relentless, underground,
And again and again and again,
It is protecting something,
Which turns out invariably
To be "ME."
Then comes the grace, the mindfulness, the compassion.
Warm attention to the frozen and contracted, tender light on the
        shadows of delusion.
And then a moment of freedom.
Relax the heart.
You are home.

Empty
Happy
One.

I am reminded of a verse in the Sabbath prayer book: *"V'taher libaynu l'avdecha b'emet"* (prepare or purify our hearts to serve you truthfully). We ask that our heart be purified, the obstacles removed, the blockages melted. In yoga we would say, may all hindrances to the flow of *prāṇa* be removed. Breath is the grossest manifestation of *prāṇa*, the life force. In Hebrew we call this *chiyut*. We must be able to train our attention in order to see what the blocks are. We must become sensitive in order to notice when we are constricted. To the extent that these knots can be loosened, our potential is released to do the work of service to creation. This comes out in our unique creativity and in causing less harm to ourselves and others. When we are free of the blockages, we are able to manifest the Divine attributes of goodness, love, kindness, patience, generosity, and gratitude.

> *The Kaddish is about opening the window*
> *Not looking through the glass, but opening the window.*
> *The window of the heart, the window of not knowing.*
> *Opening the window on fear and love.*
> *Opening the window on all time and space—l'olam ulolmei*
>   *olmeia.*
> *Just that.*
> *Opening the window*
> *To the kingdom that is just this.*
> *Opening the window to the name. The great name.*
> *No name.*
> *Amen.*

The Kaddish is probably the most well-known Hebrew prayer, and it is not even in Hebrew. It is in Aramaic, the vernacular of two thousand years ago. The prayer begins with the hope that the great name of God be made greater and holier in all the dimensions of time and space. It ends with an aspiration for peace in all the worlds. The practice of mindfulness allows one's mind to grow more spacious. This invites a connection with a wider and broader way of seeing. I identify this with the mind of God or the name of God that can never really be known. Mindfulness practice is about expanding beyond pettiness toward relationship, beyond self-centeredness toward peacefulness, and beyond duality to a wholeness that holds multiplicity and paradox.

Nowhere to run from these feelings.
Watching them spill into tears and sobs and then make their way
    to the great open sea.
Hoping to be cleaner and emptier from the secrets—Menistarot
    Nakayni—
I have asked for this and now there is no place to hide, no place to
    run.
This too is part of your kingdom.
This too is a face of your light.
This too is arising and ceasing in your realm.
This too is ready for your mercy, in your transparent gaze that
    makes all the difference.
Vayagale libi b'yeshuatecha—
My heart rejoices in your freedom, oh merciful one.
All I can do is sing praises.
L'maan shemecha
For Your name's sake.
Because this is who You are.
Because the essence of existence is one.
And we are called upon to be unifiers of the name.
Opening in our small and feeble way in whatever way we can to
    the underlying relatedness, oneness.
Call it whatever you like—trust, love, generosity, surrender.
You are One.

Your name is One.
For Your name's sake.
There is no other possibility,
However we might rebel, resist and run.
We come back to this.
Shma Yisrael Adonai Elohaynu Adonai Echad.

We are told that Judaism and Buddhism stand in conflict over the existence of God. Judaism says yes and Buddhism says no. However, when I am quiet, whether in prayer or meditation, I recognize that everything is arising and passing. Not only is this so, but everything is caused by something else and in turn causes something else. This means that everything is connected. The whole of this is without beginning and without end. And it is mostly empty space. The fact that my tiny dot of consciousness can connect with this much is an occasion for deep amazement and gratitude. The Jewish God that I know is called— IS/WAS/WILLBE. It cannot be named or pictured. Any effort at depiction or final naming is considered idolatry. Idolatry is attachment. The Buddha taught that attachment is the source of suffering and ignorance. Human liberation is tied to a sense of the unlimited, unpossessable nature of this mysterious, ever-changing existence. This was what I was seeing when I wrote this reflection on the verse used in Jewish prayer services when we replace the Torah scroll in the ark—"She is a tree of life to all who cling to her"—

Etz Chayyim He.
It does matter what you cling to
What you hold on to. (It doesn't matter what you call it),
Call it God, Life, Torah, Dharma, Wakefulness, the One.
And when you truly connect, hold on, trust,
Then all other clinging is revealed
As a shadow, a garment, an echo.

❖ T'shuvah—Returning to Our Intention

Among the many extraordinary gifts I have received from mindfulness practice is a deeper understanding of the concept of T'shuvah. This is the process whereby we set an intention, and, when we invariably stray, we remember and return to the initial intention. This is the basic instruction in sitting or walking meditation that I was introduced to at IMS. I find that it is a paradigm for all spiritual work, all training of the mind and heart, all education of self and others. T'shuvah makes human life, beset by so many mistakes and missteps, truly possible. The Jewish tradition expresses this idea by teaching that T'shuvah existed before God created the world.

T'shuvah is a Hebrew noun derived from the three-letter root that means "turn or return." It presumes that our lives have a direction and a purpose. It also presumes that we frequently forget this truth, lose our way, or actually move in the opposite direction. The days surrounding Rosh Hashanah and Yom Kippur ask us not only to reflect on the meaning of T'shuvah but to do some actual turning and returning—to put our lives on course.

Several questions immediately arise: What indeed is the desired direction of a life? What keeps us from moving in that path? How do we reorient the vehicle of our lives? Jewish language speaks in terms of dwelling in the presence of the Divine, purifying our hearts, harmonizing our will with God's will and rectifying the harmful acts that we do to others and to ourselves. Ultimately, we are intended to become ever more openhearted, generous, patient, loving, wise, and caring. As we touch these expansive qualities we feel deeply connected to the great web of existence. In this genuine belonging, we discover true happiness and peace.

In order to accomplish T'shuvah, we need to see and touch the patterns and habits that have been constructed in the scaffold of our minds, that turn us around and lead us astray. One way to encounter our own minds is through meditation. It is easy to ignore or evade one's inner life in the daily rush of life. We tend to fill all pauses and spaces with activity and chatter, electronic or human. When we take the time to pause and be still, the mind settles like a muddy pond. The simple practice of silence reveals an unfamiliar terrain. It can be surprising and frightening. It is a powerful tool for the practice of T'shuvah.

I have often marked the few days prior to Rosh Hashanah by going on a mindfulness retreat. The goal is to simplify one's life as much as possible and avoid distractions. This can best be done in the context of a structure where silence is embraced. The schedule consists only of periods of sitting, walking, eating, sleeping, and personal hygiene—the basic rudiments of life. The teachers offer instructions that consist mostly of telling us to pay attention to our experience in the present moment. "Just notice the breath as it enters and leaves the body," they will say, or "Pay attention to the sensation of each step as you lift, move, and place it on the ground," or "Allow the various pleasant, unpleasant, and neutral sensations to arise and pass through your body. Watch them change." Our thoughts are treated in the same way as our breath or bodily sensations, and we are encouraged to watch them arise and disappear. Amazingly enough, I have experienced a profound process of T'shuvah in just such a setting.

In the absence of external stimuli and distractions, after a while, one begins to notice the content of one's own mind. I have been shocked, dismayed, and outraged by mine. On one retreat I kept noticing a man who particularly annoyed me. Bear in mind that I had no contact with and no knowledge of this person. I just did not like the way he looked or acted. Every time there was a chance to ask a question, he invariably had a question. This annoyed me. He seemed restless when sitting and made more noise than I thought necessary when he breathed. I also noticed him in the dining room pouring huge quantities of honey on his cereal. This annoyed me as well. While there was no smoking on the retreat, there was a smokers' hut. I would see this man frequently going in or out of the hut. He always smelled of tobacco. As a former smoker, I disdained this behavior.

Meanwhile the teacher urged us to focus our attention on our experience in the moment. As my mind settled, I realized that my experience was one of annoyance and judgment. Perhaps hate is too strong a word. But I was having an aversive reaction to a person who was not only a total stranger but someone who was not hurting me at all. I came to realize that this man stimulated my irritated feelings because he made me afraid. I was most afraid that I was like him—out of control, hungry, addicted. I saw and felt my own fear under the irritation. I could explore how painful that felt. The structured and safe, silent environment allowed me to explore this rocky terrain without another reaction of guilt and punishment—"Bad girl for having such thoughts." Rather, my mind was spacious enough to hold these thoughts and feelings and the grief they contained. Again and again, returning, turning to the simple truth of the moment brings a soothing wind of calm. Awareness of the truth allows for mercy to arise. Call it the sweetness of Divine grace and forgiveness. Call it release from a habit born of fear and separation.

One thing became clear. My reactions had nothing to do with the man I disliked. I had uncovered the process in my mind that casts blame outside myself. I had explored its raw edges and its oozing heart. In the light of that quiet, loving awareness it began to melt on its own. As it melted, I returned to my purpose. I regained my footing on the path to wholeness and connection. Again and again, this kind of movement is T'shuvah. That is the point. Again and again I witness moments and patterns of mind and heart that have hurt myself and others. Again and again I try to unlock incidents where wrong was done, where amends are in order. How different this is from believing that the man was indeed evil or hateful or the cause of my pain in some objective way. Moving to this recognition feels like bold and courageous work.

However, this work cannot be done effectively if I judge myself unworthy. Just as the liturgy of the High Holy Days repeatedly urges us to experience a God who is gracious and filled with compassion, kindness, and patience, so the process of T'shuvah, moral transformation, assumes an unceasing source of love and forgiveness, contained as a seed in each moment of pure awareness.

❖ Jewish Feminism and Spirituality

I am a daughter of the second wave of feminism. When I finished college in 1967 it was inconceivable to question the fact that women could not be rabbis. I had the second bat mitzvah in my synagogue without any of the boys' privileges, and I fought for that. In 1983 when my daughter Abby became a bat mitzvah, I was in rabbinical school, and she could not believe there was ever a time when there weren't women rabbis.

I love being a woman rabbi. I see women's contribution to all religious life as beyond measure. The life experiences, voices, approaches, minds, and hearts of women are transformative. I think my willingness to see the connections between dharma and Judaism is connected to my life as a feminist and a woman in a public religious role. I want to tell people: it is about practice and about the heart, not just about what you think or know. Spirituality is about being alive and knowing that— being awake in the world, not just in the mind or the book. Spirituality is about telling the truth, talking about what you feel and know. It is about bringing in the margins, taking in the lost, forgotten, and weak, not just pretending to be sure and certain. I don't reject the learned, the rational, and the linear. I just want to bring in the possibility of dancing in prayer, crying out to God with real tears, and not being sure what I am going to say before I say it because I am so in this moment. The inclusion of women is the inclusion of the earth that has been rejected. It signals the inclusion of the body that has been scorned. It is the inclusion of the nonwhite, the nonstraight, the nonrich, the nonprivileged. It is the heart of the dharma, the Torah, the wisdom of life. It is the goddess aroused and filled with juice.

In her essay in this volume bell hooks observes that every woman engaged with Buddhism is asked at some point how she can support a patriarchal religion. The same can be said of Judaism. I am not blind to patriarchy. I see it everywhere. But I do not surrender to it. I realize that our cultures and our conditioning emerge from dualism and hierarchy. I know that our world is riddled with unspeakable gaps of wealth and resources, degradation, and oppression. As a Jew I am heir to a past heritage of marginality, suffering, and victimization and a contemporary situation of power, wealth, and privilege. That makes for some complex choices. I am also aware that all religions—including Buddhism and Judaism—can build bridges of the heart to one another or be vehicles of hatred and violence. I do not turn my back on the light and wisdom of the past. But I am emboldened to challenge what I have received, especially as a woman, and ask: Is this practice sacred? Is this sacred community? Is this for the sake of healing and wholeness or for the sake of power, possession, and prestige?

What do I have to offer as a woman, as a Jew, and as a lover of dharma? I have each moment the willingness to live with an open heart. I have the capacity to love and to forgive. I have the wish to pursue the truth and not to hide or pretend or deceive. I have the goal to remember the stranger, the one who is different from me, and know we are not separate. I aspire to honor the earth as I enjoy her bounty. I can try to be gentle with myself for not knowing as much as I would like to know, or being as good at some things, or remembering all the things I would like to remember. For wholeness is not about reaching perfection. And above all I can keep practicing. I can practice qualities of heart that I associate with the divine abodes or with the image of God—loving-kindness, compassion, joy and peace, generosity, gratitude, equanimity, courage, and patience. And when I am lost, and I know I am lost, I can come back.

Notes

1   *Ehyeh: A Kabbalah for Tomorrow* (Woodstock: Jewish Lights, 2002), p. 134

2   *Faith: Trusting Your Own Deepest Experience* (New York: Riverhead Books, 2002), p. 62

Race, Ethnicity, and Class

A conversation with Hilda Ryūmon Gutiérrez Baldoquín, Sharon Suh, and Arinna Weisman; moderated by Carolyn Jacobs.

CAROLYN JACOBS: *Welcome. My name is Carolyn Jacobs. I am the dean of the School for Social Work here at Smith College. I have long had an interest in spirituality and social work, which is the area of my scholarship. Currently I am a spiritual director for those who are interested in exploring religious and spiritual themes in their lives. I'm delighted to have the honor to moderate this panel on race, ethnicity, and class. Let me begin by briefly introducing Hilda Ryūmon Gutiérrez Baldoquín, who was born in Cuba of African and Spanish heritage and who is a Sōtō Zen priest in the lineage of Shunryu Suzuki Rōshi. She's the founder of the People of Color Sitting Group at the San Francisco Zen Center and cofounder of the Buddhist Meditation Group for the LGBTQ community at The Center, also in San Francisco. She leads retreats for people of color at the Insight Meditation Center of Pioneer Valley [Dhamma Dena] in Easthampton, Massachusetts and is a practice leader for the Zen Sangha at the Cerro Gordo Temple in Santa Fe, New Mexico. She's the editor of* Dharma, Color and Culture: New Voices in Western Buddhism.

Arinna Weisman has studied insight meditation for twenty years and has been a teacher for twelve years. She teaches insight meditation throughout the United States and is a founding teacher of the Insight Meditation Center of Pioneer Valley [Dhamma Dena] in Easthampton. She is coauthor of A Beginner's

Guide to Insight Meditation. *Her dharma practice and teaching have been infused with her political and environmental activism. She has led insight meditation retreats for the gay, lesbian, bisexual, and transgendered community, and she also leads retreats focused on racism and multiculturism.*

I'm also delighted to welcome Sharon Suh, who is the director of the Asian Studies Program and associate professor of world religions at Seattle University. She received her Ph.D. in Buddhist studies from Harvard University in 2000 and is the author of Being Buddhist in a Christian World: Gender and Community in a Korean American Temple.

I welcome these three very talented and gifted women to our presence and look forward to hearing and sharing their wisdom.

Hilda Ryūmon Gutiérrez Baldoquín: Buenos días. Good morning. It's wonderful to be here. I want to express my appreciation to everyone whose innumerable labors brought us to this moment. When I first saw the title of this panel, "Race, Ethnicity, and Class," I thought, And we only have ninety minutes! This is a topic that is very close to my heart. After spending twenty-five years of my life working very deeply with these issues in different contexts—both secular and non-Buddhist religious contexts—I made the decision to step away from these so-called mainstream contexts to see how we can do some of this work within our dharma communities.

As a Sōtō Zen priest, when I am asked to facilitate work around the issues of privilege and race in mainstream contexts, I often leave feeling that I haven't given the best I can offer—and that best is the dharma. At the same time, there is a belief in Western dharma communities that the inequity of privilege and race is less of an issue there than in mainstream communities. But personal experience tells me that this isn't true. It's just an illusion. It's a desire on the part of practitioners to be beyond social/political concerns, to be free from conditioned beliefs and behaviors. This is a wholesome desire but, unfortunately, one that sometimes masks a refusal to own up to the ways in which privilege and race impact our communities. As committed dharma practitioners—who, in convert centers, are predominantly white, educated, middle-to upper-middle-class individuals—we are challenged to look deeply at how multiple forms of privilege and oppression are alive today in our dharma communities. If anyone of us here—and not just folks of color—walks into a dharma community that is predominantly white and doesn't say, "How come?" we're not awake.

When your location is historically on the margin, a critical eye comes with your mama's milk. Some of the things I will say today might not sound like right speech. Yet, in my sixteen years of formal practice, I've begun to observe the importance of differentiating between right speech and "nice speech." Right speech is motivated by fearlessness. When we use right speech we speak the truth with relent-less honesty. Nice speech is just the opposite of right speech. Nice speech is motivated by fear. Sometimes we don't speak the truth because we are afraid of hurting other people's feelings. The differ-ence between right speech and nice speech is a bit like Chögyam Trungpa's distinction between "true compassion" and "idiot compas-sion." True compassion requires relentless honesty because that's the only way we can actually learn and grow as Buddhist practitioners. Idiot compassion is much more concerned with protecting the ego so, in the end, it doesn't help anyone, whether the person speaking or the person listening.

There are a couple of quotes I'd like to share with you from the anthology *Dharma, Color and Culture: New Voices in Western Buddhism,* the first anthology to be published in the United States in which both dharma teachers and students of color from different Buddhist tradi-tions speak about the impact of the dharma on healing the wounds of racism. One of the contributors to this volume is Sister Chan Chau Nghiem (True Adornment with Jewel), who is of both African Ameri-can and European American heritage and a nun in the Vietnamese Zen tradition of Master Thich Nhat Hanh. Sister Jewel, who lives in Plum Village, France, concludes her essay "Coming Home" by stating: "If Buddhism is to really make a contribution to Western society, it must use the insights of the dharma to heal the suffering of racism" (p. 123). One simple sentence says it all. Thus, so-called "American Buddhism" cannot come to fruition without embracing the issue of racism in the convert Buddhist sanghas.

Jan Willis, another contributor to the volume and an acclaimed Buddhist scholar at Wesleyan University, writes in her essay, "Dharma has No Color":

> I believe that people of color, because of our experience of the great and wrenching historical traumas of slavery, colonization, and segregation, understand suffering in a way that our white brothers and sisters do not and, moreover, that this understanding is closer to what is meant by the Buddhist injunction. Hence, I believe that—in this regard and without putting suffering on a scale—we people of color are actually already "one-up" on other convert Buddhist practitioners. We come to the practice with this deeper understanding. And this understanding, I believe, makes it easier for us to actually "get it" when we're told that we need to understand the Noble Truth of suffering (p. 220).

These are just a couple of gems I want to highlight in order to generate a bit of energy—a little Sunday morning dew—for us today.

In my practice the meeting of the pure teachings of Shakyamuni Buddha with the conditioned reality of oppression in all its manifestations is quite an exciting phenomenon because, as dharma practitioners, we are being challenged to fully understand what the Buddha taught in terms of our contemporary lives. The latest turning of the dharma wheel in twenty-first-century United States challenges us to learn how to realize these teachings as we embrace the issues and concepts alive in the world today, such as race, ethnicity, and class. Our society is based on these concepts. Each of us, regardless of our social location—whether in a "one-up" location (a member of society's dominant groups) or a "one-down" location (a member of society's disadvantaged groups)—has been conditioned to live our lives in relationship to these concepts of race, ethnicity, and class. This is not new to the dharma. During

Shakyamuni Buddha's times, the caste system, class differences, and the oppression of women were all very present.

In the professional work that I've done, we look at any manifestation of oppression in terms of four levels. Here I want to pay honor to my friend and colleague, Dr. Valerie Batts, a Massachusetts-based clinical psychologist, who founded VISIONS, Inc., an international multicultural organizational development firm that focuses on anti-oppression work. As executive director of VISIONS, Dr. Batts was one of the first people in the field of multicultural change to look at the multiple and interconnected levels of oppression: personal, interpersonal, institutional, and cultural. The personal level pertains to our deepest conditioning, our basic attitudes, values, and beliefs—whether taught or caught—in other words, our prejudices. In Buddhist terms, these prejudices are the seeds that incline us to act one way or the other. Often we remain unaware of our conditioning until we come into contact with people about whom we carry this conditioning. The interpersonal level of oppression is where our conditioning impacts the way we behave when we come into contact with others. The seeds of our conditioning start to bear fruit here. Once we reach the institutional level, the seeds have grown into vines that shape the way we do business. In dharma contexts, these vines shape the way we run our dharma centers, how we live our lives, with whom we are comfortable associating. Switching metaphors, we can liken the cultural level of oppression to the water in which fish swim. If you ask a fish to describe its home, it might leave water out. Similarly, when I ask groups, "What do we need to live as human beings? What is the basic thing we need?" the first thing people often will say is "food." Well, we actually could live quite a while without food as we see from those who take up the practice of fasting. We usually don't mention air. So when we're swimming in the midst of the conditioned waters of our culture it is difficult to see what we're in the middle of. As Master Dōgen tells us in *Genjōkōan*, "when we are in the middle of the ocean, the ocean looks circular." When we look at the issue of race in our Buddhist communities, we need to go beyond the personal and interpersonal levels of oppression. We need to examine the institutional structures that have been created in our dharma centers. We need to illumine the culture in which these structures are embedded. We need to look more broadly at where we're located in our privilege and in our power. And we need to do all this with deep kindness and compassion.

In my practice I ask the question: How do I embody my contemplative practice within a framework of multicultural change? I have begun to find "fingers pointing toward the moon." The dharma gives us lots of resources to work with. First of all, I am inspired by the teachings of women dharma teachers who have come before me. One of those teachers is Charlotte Joko Beck, teacher at the Zen Center in San Diego. Joko's description of the stages of practice help me understand how to bring the lens of contemplative practice to bear on my work on the inequity of privilege and race. Joko writes in *Nothing Special: Living Zen*, that the first stage of practice is to become aware of the fact that we have been sacrificed. She writes that

> the first layer we encounter in sitting practice is our feeling of being a victim—our feeling that we have been sacrificed to others. We *have* been sacrificed to others' greed, anger, and ignorance, to their lack of knowledge of who they are (p. 41).

The second stage of practice is "working with the feelings that come out of the awareness: our anger, our desire to get even, our desire to hurt those who have hurt us," and our desire for somebody to recognize that we have suffered (p. 41). The third stage of practice—and this is the one that really got me—is:

> if we continue to practice (maintaining awareness, labeling our thoughts), then something different—though also painful—begins to arise in our consciousness. We begin to see not only how we have been sacrificed, but also how we have sacrificed others (pp. 41–42).

This is especially the case when we act out our anger and resentment in a desire to get even.

When I first read this, I realized I had never heard anyone talk about sacrifice in this way in a dharma context. Joko's dharma teachings resonated with the work I do on oppression and race. As a result of oppression, we're systematically divided into victims and perpetrators. This isn't helpful. If we are walking on a path to awakening and still maintain a worldview in which people are divided into victims and perpetrators, we carry deep suffering with us because we see everyone as separate rather than as interconnected. We haven't fully understood the Buddha's teachings on interconnectedness.

Another great resource is the five lay precepts common to all Buddhist traditions: to refrain from harming others, stealing, misusing sex, lying, and taking intoxicants. Here is how I interpret them in terms of the inequity of privilege and race.

Whenever, as a member of a dominant group,

I stay separate from others out of fear, I am denying the goodness in others, and therefore killing their spirit, as well as mine. When I do this, I violate the precept not to harm others;

I deny others the right to have their own experience, I rob them of their dignity, and whenever I don't question the source of the everyday privileges I enjoy, I violate the precept not to steal;

I objectify or project onto others and do not see how this objectification and projection contributes to oppression and lack of respect and dignity, I violate the precept not to misuse sex;

I say that "we are all one" and assume thereby that everyone is part of the same dominant culture, and whenever I say that things, as they are, are not injurious to the majority of the world's population, I violate the precept not to lie;

I numb out to suffering and do not allow myself to see clearly what's really in front of me, I violate the precept not to take intoxicants.

Another important resource is the teachings of Nāgārjuna, an Indian Buddhist monk and philosopher who lived in the second century C.E. Nāgārjuna distinguishes between two ways of perceiving reality, which he calls two "truths." From the standpoint of ultimate truth, distinctions such as those of race, ethnicity, and class have no meaning. From the standpoint of conventional truth, however, they do. The challenge is for us to recognize that the world as we know it is far less solid and fixed than we think it is. Concepts like race, ethnicity, and class are merely conventional concepts and lack any ultimate meaning. But this doesn't mean they don't matter. Nāgārjuna was careful to say that ultimate truth does not negate conventional truth: instead it teaches us to see the conventional world with a more open heart and mind; it encourages us to let go of our prejudices because we see that they have no ultimate meaning. Unfortunately, some dharma practitioners use ultimate truth as a way of denying the reality of the pain of racism and oppression, but for something that supposedly isn't real, it sure as heck hurts. Ultimate truth isn't supposed to make us stop caring about the pain of others; it's supposed to inspire us to stop that pain.

I've seen something dangerous happening in predominately white, convert Buddhist sanghas. What I've observed is that if a white dharma practitioner has not looked deeply at the racist conditioning in his or her heart and mind, the teachings of Shakyamuni Buddha can actually enable the perpetuation of racism. This can happen when a white person denies racism by emphasizing ultimate truth over conventional truth or when a white person emphasizes the interconnectedness of all beings. Similarly, when a person of color continually stresses separation and a "we/they" paradigm, we are solidifying the suffering in our lives by not seeing or experiencing anything beyond conventional truth. Finding the delicate balance of being present with "what is" while simultaneously challenging the inequities in the world (i.e., conventional reality) is our practice and is supported by the teachings of Buddhist philosophers such as Nāgārjuna.

Arinna Weisman: Thank you all for coming. We are challenged by the dharma to love. To love not with a deluded romanticism that paints positive Hollywood colors over our lives but in order to challenge suffering, to see it, and to refrain from building it. I call on that love, and I call on all the buddhas and bodhisattvas and all the enlightened beings to bless each one of us with the strength and openheartedness to look at the dynamics of racism and oppression in general. As a white, middle-class person, I call on the powers of generosity and of renunciation that I and we as white people might free ourselves of identification with the patterns of ownership, resources, and power that exclude on the basis of race and class.

I am a racist. I don't think it's possible for us to live in this culture as a white person and not be racist. I also think it is this continued acknowledgement that makes visible what has often been invisible and makes it possible to take an antiracist stand. One of the ways racism manifests is described as white privilege. It points to how we as white people hold more resources and power without always being aware that this is happening. As Ryūmon has already mentioned, it is important to understand how racism and white privilege manifest by naming their expression on all four levels of the personal, interpersonal, institutional, and cultural.

White privilege is expressed on the cultural level as the intense predominance of white people in TV shows. I see myself reflected when I go to the movies. I see that it is mostly white people who are recognized for the Oscars or the National Book Circle Award. When I go to the opera, I see primarily white people.

On the structural level, I experience privilege when I go to my senator or representative in Massachusetts and assume he or she will listen to me and understand my experiences because we are both white. When I go to any of the city councilors in this town, Northampton, they are all white. If I go to the people who are on the boards of the corporations in this town, they are all white. We can easily generalize that throughout this country and in much of the world most of the wealth rests in the hands of white people. With regard to the legal system, it means that there is a systematic imprisonment of people of color for crimes that have less impact on society than the crimes that white people have committed. That's how these dynamics work on the cultural and the institutional levels.

On the interpersonal level, white privilege expresses itself as visibility. For example, when I raised my hand in class, I not only had the expectation that my hand would be seen, but it often was. It expresses itself as safety; for example, it is safe for me to drive my car at night, I'm not scared that I will be stopped by the police, I'm not scared that I will be searched, and I'm not scared that I will be arrested. It is going into a store and not having to face the assumption that I will shoplift. It is the expectation that I will be treated fairly. I assume I will not be immediately seen as stupid, ignorant, incapable, or a victim.

On the personal level white privilege expresses itself in the negative ideas and judgments we have about people of color that we have taken to be accurate descriptions and true. A number of years ago I was walking down Main Street in Springfield when I noticed an African American driving past me in a very new and shiny red sports car. The thought arose in me that the car was bought with drug money. I didn't assume this man had made a lot of money in the computer or software world, something I might have assumed if he had been white.

I want to acknowledge that as I started to write these comments, my mind immediately went to the places where I have not experienced equality and have not been acknowledged as a woman, as a lesbian, and as a Jew. What I've noticed over and over again in this exploration of white privilege, is how easy it is to go to the place where I am not privileged and how hard it is to stay in a place where I am. There are these voices that say, I'm not reflected here, and I'm not reflected there. It's a particular discipline for each of us to stay in the place where we are privileged because we actually find ourselves in both groups all the time. For example, if we're white, we're privileged; if we are not Jewish, if we are able-bodied, if we are middle class, or upper-middle class, or upper class, we are privileged; if we are heterosexual, if we are U.S. born, if we are English speaking, we are privileged. If we are people of color, working class, Jewish, gay, lesbian, bisexual, or transgendered, if we were born outside of this country, if we are disabled or do not speak English, then we live these parts of our lives as unprivileged.

I suspect our identification with the comfort and control of privilege is stronger than our aversion to the pain of belonging to a disenfranchised group. And so it becomes more difficult to investigate this area of our lives. Ryūmon spoke about how these unexamined dynamics can play out in our dharma communities. Our practice of liberation will remain only partial unless it embodies this exploration of privilege and a commitment to end it. We will continue to build centers in primarily white suburban areas with token diversity committees, and we will refrain from demanding that the whole sangha, especially our guiding teachers, enter into a real exploration and transformation of these issues.

When I lived on Brookwood Drive in Florence, Massachusetts a number of years ago, I lived across the street from a heterosexual working-class woman with whom I had developed a real friendship over the years. We had tea together, we shared bulbs and cut flowers and our love of gardening. After we became good friends, there was a referendum for Domestic Partnership Rights in the City of Northampton, and I asked her if she would sign a petition to support it. She said, "No. I don't really support that kind of thing." This really brought home to me how our true friendships cannot rest on only our personal connections with other people across difference. True friendship needs to be expressed in cultural, structural, and political ways as well. She could call me her friend and not sign the petition because she does not have to experience the pain of discrimination as a lesbian. She can slide over the issue into the notion of universality, pretending that we are all the same. I don't want to single her out, because we can all easily do the same thing when we are situated in our spaces of privilege. It's easy for us to say we're someone's friend and not actually make the effort to take a stand for the civil rights of that friend. I want to take the stand for the civil rights of my friends, of my community, of people of color.

As I take a stand I say this without the expectation that I will continue to remain in the protection of my privilege. I grew up in South Africa, and my parents were politically active against the apartheid state and the apartheid system. As long as their activities weren't known, it was okay, but when they actually started to take a physical stand to end apartheid, they suffered through police raids, all kinds of harassment, and imprisonment. Friends of my parents were murdered and resistance was seen as "terrorism." The anti-apartheid movement experienced the full force of the military and police state. Taking a stand to end racism and classism can be dangerous. It often means we find ourselves being targeted, ostracized, or isolated in our organizations and communities, and we also sometimes face the power of the police force and the military.

This is where we are called on to be courageous beyond the places where we've learned how to be courageous and to love beyond the places where we've learned to love. I believe that the happiness we are all seeking rests not in power, control, or comfort but rather in opening our hearts. I understand this opening requires a diligent inquiry into all the places that are closed, defended, or unexamined. It also demands of us a tremendous effort not only to abandon what is unwholesome within our own minds but also to cultivate the good. This necessarily means making an effort to change the existing inequalities in the culture and structure of our country. For those of us on the path, realizing the immeasurable preciousness of the Buddha's teachings, we are called to this transformation work, so that we can create the best conditions possible for all hearts to open. May all our hearts be liberated from suffering, ignorance, and blindness. May we live with kindness, wisdom, and equality.

Sharon Suh: Thank you all for coming to this conference panel. I wanted to first thank Ryūmon and Arinna for their eloquent commentary on the issue of race, gender, and ethnicity in the context of Buddhism. In particular, I wanted to express gratitude to Arinna for her courage and honesty in critiquing white privilege. It's easy to talk about racial equality and our own commitment to it; however, it's much more difficult to implicate ourselves within that privilege. In thinking about Buddhist women in America, I wanted to interrogate what we mean by Buddhism, women, and America. What forms of Buddhism are we talking about? Which women get to define the nature of Buddhist practice? Whose America do we have in mind here? I have been thinking quite a bit about these questions since coming to this conference and wanted to note that while it is important to acknowledge white privilege, we need to be careful not to stop at acknowledging privilege and feeling guilty for having that privilege. We need to go a step further and begin to change our everyday encounters with the "other." Too often guilt becomes a way of objectifying the other as someone who needs to be saved. Instead of treating the other as someone who needs to be saved, let's invite the other to the table for conversation. By listening to what she has to say, we avoid objectifying her and rendering her invisible. When we talk about the new forms of Buddhism emerging in America today, we need to bring to the table the voices of those who have been largely left out of the conversation so far—Asian American women. Instead of focusing primarily on white privilege, let's bring Asian American women, who are perhaps the largest supporters of Asian sanghas, into the conversation and the process of constructing new forms of Buddhism in America.

Many contemporary feminist scholars of American Buddhism maintain that women are responsible for transforming and revitalizing the Buddha sangha in the United States. Although the active presence of women in American Buddhism has been well documented, there is often an assumption that the transformative work is done primarily by Euro-American women. This assumption results in a separation between Asian American forms of Buddhism, also known as "ethnic" Buddhisms, and what is commonly understood as American Buddhism. Ethnic Buddhisms have come to denote that which is "other," "foreign," and "unassimilable." Consequently, the contributions of Asian American women to the development of Buddhism in America are overlooked. Additionally, Asian American women are left out of any meaningful discussion of the intersection of Buddhism and feminism in America. I would like to raise the following questions for us to consider as we explore women's Buddhist practice in America:

- What groups of individuals constitute this concept of America and what forms of Buddhism are considered authentic?
- Where do Asian American women fit into American Buddhism?
- How does looking at Asian forms of Buddhism in America challenge our understanding of American Buddhism?

Although the majority of Buddhist dharma teachers have historically come from Asia, most of their students have been white, Euro-American converts. The process of conversion has been well documented in works on American Buddhism, but there is little written about the Asian American Buddhist women in the United States who have transplanted and, as a result, transformed the tradition. Women do much of the work of maintaining and transmitting Buddhist traditions to younger generations in Asian American Buddhist communities. Therefore, we need to focus attention on the specific work done by Asian American women in diverse communities of Buddhists such as the Cambodian, Chinese, Japanese, Korean, Thai, and Vietnamese sanghas.

The Asian American women that I am talking about are largely laywomen. For many, their primary form of practice is lay devotion rather than meditation. This is another reason that their presence is often effaced in discussions of American Buddhism. Western Buddhist feminists often overlook laywomen's devotional practices, in spite of the fact that they have long argued for the equality of women in this religion that is over twenty-five hundred years old. Most books on American Buddhist women reflect a fascination with meditation at the expense of lay devotion. Nonmeditative practices are characterized as "popular religion" and, therefore, as less authentic forms of Buddhism. The problem with this hierarchy of practices is that for many Asian American lay Buddhist women, devotional practices are their main forms of practice. Hence, Asian American women's practices are devalued as less worthwhile endeavors. I argue for a reconceptualization of Buddhist practice. We need to take seriously the centrality of lay devotion in Buddhist women's lives. If we fail to do so, we distort the nature of Buddhism in America. Additionally, valuing meditation over lay devotion reinforces a mind-body dichotomy that values the mind, which is the locus of meditation, over the body, which is the locus of devotional practices such as bowing. I suggest that we take this conference on "Women Practicing Buddhism: American Experiences," as an opportunity to interrogate the assumptions behind our concepts of Buddhism, women, and America.

CJ: *As I listened to the presentations at this conference, I wondered how our conversations about women practicing Buddhism would have been different if they had engaged more fully the intellectual and lived experiences of people of color.*

First of all, race, ethnicity, and class are social constructs rooted in European and American social and political thought; it is these constructs that give language and the power of belief to behaviors that enact, and policies that support, separating human beings from one another. Such separation has resulted in economic and political power differentials as well as in social, educational, and health disparities. These constructs have resulted in categorizing human beings into groups that are separated into hierarchical structures, each embedded with relative privileges and power. While there are efforts to deconstruct these constructs, they still have great influence and power over the opportunities, exercise of potential, and freedom of large numbers of human beings. The challenge before us is to restore all beings to freedom without creating additional hierarchical structures or shifting human beings from one category to another; this is the opportunity before us.

The essence of sitting in silent meditation allows human beings to move away from the enslavement of the internalization of those constructs. Sitting entails a commitment to being present and allows one to no longer be captive to existing constructs and one's own interpretations of those constructs. I feel a deep commitment to paying attention to the ways in which sitting allows one to be aware of one another's personal stories. Paying attention allows a gentle holding and awareness of others and our experiences of the unfreedom of race, ethnicity, and class constructs. Paying attention enables examination of the illusions we have about the other and the kind of social constructs that limit our freedom to fully be who we are in this universe.

What people of color bring to a conversation on race, ethnicity, and class is very much connected with who we are because our definition of self is intimately linked with our ancestors, our elders, our history, and our place in our community. For many people of color, our task is not to separate from our community but to find ourselves in the fullness of the community. The community is the primary definer of self. Life occurs when you are present to the community. The highest value is placed on interpersonal relationships. The quality of paying attention to others is a clear expression of the value placed on relationships. Once you meet on the ground of "being with," there is a shift, affectively, into spaces of comfort and acceptance. One experiences the life force that pervades and permeates all things, all relationships, with a particular historical and ancestral configuration for each group. Silence or the spaces between words, looks, and movements give expression to the importance of self defined in relationship, of self that is lost and found in all selves and in no self.

There is no dichotomy between sitting practice and engaging in other traditions for people of color. We have the capacity to hold what are perceived of as diametrically opposing worldviews and navigate connecting and seemingly disparate communities and beings. If there is a tension, then it is a point of healing or resolution as one continues the journey. Forgiveness of self and others may be important for the process. Conversations regarding race, ethnicity, and class often lead to moments of tension. Such moments demand justice and beg for compassion. They invite a quality of attention that comes from a deep connection born of centeredness, allowing pain, suffering, and oppression to surface through layers of social construction and psychological experiences. Compassion and openness to transformation require an authentic letting go of self, not out of a privileged letting go but out of a surrendered reality that being closely with the other is the true privileged position for all beings.

References

Hilda Gutiérrez Baldoquín, ed., *Dharma, Color, and Culture: New Voices in Western Buddhism* (Berkeley, CA: Parallax, 2004).

Charlotte Joko Beck, *Nothing Special: Living Zen* (HarperSanFrancisco, 1993).

Fashioning New Selves: The Experiences of Taiwanese Buddhist Women

Carolyn Chen

PATRICIA CHIU, an immigrant from Taiwan, tells me that after spending her entire life trying to please her family members—first her parents and now her in-laws—she finally realized that she was deeply unhappy with herself. Despite her own professional success as a doctor, she lived her life aspiring to meet the expectations of her family without ever bothering to know who she really was or what she really wanted. She claims that it was only after converting to Buddhism that she "awakened" her true self—a self that escaped the bounded definitions that her family had imposed on her.

Religious converts from various religious traditions and historical periods have often narrated their salvation experiences as the liberation, or the recovery, of the authentic self. Taiwanese women are no exception in this regard. Most striking is *from what* religion liberates them and *who* they describe their new selves to be. Patricia Chiu describes her religious conversion as freedom from the restrictions of traditional Taiwanese womanhood—a womanhood that she sees as hemmed in by familial obligations—and the freedom to follow her individual spiritual calling independent of her family's demands. This personal account of religion as a liberating force calls into question a scholarly literature that describes immigrant religions as reinforcing traditional patriarchy. When we look at how women interpret and practice religion in their daily lives, however, we can see how religion *challenges*, rather than preserves, traditional patriarchal understandings of the self in relation to the family.

Many Taiwanese women claim to become Buddhist only after migrating to the United States. Having participated in Buddhist religious rituals only nominally in Taiwan, these women rediscover the tradition in the United States. They now incorporate Buddhist practice in their daily lives and embrace a new Buddhist identity. This essay explores how Taiwanese immigrant women use Buddhism to fashion new selves in the United States. Whereas self is subsumed by kinship in Confucian tradition, Taiwanese immigrant women use Buddhism to negotiate spaces of independence from the family. In many ways, the experiences and strategies of Taiwanese immigrant women resemble those of other immigrant women who have carved out some measure of autonomy through working outside of the home. Yet these women still struggle to reconcile traditional Confucian conceptions of womanhood with realities of living in the United States. Buddhism can encourage women to consider alternative conceptions of selfhood, conceptions less tethered to traditional notions of womanhood that are largely defined and bounded by the familial roles of mother, wife, or daughter. Religion offers Taiwanese immigrant women a new identity and sense of purpose beyond the family, although these new religious commitments may cause tension within extended and nuclear kin relationships and even restructure them.

❖ Methods and Setting

My findings are based on fifteen months of ethnographic fieldwork at a Taiwanese Buddhist temple in Southern California between January 1999 and March 2000. To maintain the anonymity of the institution and the people involved, I have given them pseudonyms. I call the Buddhist temple, "Dharma Light Temple." Most of my findings in this essay are based on interviews with fifteen Taiwanese Buddhist women. The respondents are between the ages of thirty-three and fifty-five. All but one are married with children. Although some Taiwanese immigrated to the United States as early as 1969 and others as late as 1997, most came in the 1980s and early 1990s. Many came to the United States to pursue advanced degrees and then decided to settle here. Over half of the Taiwanese women in my sample are college educated. More than one-quarter have advanced degrees, all earned in the United States. At the time of the interviews, just over half of the women worked outside of the home. Of these, approximately half worked in non-Chinese businesses, while the other half worked within the larger Chinese American community. The majority of the women have worked at some point during their residence in the United States.

❖ Becoming New Selves

Amid the unsettling changes that migration brings, the Taiwanese immigrant women I interviewed use religion to negotiate old traditions and to construct new traditions of gender and selfhood in the United States. In migrating to the United States, Taiwanese women face a number of contradictions and tensions between their present American realities and the Confucian ideals of womanhood with which they were raised. The Western conception of the self as an autonomous unit is foreign to most Taiwanese. Like other traditional Confucian societies, a Taiwanese person's identity is deeply embedded in a communal context. Individuals are always defined relationally, according to their location in the kinship structure. For Taiwanese women, this traditional structure is a patriarchal one. Being a woman means belonging to, and hence subjugation to, men—first her father, then her husband, and then her sons. A woman is expected to marry out of her own family and devote her life to her husband and his family. Even the figure of the domineering mother-in-law participates in this patriarchal institution, since she wields her power by virtue of her relationship to her son.

In their upbringings in Taiwan, the women I interviewed were encouraged to cultivate the womanly virtues of obedience to, and dependence on, male relatives. Comparing the differences between American women and Taiwanese women, one respondent said, "Chinese women are more obedient. At home, we listen to our husband. My mom always said, 'Whatever the husband says, you must go along.'" Suzanne Wu, a woman in her midforties with an M.B.A. degree, remembers how her parents would tell her "it's not good for a woman to think too much." Although expanding economic and educational opportunities in Taiwan have challenged some of these concepts of womanhood and gender relations in the last few decades, the immigrant women that I interviewed continued to characterize womanhood in Taiwan in these traditional Confucian terms.

Their situations as immigrant women in the United States, however, required different and even contrary qualities to those they learned as women in Taiwan. Like other immigrant women in the United States, these Taiwanese women adapted to the financial demands of raising a family in the United States by working outside of the home. At the time of the interviews, more than half of the respondents worked outside of the home. Nearly all of the respondents worked outside of the home at one time in their lives in the United States. Several of the women have devoted years developing their professional careers as dentists, computer programmers, and nurses. These careers give them a sense of status and identity outside of the family. By working, these women gain a degree of economic independence and financial power in household matters that their mothers did not have. For example, consider how employment changed the gender dynamics in the home of Yi-Ming Lee, a working-class woman who has lived in the United States for seventeen years:

> In Taiwan he [her husband] used to take care of all the financial matters, and I didn't know how much money he made. All of our money was in his control. It's not like that here in America. There, he was working and he took care of all the

payments. I had to ask him for money. Now because I work we have a joint bank account. Financial matters are joint decisions. My name is on those documents so he needs to ask for my permission. Before, in Taiwan, he bought two houses without even telling me. Now he can't do that.

Even those women who do not contribute to the family income agree that living in the United States enlarges women's traditional sphere of authority compared to that in Taiwan. For example, Arlene Su, a housewife, makes the decisions regarding financial investments in her household:

When we deal with financial investments I often make the inquiries because he's at work. I have the time to look at things. He consents with the decision that I've made.

Because of these new responsibilities in the household she is "forced to learn" so that she can "contribute to the decision." Arlene adds that the survival skills she needs in the United States clash with the traditional Taiwanese womanly virtues of submissiveness and obedience. "If a wife is trained to be submissive," Arlene says, "she will be submissive no matter what. She won't fight back. It's very tough. In this country you need to learn to speak out for your own rights and fight back."

As Taiwanese immigrants, women see firsthand how American women live in the United States, and they question the hierarchy and patriarchy of their own traditional culture even more deeply. Comparing their own situations to those of Anglo-American women, Taiwanese women remark with envy on the equality between American women and men. As one respondent puts it:

In America, women and men are on the same level. If men do it, then women do it, too. Men and women earn money and go to college. In America women are better off. In the house, men also help out. In America, it is more equal.

Taiwanese women also feel that American women are more independent. When asked to describe a typical American woman and a typical Taiwanese woman, Sharon Wang, a woman in her early thirties
with a bachelor's degree from an American university, says:

> American women are independent. They have a lot of space
> to do things that they really enjoy. The typical Taiwanese
> woman is not independent. She will look upon marriage as
> the most important thing in her life. She will try to secure her-
> self financially through their marriage.

Many of the respondents admire the qualities of American women
while they criticize their own Taiwanese ideals of womanhood. They
claim that their normative Taiwanese traditions feel static and confin-
ing when their realities are so different in the United States. Their new
American lives cultivate and even require a new independence from
men (and the family) that challenges their traditional Taiwanese notions
of womanhood. The development of separate careers and income from
men, the example of independent American women, and the need for
immigrant women to "fight for [their] rights" in the American public all
nurture a new notion of womanly selfhood in contradistinction from the
traditional Taiwanese self. Since women are traditionally defined by
their relationships to men in the family, it is no surprise that it is also
within the family that these tensions of negotiating a new self are most
pronounced.

It is in the context of these everyday familial negotiations that Taiwanese immigrant women use religion to work out the contradictions
between Taiwanese traditions and their new American realities. These
tensions are dramatized in their conversion narratives in religious language that gives voice to their experiences and offers a vocabulary to
declare a new kind of gendered self that transcends old traditions. Taiwanese immigrant women use their new identities and obligations as
Buddhists to carve out spaces of independence from their roles and the
expectations of family—or even to subtly redefine them.

⁖ A Self Separate from the Family

The story of Tina Tseng's spiritual awakening as a Buddhist illustrates how religious conversion liberates some Taiwanese women from traditional gender roles in the family. Her experience embodies the familiar Chinese trope of the long-suffering daughter-in-law in the face of the oppressive mother-in-law. Tina's career as an accomplished doctor gives her an independent and high-status identity beyond the family. And yet Tina, who is forty-six years old and married with one daughter, claims, "I didn't like myself deep inside my heart," before her conversion to Buddhism seven years ago. A self-proclaimed perfectionist in both her professional and personal life, she aimed to win the praise of others. She had attended the top medical school in Taiwan and been awarded a prestigious research fellowship at an American university. She was adored by her husband and daughter as a devoted wife and mother. But she still did not like herself deep inside her heart, she explains, because she could not live up to the expectations of her overbearing Christian mother-in-law. Although none of the respondents were living with their in-laws permanently, many, including Tina, had in-laws from Taiwan visiting for months at a time. Tina says:

> I tried my best to please a lot of people. I tried to be a perfect daughter-in-law, but my mother-in-law would tell me that I wasn't good at this and I wasn't good at that. And I believed her, and I started to blame myself. I didn't like myself deep inside my heart.

Although Tina had converted to Christianity to marry her husband, it was not until she encountered Buddhism, when dealing with her own mother's death, that she claims she started truly to know and like herself. To Tina and other Buddhists, knowledge of self is one of the first steps to enlightenment. In Buddhism, ignorance enslaves humanity to an endless cycle of suffering. The human condition is one of perpetual delusion, whereby humans regard the empirical world as permanent and real, when in fact it is impermanent and illusory. As one monastic described it to me, "We are living in an eighty-year dream state." As humans, we are socialized into regarding this world as ultimate reality. Suffering and unhappiness arise out of the tendency to become attached to finding fulfillment in things that humans think are permanent and real when in fact they are not.

To Tina, knowledge of self means knowing that the empirical self, the self who is attached to meeting the expectations of others, is also illusory. In contrast to the empirical self is the awakened self, the self that possesses buddha nature. One's buddha nature is the innate capacity for all sentient beings to become enlightened, but it is obscured by the attachment to this illusory world. Speaking on the empirical self at Dharma Light Temple, Ven. Man-yi compared the self to an onion. She instructed the devotees, "You strip the empirical self down and there is no core. The empirical self is conditioned by the environment. It is not the ultimate self, so let the empirical self go."

In letting their empirical selves go, Buddhists devalue their social identities to the enhancement of their buddha nature, their true nature that transcends their socially ascribed selves. Tina articulates this when she says:

> Buddhism enhances you as a person. You as a person are responsible for yourself. And you find yourself from within yourself. Through calm or chanting time, it gives you space to think about yourself and refine yourself as a human being. *It's not about being liked by other people but about letting your true nature come out.*

Salvation, for Tina, is the realization that she was mired in a world of illusions where she believed that happiness would come from meeting the approval of others, especially those in positions of superiority to her. Her attachment to pleasing her mother-in-law was preventing her from true happiness and fulfillment.

Buddhism not only gives Tina a sense of peace and calm, it also grants her new independence from traditions. By prioritizing the awakening of her buddha nature over meeting the demands of her mother-in-law, the boundaries of kinship expectations no longer define her existence. She realizes that who she should be is not who others think she should be. Buddhism teaches her that there is no one that she "should" be, but that she only needs to discover who she really is. This does not mean that she totally disregards her obligations to her mother-in-law; rather, she now approaches them with a new perspective. Before, she would hide her Buddhism from her mother-in-law for fear of disapproval and would leave home early to practice her chanting and bowing in her medical office rather than at home. Now she is open and unapologetic about her Buddhism. She will still accompany her mother-in-law to Christian church services. However, she maintains the Buddhist altar in her home despite her mother-in-law's strong disapproval. Through her Buddhist identity, Tina carves a space of independence from her mother-in-law. She will continue to fulfill her obligations as a daughter-in-law by accompanying her to church but limits these obligations when they infringe on her own personal religious practice. She holds her religious obligations sacred, so to speak.

Like many of the women at Dharma Light Temple, Tina devotes one afternoon a week to volunteer work at the temple. Volunteers serve in a variety of capacities, such as answering the phone, translating Chinese documents into English, maintaining the grounds, and so on. Volunteering at the temple offers Tina the freedom to be more than a mother, wife, and daughter-in-law. At Dharma Light Temple, her identity revolves around her buddha nature, rather than her kinship obligations. Little else has changed in Tina's situation with her mother-in-law, who continues to nag and criticize her. What has changed, however, is that these kinship obligations no longer determine her existence. Buddhism, according to Tina, has freed her to seek her true happiness and to be who she believes she really is.

Tina Tseng's story illustrates how Buddhism can offer women alternatives to traditional kin-centered definitions of self. What is significant is how women use their religion in the contexts that they are in. In traditional Taiwanese culture, religious and familial duties are inextricably linked. The cult of the family, or ancestral worship, is not about personal piety but about offering provisions for one's ancestors in their next lives. Daily rituals of ancestral veneration both provide links to one's past and foster moral solidarity among family members in the present. As a woman who has married into her husband's family, Tina is expected to maintain the family's religious tradition, whether it is traditional Taiwanese religion, Buddhism, or Christianity. For example, Tina converted to Christianity in order to marry her husband.

In this context, religious conversion represents an act of independence from the family. To Tina, religious conversion is as much about converting *to* Buddhism as it is about converting *from* Christianity, the religious tradition of her in-laws. It is precisely because religion holds such symbolic weight within the family that religious conversion produces such dramatic consequences for women who are so defined by the family.

❖ Religion and Family: Competing Commitments

The example of Tina Tseng illustrates how women can use religion to fashion new self-identities from which to limit their kinship obligations to their in-laws. Their new religious commitments also offer women the leverage for greater autonomy and authority within the nuclear family. Women rarely use their religious license to abandon or reject familial responsibilities altogether, however. More often, women fulfill competing religious commitments within the constraints of the family.

Although Buddhism has made her life more joyful and meaningful than ever before, Mei Hwa Huang claims that Buddhism is also a source of strain and tension in her marriage. Mei Hwa is a former computer programmer who is now a housewife and mother of a nine-year-old girl. Before converting to Buddhism, she was, in her own words, a "typical society lady." Always impeccably dressed in the latest designer fashions, she was a socialite who flitted around from one party to the next, making the necessary social appearances to build her husband's expanding international software business. After a friend of hers introduced her to some Buddhist books, she started to question the meaning of her life. Her beautiful things lost their luster and her endless parties became monotonous. She was increasingly disillusioned with how shallow her life had become. She turned to Buddhism to fill this void and started to devote herself to Buddhist practice. Instead of attending glamorous parties, she now attends chanting ceremonies. Instead of hosting charity events, she volunteers as the telephone receptionist at the temple. Her friends and family worried that perhaps she had lost her mind.

This transformation in Mei Hwa created problems in her marriage. Her husband relied on her to host and accompany him to social events where a great deal of his informal business dealings took place. Now her time is occupied by activities at the temple. Even when she has the time to attend her husband's events, she quite often refuses because they do not accommodate to her new vegetarian diet. As Mei Hwa says, "Buddhism changed our lifestyle." Now even what used to be the most basic decisions of where and what to eat have become points of tension in their marriage because Mei Hwa's Buddhist vegetarian diet precludes even onions and garlic. Equally, if not more, disconcerting to her husband are the times she insists on practicing sexual abstinence for religious observance. She knowingly admits, "During times of intense ceremony and ritual, I'll separate myself from my family and husband. That's changed our relationship a lot." Her husband is not a practicing Buddhist, but at his wife's urging, he has agreed to "take refuge," a practice similar to the Christian ritual of baptism. Commenting on the effect of her conversion to Buddhism on her husband, Mei Hwa says, "I'm more my own. I make choices differently from my husband. This creates some distance, but gradually he's become more supportive."

As the case of Mei Hwa illustrates, religious conversion creates new moral obligations and commitments that compete with those of the family. Many women have similar experiences of balancing their familial and religious commitments, especially when their husbands do not share in the same religious enthusiasm. For example, after becoming a practicing Buddhist, Suzanne Wu, a business executive, started to attend the activities at Dharma Light Temple more regularly. She tried to bring her husband and son along. Her son willingly accompanied her and is now actively involved in the youth group. Her husband, however, refuses to attend the temple. This has created rifts in the family because now her husband must compete with Buddhism to spend quality time with his wife and son.

Among the Buddhists I interviewed, women tend to be more religious than men. This is obvious at the temple, where women participate in greater numbers in chanting ceremonies, dharma classes, and volunteering. At the Taiwanese immigrant Christian church, men and women are more equally represented than at the Buddhist temple, where fewer of the women report their husbands sharing their level of religious devotion. This may be due to greater opportunities for lay leadership positions (which are predominantly male) in the church than in the temple. In my study, religion tends to be a greater source of marital tension for Buddhists than for Christians, perhaps because the husbands of Christian women tend to share more in their religious commitments.

Where husband and wife are equally committed, my findings suggest that religion can challenge traditional arrangements by granting women more autonomy from their husbands. In the case of Ann Lee and her husband Tom, for example, a shared commitment to Buddhism has radically changed their lifestyles, moving them both away from traditional family-defined roles. Ann has decided to stop working and contributing to the family income so that she can devote more of her time to Buddhist practice. Ann and Tom no longer engage in what used to be family activities, such as going to the movies or watching television, because they both agree that these are not conducive to their Buddhist practice. They have also decided to stop having sex because this only cultivates what Ann regards as misguided desires. As devout Buddhists, the Lees subjugate the expectations of a traditional marriage to the cultivation of their buddha nature.

The example of Ann and Tom Lee is an extreme case of how new religious commitments may subvert traditional familial relationships. For most of the Taiwanese women I interviewed, however, the changes are far more subtle and incremental. Many women want to honor these new religious commitments, *and* they want to maintain the integrity of the family. Women want to reject some traditional kinship obligations, like the absolute authority of the husband and his elders, while preserving other traditional familial responsibilities. In none of the cases do religious commitments actually lead people to reject their families, much less the institution of the family. Rather, religion is a way for women to negotiate or "bargain" for more autonomy *within* the constraints of the family. New religious commitments offer women wiggle-room to fashion new priorities, often leading to the formation of religious obligations that may compete with traditional familial expectations. But Taiwanese women are still wives, mothers, and daughters-in-law, and their religious commitments are tempered by their familial responsibilities. Religious license is constrained by the desire to keep intact the nuclear family and, to a lesser degree, the extended family. Women pursue religion to the extent that it does not compromise the integrity of the nuclear family.

The case of Diana Chen, a homemaker who immigrated nine years ago, illustrates how a woman may alter her religious practice to preserve a peaceful relationship with her husband. Knowing that her husband strongly disapproves of her "superstition," Diana tries to hide her Buddhist practice from him. Unlike other Buddhist homes, hers has no religious icons. She strategically performs her morning practice of chanting and meditation after he leaves home. Unbeknown to him, she meets with a sūtra study group one afternoon a week. She participates in temple activities only rarely when her husband is out of town at business meetings. Diana's husband knows that she is religious. After all, he sees her Buddhist books sit on the bookshelf. But she feels he is less tolerant than the husbands of other women who openly practice their religion. His disapproval of Buddhism is so strong that Diana thinks that it could seriously damage their marriage and family. Weighing such severe costs to the family, Diana chooses to tiptoe around the tense issue of religion and render it as invisible as possible.

Although Diana Chen is someone who takes great measures to alter religious practice, many Buddhist women, like her, will strategically compromise their own religious commitments for the sake of the family. Many Buddhist women want to prepare only vegetarian meals in order to obey the religious teaching not to kill. However, as the family cooks, few women actually do this because of their husbands' eating habits and the concerns for their growing children's dietary needs. Women also mentioned that family responsibilities keep them from participating in Buddhist retreats that run from one week to ten days. More specifically, women were concerned about neglecting their responsibilities as mothers. Where religious commitments conflict with family obligations, women curb or hide their religious activities—as they see it, "for the sake of the family."

The women in my sample want to maintain their religious commitments but not at the cost of radically threatening the family. The religious and cultural stigmas against divorce discourage it among these women. Equally significant is the fact that as immigrant women they may not have kin to rely upon, and some may not have the language and skills to be financially independent. For example, one woman who is in an unhappy marriage admitted that she would get divorced were it not for the fact that she could not support her children and herself in the United States.

Short of threatening their families and marriages, most of my respondents are willing to challenge some traditional familial expectations to fulfill their own religious commitments. Respondents vary, however, in the extent to which they will go against their husbands. With the relatively small sample size, I cannot comment conclusively on how women's education and income influence their bargaining power with their husbands. In cases such as Diana Chen's, women who must accommodate their religious practices around their husbands are not working. The lack of a separate income may hurt women's bargaining power over religion. But the evidence also suggests that both working and nonworking women expect their husbands to accommodate in varying degrees to their religion.

⋄ Conclusion

This essay offers a glimpse into the ways that Taiwanese immigrant women use religion to resituate themselves in the United States. For Taiwanese immigrant women struggling with the discrepancy between their new realities in the United States and the normative traditions of Taiwanese womanhood, religious language gives voice to their experiences and offers a vocabulary to declare a new kind of gendered self. My findings suggest that even though immigrant women's participation in the labor market may lead to greater independence and equality, some women may still need the symbolic and moral resources of religion to legitimate the departure from the old kin-centered self to a new independent self. Religion is a catalyst for transformation, as its rejection of "this world" becomes a metaphor that these women use to reject certain kinship expectations that they now find constraining in the United States. At the same time, religion helps them make sense of the changes by offering conceptual resources to frame who they were, who they are, and who they are becoming.

By claiming that religious commitments may compete with family commitments, I am not arguing that religion and family are inherently opposed. There is no doubt that religion sanctifies certain family roles. To my respondents, being good Buddhist women also meant being good mothers, wives, and daughters-in-law. Rather, the issue is *what kind* of womanly self does religion sanctify in relation to the family? Is it a self who is only mother, wife, and daughter-in-law, as in the traditional Taiwanese model of womanhood, or is it a self who has purpose and meaning outside of kinship? For my respondents, religion offers the possibility of an ontologically and empirically separate self, whose purpose and commitments may converge with the traditional Taiwanese family but may also diverge from the traditional kinship expectations. It is through the pursuit of these extra-familial, religious goals that most women carve spaces of independence and authority for themselves, albeit never at the cost of radically threatening the nuclear family.

NOTE

This essay is adapted from my previously published journal article, Carolyn Chen, "A Self of One's Own: Taiwanese Immigrant Women and Religious Conversion," *Gender & Society* 19:3 (2005), pp. 336–57, in which I discuss religious conversion among Taiwanese immigrant women in greater detail; the article also includes an analysis of the appropriate secondary literature on immigration.

Growing Up Buddhist

Alice Unno

❖ Family Background

I'M FROM a lay Buddhist family. My father was born and raised in Japan; he came to the United States at the age of sixteen. My mother was born in the United States, but when she became of education age, which must have been around first grade, her family sent her back to Japan to study. Later she returned to the United States and married my dad. They both came from the Hiroshima area, which is a very strong Shin Buddhist region. All I really remember is that it meant everything to my parents to go to the Shin Temple, to contribute physically and financially, even to the point where that was more important than keeping the family in fancy clothes. Their lives were very difficult, as kind of semi-immigrants. Although my father spoke perfect English, the only work that he could get was as a laborer. My father was very much one who believed that living in one place was important for his children's education, so he became a foreman of a vineyard. He couldn't own land because there was a law on the books that if you were Asian, you couldn't become a naturalized citizen, and if you weren't a citizen, you couldn't buy land. Although my mother was a citizen and could have bought the land, I think that it wasn't possible given his pride as the man of the house, so he worked for other people instead.

We lived in a small town in California called Lodi, where I was born and raised, along with an older brother and a younger sister. Every Sunday or whenever they had any activity at the Buddhist temple, all of us piled into the car and went. It was really important to my parents that we had an *obutsudan* (Buddhist altar) at home. My parents always told us that if ever there were a fire, the altar was the first thing we had to take out of the house—that and the drawer underneath it, which contained the sūtras and important papers like birth certificates. I was always scared dusting the altar because it was so special and sacred. My mother always said you shouldn't just use an ordinary rag. There was a special cloth to clean it with. We bowed to it in the morning and in the evening before we went to sleep. We also had a premeal ritual where we thanked the vegetables, rice, or other food for providing sustenance so we could live. The Japanese phrase is *itadakimasu* (may we respectfully receive this food)—it's like grace. When we finished eating, we thanked everyone and everything again for the food. That's the basic Buddhist practice that I remember from childhood.

The Shin Buddhist temple where I grew up was like the community center. It was a support system for all of the Japanese immigrants and those born in the United States, because we were still segregated. There wasn't obvious discrimination, as there was so clearly against Black people, but Asians were not easily integrated, although I never really felt different in the public school system. My father always said, "Be honest. Be good. Study hard to be an American." There weren't a lot of Japanese American children at my school. There was a sprinkling of Mexican American children, but I think I was the only Japanese American in my classroom. I really didn't feel different. My best friend in first grade was an Italian American girl, and we'd even wear the same dresses to school to be like twins. I had a very happy, stable childhood until World War II.

❖ Experience during World War II

World War II was devastating for me. It really changed my whole life. I was only eight years old when it started, and it was very difficult. The

FBI came in black suits and went through the house. My mother packed my dad a small suitcase, and I still remember him trying to reassure us that he'd be back "soon" but not right away. My father was born in 1902, so he was in his late thirties when he was taken away in 1941. Japanese and Japanese American families didn't usually kiss their children to say goodbye, but he kissed us goodbye, so I knew something was desperately wrong. He disappeared out of our lives, and I didn't know where he was for three or four weeks.

My father was singled out because he was bilingual and was probably considered a potential leader in the Japanese American community. He had helped many of our friends who couldn't speak English do things like open a bank account, or get insurance, and even with shopping, because he spoke very good English. After the war was over, my father told me that when the FBI picked him up and took him away, they put him in the county jail. He refused to eat or drink for three days in protest. He said he was so angry because "I hadn't done anything, and they were accusing me of being the enemy." He was incarcerated at the Army Presidio in San Francisco. I remember visiting him once or twice there before we were sent to an internment camp. My mother must have visited him more often—I remember that the shades would be drawn sometimes when I came home from elementary school because we had to observe a blackout order. The drawn shades were a sign that my mom and my younger sister weren't there, so I'd have to wait more than half an hour until my brother came home. That for me was a terrible, terrible time. I hated being alone waiting for my brother to return home. I didn't realize for the longest time after the war why drawn shades bothered me, but when I remembered and put the two together, I realized, That's why I don't like shades.

I cried every day at school trying to figure out why I was, in my particular class, the only one who was now becoming the enemy. One friend of mine had dark hair and dark brown eyes like I did, but I was singled out as being the enemy, and I hated Japan for starting the war. I hated the way I looked and who I was because of that. It never left me, the idea of having to learn to like myself, because I always wanted to be blue-eyed and blond. I used to draw all the time, and blond-haired, blue-eyed girls were all I ever drew. I still remember the teacher trying to reason with me, but I don't remember what she said; there was just no way to console me at that point. And so, I carried that with me for a long, long time. Many of the children who went into the internment camps remember it as a fun time because they had a lot of friends, but I don't remember it that way. I always wondered, Why, *why* was I born with this face? I'm an American and I still became the enemy. There was no way to rationally erase that for me.

When the U.S. government ordered my mother, my siblings, and me to go to the internment camps in May 1942, we were first sent to the county fair grounds in Stockton, California, a town about ten or fifteen miles away from my hometown of Lodi. That was the place where my dad used to take us every year for the exciting and fun county fair, as far back as I could remember. Now those grounds became our prison—they had barbed-wire fences around, and the water fountain that I used to love to go and watch was now dry. We were constantly told not to go near the barbed-wire fences because there were guards with guns pointed inward at us to prevent us from trying to escape. None of that made any sense to me—why would I want to escape? And why was I in this place? This was the place I used to love, and now there were adults crying, people scared to death, and my mother trying to hold us together as a family. They didn't take my citizenship away, but I saw my mother trying to take care of everything so that we could go into the camps with the luggage we needed, and I deeply felt her fear. She didn't have answers for us. Later in life, my mother said she had thought I was okay with the whole scene. I was very quiet, and I seemed to handle things fairly well, so she didn't realize at the time what turmoil I was going through on the inside.

We used to line up to go to eat at what we called the "mess hall," and a lot of the food was very unfamiliar because, as we know, we're spoiled by our mother's cooking. The bathroom was just like a warehouse, with no partitions. I remember a lot of those kinds of things, as well as always feeling insecure, uncertain, and frightened.

Even in the Stockton Assembly Center, they used to have Buddhist services in the grandstand of the racetrack, and I remember my mother insisting that we kids go together. So a bunch of the older kids would round up us little ones, and off we'd go. I used to be a little bit of a rascal, so I'd climb way up to the top in the last row, and that's actually where I learned sūtra chants. They gave us a piece of paper with the *Junirai* (The Twelve Adorations) written on it, and every Sunday we were supposed to chant it. If we talked during that time, the older people would turn around and hiss at us. So we learned to keep our mouths shut, and the only thing we could do was just read the darn thing, and we soon memorized the sūtra. That's my memory of learning how to do the sūtra chanting.

I don't know when they sent my father to Santa Fe, and I don't know how long he was there, but they eventually allowed him to join us at the assembly center just before we were shipped to Rohwer Detention Camp in Arkansas. I still remember how a young soldier in the train was very kind to my mother, asking if she needed anything. She turned around and said to us, "He feels very badly for us." She acknowledged his kindness by putting her hands together and bowing. I was never really scared of the soldiers, but I knew that we weren't supposed to do anything nasty or mischievous—you really had to behave yourself around them. That's kind of hard on a kid, you know.

I think there were fewer than ten thousand people in the Arkansas camp. Putting people into camps was one way of making sure they wouldn't be doing whatever negative thing we were suspected of possibly doing. The intent of the camps was not to torture us but just to house us, so they had to provide things for us. We were in these camps with barbed-wire fence surrounding us and high towers with the soldiers and guns, but they fed us three meals a day. The men were allowed to make vegetable gardens, so they banded together and grew vegetables to provide for their respective camps. My father got a job, nineteen dollars a month, monitoring the water pumps in the camp. My mother worked in the mess-hall kitchen and earned twelve dollars a month.

We children all went to school in the camp. At a conference I attended in 2004 in Arkansas about internment, sponsored by the University of Arkansas and the Rockefeller Foundation, I found out that the U.S. Government had offered to pay teachers two thousand dollars a year if they'd teach in the camp. Teachers in Arkansas weren't being paid that much to teach in the public schools, so the good teachers who should have been teaching in Arkansas came instead to teach in the camp. Ironically, we had the best education, the highest level of scores in testing in the state. Isn't that amazing? That was an eye-opener.

The other heart-wrenching thing that I found out at this conference was that there were very poor Arkansas people, both African American and Caucasian, who lived near the camps. There were always some garbage and leftovers from our meals, so the government permitted people on the outside to come with trucks or buckets or whatever and haul it away to feed their pigs. When we went to this conference, the local people told us stories that their parents had told them: There was food they had never seen before in their lives. It was so much better than anything they had ever eaten, and they couldn't believe that it was being thrown away to feed their pigs. One of the big problems, however, was that the food they served us—like mutton stew—was very hard for us to eat. So whenever they served mutton, I could never eat it. I would always throw my portion away. When we finished meals we had to bus our own plates, and we dumped the garbage and passed the dishes down. I'm sure that's the garbage that supposedly went to the pigs. That shocked me—you know, *really*. I had never thought about people on the outside being even worse off than we were in the camps. It just broke my heart when I heard about it. You see, my experience was colored by my own personal little-girl perspective, but it puts a whole different kind of complexion on everything to hear, as an adult, how others were suffering at that time too.

We were in the camps for a total of three-and-a-half years. That is where I would say my search to find a reason for living and meaning in life began, because I turned the hatred I had experienced toward myself. My husband Ty thought I was the happiest person when we met, but when he married me, he found out I was a pretty unhappy woman inside. It took a long time doing my own seeking, through Buddhism, to find out what life is really about—you can't keep hating yourself. I've never felt bitter against the United States, because it's my country. But I could never understand as a child, even though as an adult I did rationally, why my own government turned against me, and all I could think of was that I looked wrong. That was basically the reason I turned toward a spiritual path, hoping to find some kind of meaning. I can honestly say that if it weren't for Buddhism, I wouldn't be who I am today. It anchored me in reality.

❖ Coming to Buddhism

Before I started seriously studying Buddhism, I went to the Methodist Church, because I really wanted to go somewhere where English was spoken and I could understand the teachings. I asked my parents if I could become a Methodist, and they were very wise. They said, "Well, you know, we would be very sad if you changed to Christianity, but if you would, do us the favor of studying Buddhism first, and if you really find that it doesn't have meaning for you, then even though we'd be sad, you would go with our blessings if you became Christian." That's when I started to ask people for books on Buddhism. There are a lot of good books now, but at that time when I first started off, all they had were things like the anthology of translations put together by Dwight Goddard, and it was all just words to me. It just didn't apply to my life. The Japanese-speaking ministers, especially in our tradition, say the whole teaching is contained in the phrase *Namu Amida Butsu*. I was really impertinent by asking the minister, "You say this so seriously, but what does it mean to you personally? Can you tell me?" And they really couldn't explain it because it is a personal experience. There are words that can explain it, but they didn't have the English skills. Daisetz Suzuki's book, *Introduction to Zen Buddhism*, really helped me. I read that so many times back and forth. Even though it didn't always make sense, there was phrasing in it that would somehow almost make sense. And his way of explaining was more intuitive, so that I could feel what meaning might be there, but I didn't know what it was. I read most of his books, and that's how I got into Buddhism.

Most of the ministers before, during, and even immediately after World War II conducted services in Japanese. My husband Ty was the first English-speaking person I could ask about Buddhism. That's how we originally met. He had been studying in Japan from 1951 to about 1956, when he came back to the U.S. At that time, I was at a Buddhist conference in Los Angeles and was desperately in need of some answers, and so I started to talk and write to him, asking him questions. That's how we became friends.

The Buddhist services were in Japanese, but pretty soon the phrases, even though I didn't know the exact translations, began to make sense. My parents spoke to each other in Japanese, and since I had some hearing ability, I could understand a little. I'd pick up the intuitive sense of what they were talking about, and then I'd ask Ty to give me a summary of what had been discussed. I was lucky I had a firsthand teacher so willing and available to explain things to me. When I was beginning to ask questions about Daisetz Suzuki's writings and the sūtras, Ty would try to explain them, so that they would have more meaning for me in my life. Meeting Ty was the reason I stayed in Buddhism. Yasutani Rōshi was also important for me because even after I married Ty, it still wasn't clear to me what life really was about. I remained a seeker.

❖ Studying with Yasutani Rōshi

As part of my Buddhist training, I did Zen meditation with Yasutani Rōshi in Japan. I went to my first *sesshin* with him for a whole week in 1965. There I found out that I apparently have a great capacity for sitting still. The reason is that I grew up on the farm, and my best friends were little ants and animals in the wild, and I'd sit there and watch them. Without my even realizing it, my body learned to be still and to breathe naturally, and that's all meditation really is. When I went to

Yasutani Rōshi's sesshin, the first time I really met him, I had the answer to my kōan and was able to give it to him. I went in alone and bowed, and then he asked me, "Well, what is your answer to MU?" When I described my experience to him, he accepted it. I was so surprised that I almost fell over.

Yasutani Rōshi's sesshin was for foreigners. A few of the students had apparently been practicing with him for a while already, and there were a few Japanese students as well. The reason they invited me to the foreigners' sesshin was that my husband told them that my Japanese was not all that great. I was picking up the skill, but it's not my first language. Yasutani Rōshi actually spoke to me in Japanese, but he had enough English that if I gestured that I didn't understand, he could use English with Japanese so that I would understand.

Yasutani Rōshi was most important and helpful for me because of who he was. It was the way he interacted with his main disciples, who were helping to run the sesshin, and how he shared his ordinary side. When some of them would complain about how things were going, he'd be very ordinary in his response and say, "Well, those are things we can't control, and it happens." Not having a solution for such problems was, to me, so enlightening. It was just an incredible experience to see. He was such a *human being*, so genuine and so kind and yet very eager to help me in my meetings with him.

Yasutani Rōshi never yelled at me in our meetings, even though he had a reputation of being fierce. I always felt totally accepted by him, and he would gently guide me through the several kōans I did with him. I don't know what I did—I really don't know what I said or did—but every time I'd go in to speak with him, he would say, "Okay. That's fine," and he'd give me another kōan. I went through about five kōans in one week with him, and he was able to accept them. I had heard that he generally didn't accept students' answers that easily, so I thought, Well, I don't know what I'm doing, but I guess it must be okay. I had to say goodbye to Yasutani Rōshi when I returned to the United States because at that point he was grounded in Japan—that was his home, and that was his practice.

I don't feel that I was discriminated against for being Buddhist. It was because we were Japanese-faced Americans that discrimination happened. I never saw Buddhism as being part of the discrimination at all. Growing up, I didn't go around telling everybody I was a Buddhist. I never had the need to. After I met my husband and went to Japan in the 60s and returned to the U.S. six years later, Buddhism still wasn't a big boom. I never felt like I needed to explain to anyone or be apologetic about it, but I studied it, and I really made it a part of my thinking, so that if anyone asked me, I could explain what Buddhism was about. A lot of my friends who grew up in traditional Buddhist families can't explain what Buddhism is because they were just steeped in the tradition. If someone asked, "Well, tell me what your practice is. What does it mean?" they wouldn't be able to articulate it; they'd just say, "Well, I go to the temple. I listen to the sermons. I listen to the dharma talks. But when you ask, what is my practice, maybe I can't really tell you." But *I* can because I've had to struggle so much in that process. I respect others to make their own choices. If they discover Buddhism and want to practice it or are just curious, I value that because in Buddhism they say even the brushing of sleeves has significance, even if you don't meet or speak to that person. If someone's interested in Buddhism, I think it's great. It's very much that attitude of this brushing of sleeves being very significant for the moment. We use the term *here and now*. And then time moves on, life's impermanent, and it's very fluid and very gentle and very open. I'm excited that Buddhism is becoming more popular. I think it's wonderful that people are discovering Buddhism. University courses about Buddhism are just fantastic. Whether the students become Buddhists or not isn't really the point. That they are curious enough to want to take the course is what's important.

·:· Current Practice

I am still a seeker, but I now have chosen the Shin Buddhist path because I like its structure. Shin, particularly, is a lay path. In Shin Buddhism, everyday experience is where you reflect on your life, using the dharma as your guide. There's no magic to it. Shin Buddhism is so honest. It really helps you to see how your ego-structure colors the way you live your life. For me, the Shin path was the one that really worked, but I would never presume to urge Shin on anyone else. It has to be an individual's choice. I really think that's what Buddhism's all about. I would love to be able to say, "Well, come, then, be a Shin Buddhist." But that would be absolutely wrong according to my experience and understanding of what Shin is.

I also have training in the Japanese Tea Ceremony, which is a very stylized form of learned motions. You first have to process from head to body. When you reach a certain point where you no longer have to think what to do, and you continue building on that, you embody it naturally, and it really becomes your own. It's no longer something that someone else has taught you. I have a lot of that kind of training in my background, including Aikidō and flower arranging. Initially you think, and then you practice, but after you do it for several years, things flow together. I don't even know how that happens, but I do remember that it happened. I struggled so much because it didn't come naturally for me. But all of a sudden, things just came together. I think what's important about this process, including the meditation, is that it centers you. I think that's what has happened as a result of my practice, without articulating it. I was a special education teacher in the public school system. In special education, you don't have a choice of children. Some of them are hyperactive, some act out, and some are emotionally really sad because they aren't successful. Amid all of this, I learned to never lose my cool with those children. I never yelled, and they are used to being yelled at. My training in Aikidō and Tea Ceremony along with meditation really helped me to center myself in working with all types of children.

Nowadays, we do quiet sitting in Shin gatherings. We call it quiet sitting because it's not formalized like Zen sitting and done for a set period of time. Ty and I have a Shin Buddhist sangha of people who, for whatever reason, found us and wanted to listen to the dharma. We have gatherings once a month for the adults. We also have monthly gatherings for the children. And Ty has a study session once a month, kind of like a seminar, for people who want to study the scriptures more in depth. At our gatherings, we always do the chanting, reading selections from the three main sūtras of the Shin tradition. Ty and I also chant at night and then do an incense offering. That's our practice, basically, but Shin is not a practice you just do at set times. It's important to do the sūtra chanting because these are scriptures that are reminders of the teachings, but everyday life is my practice. When life doesn't go the way I want it to go, and I'm blowing steam off my head, I realize it's not the other person or the circumstances that's steaming, *I* am. I say the phrase *Namu Amida Butsu*. *Amida* means the light of the teachings. And *Butsu* is the teachings. As Ty explains, we say *Namu Amida Butsu* in gratitude: Thank you for making me realize that I'm the problem. Basically, it's an awareness. It's the total foundation of understanding what life's all about. And the biggest obstacle is not out there, it's me—it's my ego. When we sit, we can brush away all the cobwebs and come to a very still point where thoughts are no longer flowing, but we can't stay there. That's okay. When that's okay, then we're liberated to appreciate our own limitations. That's what Shin works on. I was so wrapped up in myself, I was blind to my ego, but when I opened up from the darkness to the light of what life is all about, I saw why I was so miserable; it was that I was only worried about *me*. I still get angry now, I still have my ego problems and all that, but look!—at age seventy-two, look at the gifts I've got. Life and its problems keep me alive, and it's wonderful.

One of the most important teachings that I've found through Buddhism is how to live life knowing that death is a natural part of it. I can never help others through their process to death, but I can be a friend in the shadow with someone. I walk some people to death in old age. It's a very tough road for some people because it's so frightening. But if I say, "I'm always here in the shadow with you. You are never alone," it somehow reassures that person that it doesn't have to be a lonely path. I don't care which branch of Buddhism it is, I think this is what Buddhism's all about: how to live, how to *really* live and how to really die. I can't say I'm ready to die, but I also know it's a given. And if I can say, "You know, even though I ranted and raved for so long, it was a good life. It was a meaningful life," I don't think I could ask for more. I really don't think I could. That's what Buddhism has given me. What a gift.

NOTE

This essay is based on an interview conducted by Lesley Jo Weaver on November 29, 2005. After the tape was transcribed, Weaver edited the material into a coherent narrative form, which was then revised by Alice Unno.

Women
Dharma Teachers' Forum

❖ ❖ ❖ ❖ ❖ ❖ ❖ ❖ ❖ ❖ ❖ ❖ ❖ ❖ ❖ ❖ ❖ ❖ ❖

T HIS FORUM *brings together four prominent women dharma teachers representing different traditions of Buddhism in America to address a series of questions about their experience as women studying and teaching Buddhism.*

Ven. Thubten Chodron (Cherry Greene) was ordained as a Buddhist nun in 1977. She studied and practiced Tibetan Buddhism under the guidance of His Holiness the Dalai Lama, Tsenzhap Serkong Rinpoche, Lama Zopa Rinpoche, and other Tibetan masters for many years in India and Nepal. She has been resident teacher at Amitabha Buddhist Centre in Singapore and at Dharma Friendship Foundation in Seattle and was co-organizer of "Life as a Western Buddhist Nun," an educational program in Bodhgaya in 1996. In 2003, she founded Sravasti Abbey near Newport, Washington. She is involved in interfaith dialogue, conferences between scientists and Buddhists, meetings of Western Buddhist teachers, and gatherings of Western Buddhist monastics. She teaches Buddhist philosophy, psychology, and meditation worldwide, and she is active in prison work. Her books include Open Heart, Clear Mind *(1990);* Buddhism for Beginners *(2001);* Working with Anger *(2001);* Taming the Mind *(2004); and* Blossoms of the Dharma: Living as a Buddhist Nun *(2000).*

Rōshi Pat Enkyō O'Hara is the abbot of the Village Zendo in Manhattan. She received priest ordination from Maezumi Rōshi and dharma transmission from Rōshi Bernie Glassman. The example of her teachers encourages her work in the ordinary running of an urban temple and in peacemaking activities. Much of O'Hara's activism concerns the world of HIV/AIDS. An ongoing exploration for her is articulating a Zen Buddhist approach to issues of difference around race, class, sexuality, and health. Working with Bernie Glassman, O'Hara is involved in the design of the Maezumi Institute, a study and practice center for Zen and peacemaking. O'Hara was associate professor at NYU's Tisch School of the Arts, where she taught video and interactive arts for twenty years.

Ven. Yifa was born in Taiwan and was ordained as a Buddhist nun at Fo Guang Shan in 1979. She went on to receive an M.A. in comparative philosophy from the University of Hawaii and a Ph.D. in Chinese Buddhism from Yale University. She published a historical study and annotated translation of the Chanyuan Qinggui, The Origins of Buddhist Monastic Codes in China *in 2002. She has taught at Boston University, McGill University, and Sun Yat-sen University, served as abbess of the Greater Boston Buddhist Cultural Center, and currently serves as provost of the University of the West (formerly Hsi Lai University) in Rosemead, California, where she also chairs the Department of Religious Studies.*

Carol Wilson has been involved in practicing and studying Theravāda Buddhism since 1971, including a year-long ordination as a nun in Thailand in the early 1980s. She began leading intensive meditation retreats at the Insight Meditation Society, in Barre, Massachusetts, in 1986. Currently she leads insight meditation (vipassanā) as well as loving-kindness (metta) retreats, both at IMS and around the world. Wilson is particularly interested in bridging ancient and more structured forms of transmitting Buddhism with forms appropriate for modern Western practitioners. She is presently serving as one of the guiding teachers of the Insight Meditation Society, as well as on the board of directors for the Barre Center for Buddhist Studies and the Dharma Seed Archival Center. In the past two years, she has been inspired to be a part of the Metta Dana Project, which assists the people of the Sagaing Hills in Burma with education, health care, and the support of their monasteries and nunneries.

1. What kinds of challenges did you face in your path as a woman?

Thubten Chodron: I met the dharma in 1975, was ordained twenty-one months later, and have lived as a monastic since then. My path has been as a woman and as a monastic, so I would like to speak about the challenges I have faced in both areas. Any descriptions of difficulties are not meant as complaints or accusations but simply accounts of how I experienced my environment.

When I first began my Buddhist training in the Tibetan tradition, I didn't recognize the institutional bias against women. As a Westerner I didn't fit into the Tibetan institutional structures in any case. Through their teachings and their example, my teachers generated within me the wish to study the great philosophical texts, as they had done as monks in Tibet and as a new generation of monks was doing in monasteries that had been established in exile in South India. But in the middle and late 1970s this avenue of study was not open to women.

At this point I became aware of the discrimination women faced. Raised in a family of strong women, I did well in school as a child and thus was not inculcated with the idea of women being inferior or lacking in abilities. Furthermore, I idealistically believed all Buddhists would be beyond bias. Thus, I was surprised to find prejudice in Buddhist institutions—especially since the Buddha taught that all sentient beings were equal in having buddha nature and in wanting happiness and seeking to be free from suffering.

I was among the first generation of Westerners to ordain in the Tibetan tradition. At that time, the only female role models we had were Tibetan nuns, who were mostly shy, unassertive but friendly women who conducted lots of *pūjās* but studied little. Modeling myself after them, I tried to be quiet, unassuming, and polite. I tried not to ask questions or challenge views I didn't agree with.

But it didn't work. I had a Western college education and a career as a teacher before meeting the dharma. My mind was naturally curious and full of questions. Additionally, my upbringing in America led me to believe in gender equality, even if this ideal was rarely realized at home. At some point in my training, I had to acknowledge that I didn't fit what I thought others thought was the role of a "sweet nun." Thankfully, my teachers appreciated my inquisitiveness, and since we Westerners were so few in number, we nuns received the same education as the Western monks.

Nevertheless, the shortage of female role models was noticeable. The lineage lamas and merit field that we visualized each day consisted almost exclusively of male figures. When we women raised this point, we were told that Tārā and Vajrayoginī are female deities, implying that no prejudice against women existed.

It took me a while to understand that, for the most part, my Tibetan teachers genuinely believed there was no gender bias. It took me even longer to understand that most Western male practitioners were generally oblivious to gender discrimination in dharma centers. But then I learned the same lack of awareness applied to me in situations where I belonged to the prominent group. Sadly we human beings don't understand the experience of those in an oppressed group unless we are also in that group.

In 1993, I attended a meeting of Western Buddhist teachers with His Holiness the Dalai Lama. Some of us women planned a presentation that Sylvia Wetzel delivered, in which she asked everyone to imagine being a man in a society that was biased in favor of women: "You enter this room and see Her Holiness the Dalai Lama, who has been a woman in all fourteen incarnations. Surrounding her when she teaches are high lamas, all women. In fact, most of the audience is female, except for a few shy monks sitting in the back. The paintings on the walls are of the twenty-one Tārās, Namgyalma, and other female meditation deities, and you wonder if there is prejudice against men. You approach a lama and ask her. She responds, 'No, there is no prejudice, but it's good if you pray to be reborn as a woman in your next life.' Unsure about this answer, you ask another high lama, who responds, 'No, there is no prejudice. Both women and men are empty.' Still confused about why you always have to sit in the back of the room, you question yet another lama. She says, 'There is absolutely no prejudice against men. You can be a *ḍāka* and give great bliss to the lamas.'"

By this time, the Westerners were laughing uproariously, while the Tibetans sat expressionless. They didn't get it. Of course Western men in positions of power don't usually understand such concerns either. This is simply the way human beings are. I, too, don't recognize my prejudices even when they're pointed out to me.

Happily, in recent years the educational opportunities for Tibetan and Himalayan nuns have improved dramatically. His Holiness the Dalai Lama and some other lamas have consistently supported this, and many nuns and laywomen, both Western and Tibetan, have worked together to found nunneries and educational institutes for nuns.

The Tibetan tradition lacks the lineage of the *bhikṣuṇī* ordination—the full ordination for women. Almost all of the Tibetan nuns are *śrā-maṇerikās*, or novices, while a few of us Western nuns have gone to the Chinese, Korean, or Vietnamese traditions to receive the full ordination. This was a profound experience for me and a turning point in my training as a monastic. However, Tibetans have not yet recognized the bhikṣuṇī lineage as valid and thus have not authorized it to be introduced in a widespread way in their communities. On an individual level, Tibetan teachers have been supportive of our taking this ordination, but as a collective whole, they are still researching the issue after over twenty years.

In 2005 His Holiness the Dalai Lama encouraged Western nuns to take the lead in organizing conferences to discuss introducing the bhikṣuṇī lineage into the Tibetan tradition as well as into other Buddhist countries where it has not spread or was lost. In a few years some Tibetan nuns will finish their studies and be ready to take the geshe exams, which until now have been open only to monks.

I lived in the Tibetan community in India and Nepal for many years, but it was only when I returned to the U.S. in the early 1990s that I realized the extent to which my self-confidence as a woman and as a Westerner had eroded. Going back to the West allowed me to reestablish my self-confidence and to discover that, as a female monastic, I could benefit others by practicing and teaching the dharma in a Western culture.

Yet upon relocating to the U.S., I was surprised to discover additional challenges for women and monastics. One aspect is a bias against female monastics in Western dharma centers, where people give more support, respect, and offerings to monks than to nuns. This behavior is all the more startling because so many of the benefactors are women. Furthermore, many translations still reflect gender bias: "Sons of the buddhas" and other such exclusionary expressions persist.

A further bias I encountered was against Western monastics in general. Even today, many dharma centers do not see the benefit of having ordained sangha and instead see us as cheap labor—or even as a financial burden for the center. We will lead meditations, ceremonies, and discussion groups, teach, and give spiritual counseling, but in general we do not receive wide support for the lifestyle choice we have made or the vows that we live in.

While Tibetan monks are honored in dharma centers, Western monastics are often looked upon as oddities. There seems to be the thought that if one is a Tibetan monk, one is a genuine and even realized practitioner worthy of respect and offering, whereas if one is a Western monastic, one doesn't know much. While Tibetans are well cared for in dharma centers, Western monastics are expected to work long hours at the center or to pay to live there. Some are told that they cannot live at the center and must live outside. If a monastic must get a job in the city in order to support him- or herself, keeping precepts and living a monastic lifestyle become extremely difficult.

Another layer of bias is one against monasticism in general. America is a predominantly Protestant culture and thus historically has had limited experience with monastics. If people are familiar with monastics, they often think of hierarchy, inequality, and sexism, and in their wish to promote democracy and equality, assert that monastics are irrelevant. That this attitude exists even among some prominent lay Western Buddhist teachers is a cause of sadness for me.

For example, some American Buddhists have commented to me that monastics are running away from sexual relationships and are afraid of emotional intimacy. In a culture where even toothpaste is sexualized, those of us who choose not to follow this groupthink are seen as "having issues with sex." In a country where the national ethic is one of individualism and self-reliance, some American Buddhists say, "I want to practice dharma too; why should I support monastics when they could work, earn money, and support themselves?" This final level of prejudice has probably been the most startling one for me. In Asia, we nuns faced bias due to our gender. In America, where gender equality is at least nominally advocated, we nuns face bias due to being monastics.

Counteracting attachment in a materialistic consumer society is not easy; some American Buddhists denigrate monastics, saying that we are extraneous instead of respecting our efforts to live simply and devote our lives to dharma study and practice. These critics seem to discount the fact that for over 2,600 years the dharma has been preserved and passed down by monastics with the support of the lay community. As twenty-first-century Buddhists, we are indebted to those monastics, who for centuries offered their lives in service to the dharma without the pleasure and security of a job, relationship, and family. Due to their diligent practice, the Buddha's teachings that we love and their lineages exist today. It is doubtful that individual lay practitioners could have kept these alive over the centuries. Furthermore, the Buddhist teachings are included in three baskets of teachings: Vinaya (monastic discipline), Sūtra, and Abhidharma. It's essential that all three baskets be transmitted to the West. Omitting the Vinaya basket or not supporting the monastics who practice it would be a great loss for everyone for many generations to come. Therefore I urge both monastics and lay Buddhists to respect and appreciate each other's choice of lifestyles.

Being a Western nun is an interesting experience. We never know quite how we will be treated by Western Buddhists or in the larger Western society. I travel a lot to teach, and several times people have come up to me in public places and said, "Don't worry. Your hair will grow back when the chemo is over." I don't take offense at this; these people are expressing a genuine care and concern that I find touching. Other people have commented, "That outfit (referring to my robes) is very attractive," or "Not everyone can wear their hair like that, but it looks really good on you." Sometimes, in a woman's restroom, a woman will enter and gasp upon seeing me, thinking that I am a man. Having been ordained for nearly thirty years, I chuckle at these experiences. But they show that often people don't know what to make of us monastics or even what we are.

Yet being such an unusual figure in public places also has its advantages. Some people recognize the robes and approach me, asking if I know His Holiness the Dalai Lama, could explain rebirth to them, or tell them where to find a dharma center in their city. Some people, knowing only that we are a religious, will ask for help with a personal problem or confide a personal problem they have been reluctant to share with another layperson. Others are simply inspired to see someone who is practicing ethical discipline and striving to transform their mind into one of love and compassion. Monastics represent the spiritual aspect of themselves that is often neglected in their busy lives and seeing us helps remind them of that cherished part of themselves.

While some people might find this lack of anonymity uncomfortable, I find it good for my practice. I am continuously aware that my life centers around the dharma and that others' faith or lack thereof can depend upon how I act at any particular time. Thus, while irritation may arise when a flight is delayed or canceled, I restrain the wish to vent my feelings on the airline staff because it would adversely affect others and would contradict how I'm endeavoring to train my body, speech, and mind. Being in robes, we can't take time out from training and think that no one will know the difference. This spurs us to practice sincerely and constantly.

Pat Enkyō O'Hara: Oddly enough, when I reflect on my path, I recognize that the Zen I was first attracted to, is in fact the Zen I am now enjoying, after a long detour through a more authoritarian, patriarchal style of Zen. Many things can be learned on a detour; although it is less direct, it may also offer surprising insights.

As a young woman in the 1960s, I was swept along by a profound disillusionment with the conformity, lack of imagination, and brutality that I witnessed in a society that reeked of false piety. When I read a haiku or saw a piece of Japanese calligraphy, I was knocked out by the earthiness and liveliness of the spirit. The frog plopping in a pond, the bird flying out of the stone Buddha's nose—these seemed to embody the irreverent, edgy, and living spirituality that I craved. Studying the Zen principles underlying these arts, I determined to find the freedom and compassion they promised.

But the actual communities I visited were another matter entirely! To my surprise, the American Zen communities seemed authoritarian, almost militaristic in style. Open discussion was discouraged, and the strict hierarchy made real communication out of the question. Unquestioning obedience seemed to be proof of spiritual progress. To my independent, feminist eye, this was not "real" Zen. It seemed to me that any structure that silences one, would not be conducive to encountering the truth. I worried that legitimate spiritual surrender was being confused with unconscious submission.

And yet, I had such yearning for the transformation promised by Zen teachings, that eventually I put my objections "on hold" and entered an American Zen community. Like many other such communities, it was a mixture of inherited Japanese Zen tradition and a Western interpretation of the same: a fusion of boot camp, samurai myth, and sincere spiritual pursuit, plus an unambiguous hierarchical structure. There was much for me to "overlook" and yet, I still recognize, much for me to engage. The silence, the long hours of meditation, the struggle for expression through kōan study, the sincere efforts of the teacher and community, the dropping of the social mask, all did in fact contribute greatly to my growing understanding of myself, of Zen, of life itself. How, I asked myself, could I continue to support a system that exhibited this classic authoritarian style, even if it did offer lip service to gender equality? It was a precarious balancing act: on the one hand, the rich immersion of Zen study and practice, and on the other, a sense, as a woman and a mother, that this version lacked the vitality of intimate and honest dialogue and interaction, the capacity for spontaneity and freedom that would nourish me and support me to serve others.

It was wrenchingly difficult to leave that teacher and community, and yet somehow I knew that I needed a different approach to Zen. Fortunately, I began to practice with Maezumi Rōshi, a Japanese teacher who had lived in this country for thirty years. At the time when I worked with him, the forms of mid-century Japanese Zen that he had brought over seemed to have lost their resonance for him, and his way was softer and more receptive. It was strange because somehow in my years of study, I had absorbed more of the stern style than I realized. Seeing that I had internalized those older, more rigid forms, he gently helped me drop them. In fact, Maezumi Rōshi's manner with me embodied many of the attributes we associate with women: a softness, a willingness for dialogue, and a sensitivity to one's feelings, shown more than once through tears and sighs. In such a community, with quite a few remarkable women dharma teachers, I began to find a sense of a practice that was in consonance with myself as a woman. After Maezumi Rōshi's death, I studied with his successor, Rōshi Bernie Glassman, who, under the influence of his wife, Sensei Jishu Holmes, was pursuing a freer, more open style of practice and community structure. Together, we experimented with study groups and councils that were based on feminist principles of group dynamics and models of peer circle practice.

The detour I took through a more rigid and authoritarian structure alerted me to dangers I might not have otherwise noticed: the tendency of the most vulnerable seekers, not just women, to find a hiding place in the discipline and structure of a spiritual community and thereby miss the very insight they seek.

Was this experience because I am a woman? I don't know. Certainly, my path coincided with the historical period when women were examining the structures that held them in a nondominant position, and so my consciousness was alerted to the dangers inherent in the forms I encountered and persuaded me to continue seeking a path of Zen that was in harmony with being a woman.

Yifa: Even though for years I have spoken out for women and advocated extending bhikṣuṇī ordination to all Buddhist countries and traditions, I still wonder if I should call myself a feminist. In my academic training, I was educated at the National Taiwan University and continued my higher education in the West at the University of Hawaii, Yale, and Berkeley. In my religious training, I joined an order in which nuns are the majority, which is different from most Buddhist monastic orders in other traditions, which are dominated by males. I also joined the order with a prestigious educational background in law. Due to my education and position in an order with a female majority, I have always been treated with respect. With so many factors operating together, I always feel that it is difficult to think of this issue in a one-dimensional way.

I was born in Taiwan in a family with seven children: four boys and three girls. When I was young, my brothers always envied me for being a girl because it was much easier for me to get things that I wanted from my parents. In Chinese society, parents often favor the youngest child with the most attention. Being the second youngest, I enjoyed this kind of favor for at least seven years until my younger sister came along. The only way that I felt that I was at a disadvantage for being a woman during my childhood had to do with social attitudes regarding women's education. My mother was my role model in traditional virtues, but she was also influenced by the general social values and questioned whether her daughters should have a higher education. I had to have many discussions to convince her why it was important for me to continue my education, and in the end she supported me. When my sisters and I were accepted to the most prestigious university, she was the one who strove to help us financially to finish school.

In 1979 at the age of twenty I was a law student at National Taiwan University. I intended to become a lawyer and to have a career in politics. I even dreamed about the possibility of becoming Taiwan's first female president. That same year I went to Fo Guang Shan to study Buddhism for the first time. During the two-week program, I experienced an inner realization in which the old world shattered and a new world emerged. So I decided to shave my head and to become a nun and join this order.

The founder of Fo Guang Shan, the Venerable Master Hsing Yun, is the forty-eighth generation of the Linji lineage of the Chan tradition, but the Buddhism he advocates is Humanistic Buddhism, which is part of a new Buddhist movement occurring in Taiwan. It emphasizes that Buddhism should be engaged in society and not be confined to the monastery. The focus is on this life not the next, human responsibility not divine power, and education not rituals.

Even though the founder of this order is a monk, I saw that the nuns in Fo Guang Shan played an active role in running the organization. I was attracted by their life and energy. At that time Fo Guang Shan had about two hundred monastics, the majority of whom were young women. Most of the monastic offices were run by nuns. Five senior nuns were sent by the master to be educated in Japan in the 1960s. When they returned, they were put in charge of different areas: temple construction (Ven. Cizhuang), education (Ven. Cihui), social welfare (Ven. Cirong), culture (Ven. Ciyi), and spiritual cultivation (Ven. Cijiao). Their example inspired me to further my education abroad.

Master Hsing Yun encouraged me to finish my law degree and to continue my education in the U.S., while I thought that as a monastic I should have given up my secular pursuits. In 1988, the Temple sent me to study with Professor David Kalupahana at the University of Hawaii, where I received a master's degree in comparative philosophy. I later went to Yale University to study Chinese Buddhism under Professor Stanley Weinstein. His training was very rigorous and demanding, and I am proud to be the first female student to finish a Ph.D. under him.

Master Hsing Yun is a man of great virtue and wisdom. People around him feel the force of his personality. Even though he is a strict disciplinarian, he is always fair. I remember that when I was preparing to go to Yale, he instructed the abbess that I should be given the same support as Ven. Huikai, a monk who was studying at Temple University at that time. I have never felt discriminated against under my master's tutorship.

After I graduated from Yale, I was appointed provost of Hsi Lai University (which has been renamed University of the West). The challenge that I faced there was not so much gender bias as cultural norms. After our Western education, both the monk Huikai and I were criticized for not being humble and obedient to the order. Our American graduate training had taught us to speak in a straightforward way and to criticize things in a forthright fashion, which is not the way traditional Chinese monastics normally act. We were often seen, and still are, as violating the traditional protocol of proper deference.

Nuns at Fo Guang Shan sometimes feel that monks have more privileges. But this is not because the monks dominate the order; on the contrary, it is because the temple has adopted an "affirmative action" policy to protect their rights and opportunities as a minority. Many monks have a hard time working under female leadership. Accordingly, Fo Guang Shan reserves certain temples and administrative departments for monks so that monks can be led by monks. Some nuns may also feel that monks at Fo Guang Shan are promoted faster and have an easier life. Yet this can just as well be seen as the way that the temple tries to maintain a balance of power between both sides. I myself try to balance this power, and in my own temple I tend to give more privileges to monks. In a different context where nuns are a minority, I advocate for their rights. So I am not sure if I should refer to myself as a feminist activist.

Carol Wilson: I was introduced to the practice of Buddhism through the intensive meditation retreats of S. N. Goenka. These retreats were held in India, for laypeople, in English. The majority of students in the retreats I attended were Westerners. In my experience, men and women were treated equally. To be honest, the gender question never arose in my mind, either during those retreats in India or when I returned to the West and continued to practice in the lay vipassanā style. At this time, the early-to-mid-70s, I was involved in two wings, one could say, of Buddhist vipassanā meditation and practice. One wing was the retreats that were offered by three other disciples of the teacher of Goenkaji, a Burmese layman named U Ba Khin. All three of these teachers were also lay, and one of them was a woman, Ruth Denison. The other wing was led by young Americans who had begun sharing dharma teachings in the vipassanā style and who founded the Insight Meditation Society. At this time, the most well known of these were two men and two women.

Today I am so grateful to have had this introduction to the dharma. My early teachers were committed to traditional Theravāda Buddhist teachings and practice; they taught from and transmitted this inspiration and understanding. Early on I developed a great love for and faith in the Pāli teachings of the Buddha and the liberating power of a pure heart supporting the wisdom of nonattachment and no-self. As the majority of my teachers were Western laypeople, both men and women, I simply did not experience the gender discrimination that can be seen in the Asian monastic traditions as they are today. My faith— that liberation from suffering, living one's life from a compassionate motivation, is the potential of each of us—had a chance to deepen into surety. I do believe that this was supported by the environment in which I practiced—I was not in surroundings where my personal and cultural conditioning would be frequently in conflict with practices and teachings that appear to me as cultural bias yet were taught as implicit aspects of the dharma. I surely would have gone through more confusion and possibly doubt had I begun as a nun or been taught solely by monastics. Instead, I regularly saw women teachers and students modeling the path I was treading. It never entered my mind that awakening and the practices that support it were not as readily available to women as men.

My choosing the vipassanā path was not a result of "shopping around" or conscious choice to find a scene more supportive of women. I met vipassanā at a young age and resonated with it so deeply and immediately that I never wavered from that particular expression of

Buddhadharma. When I hear of the difficulties that other women have sometimes encountered in their introductions to the dharma, difficulties of perceiving a more exclusively male hierarchy and modeling of awakening, I feel doubly blessed. Sure, I am a woman, and that affects everything I do! But I can honestly say that in my first ten years of practice and service at IMS, gender was not an issue for me.

2. One of the dilemmas Helen Tworkov raises in her contribution to this volume has to do with the fact that some of the qualities that the tradition advocates as embodying its highest spiritual ideals (such as putting others before oneself) are the very qualities that some feminists claim perpetuate the subordination of women in our society. What thoughts or feelings do you have in regard to this dilemma?

TC: If we understand the dharma properly, this concern is not an issue. It becomes difficult if we do not properly understand the meaning of the teachings. The Buddhist teachings about patience do not mean that we become the world's doormat. Rather, when we free ourselves from anger before acting, our decisions and actions will be less harmful and more beneficial. The love we try to develop in Buddhism is not the codependent, people-pleasing kind, which should more accurately be called "attachment." There's a big difference between caring for others when we lack self-confidence and seek their approval and the sincere wish to benefit others because we see the advantages of cherishing others, and we genuinely care about them. In a Buddhist context love is simply the wish for sentient beings (including ourselves) to have happiness and its causes.

Similarly, the ordinary concept of compassion may involve "saving someone" by fixing their problems or giving them exactly what they ask for. This is not the Buddhist meaning of compassion. Sometimes saying no is a compassionate response, and challenging others to find their own solutions, rather than rescuing them, is an expression of loving concern.

PEO: These qualities may look the same, but they are different. True spiritual surrender, true generosity, true patience, do not arise out of a mind that is still holding fear and injury. So of course, what may look like a humble and compassionate being may well be an unexamined, fearful, angry, and injured self.

It seems to me that in a conscious spiritual community it is deeply the responsibility of the leaders to look carefully at the behaviors of the participants and help them to inquire into their nature. In our dharma center my partner and coleader Barbara Joshin O'Hara has been pivotal in alerting us to this issue. Dharma centers need to be on the lookout for that compliant, easily manipulated volunteer who is actually running in the opposite direction of awakening. To me, this is of grave importance to the survival of Buddhist principles in this country. For us to ignore the Western teachings on mind, from peace and reconciliation work, from psychology and philosophy, is foolish and, really, unconscionable. All the wisdom available to us, here and now, has the potential to shape an authentic realization of the classic *pāramitās*.

As for the reference to "putting another before yourself," it seems to me that one can only do that skillfully if one is engaged in the project of deep awareness of self and other. Otherwise, thinking we are helping, we are merely rushing to satisfy our own needs, and inadvertently we cripple or alienate others.

Just the other day I witnessed a comical interaction where an ordained person was insisting on carrying a much younger person's bag, but instead took it in the wrong direction! I had to laugh; it was so emblematic of the problem of "idiot compassion." And yet this is absolutely serious: dysfunctional rescuing is a form of infantilizing and making someone a "victim" rather than creating the circumstances for healthy growth. Much of the time the best action is to help the person help him- or herself. Watch the cow, with loving energy. This is not easy, it requires a rigorous attention to what is happening in this very moment, from all the perspectives: with me, with the other, with the situation at hand—what is needed. This attunement with all the elements of "now" can break down our knee-jerk reactions and self-aggrandizing "helping" or "putting before" strategies.

Y: Dilemmas occur in our lives all the time. In my life I have encountered the challenge of remaining filial to my parents even though I wanted to pursue a monastic life. I also deal with filial piety in relation to my teacher. I respect him, but at the same time I won't allow myself to be intimidated by him. Although I want to obey my master, I do not want to totally give up my freedom of choice. These dilemmas are not that easy for me to deal with, and they often create tension that can escalate, which ends up hurting both parties. But the most important aspect of the challenge we face is not to give up on substance while maintaining a flexible attitude that allows for negotiation and communication. The whole process is not only a mutual education but also an education of counterbalance. I still believe that the Buddhist ideal of putting others before oneself is a good teaching because it is not only a teaching to women but also to men. Men need to learn to put others, including women, before themselves as well. We must always be willing to engage in this mutual process of counterbalance in all of our relationships.

CW: While this can seem like a dilemma, or a paradox, I feel that it is a confusion based on a misunderstanding of the actual experience of these spiritual qualities. In fact, the basic misunderstanding can be seen in the very form of the question: "highest spiritual *ideals.*" Ideals are important; they show us our potential, can open us to deeper aspiration and a possibility to live in this world in a very different way; they remind us it is possible not to respond so automatically from self-centeredness, fear, and greed. What is inspirational and exciting for me is knowing that these ideals are not based on a philosophical idea of how one should be or what sounds like the "right" way to act. The qualities that embody some of the highest spiritual ideals—such as putting others before oneself or responding to suffering and even cruelty with compassionate understanding rather than anger, fear, or vengefulness—are the natural expression of wisdom and love. One of the inexpressible benefits of meeting deeply committed spiritual beings is that one has the opportunity to experience, or at least to observe, the manifestation of these qualities when they have ceased to be "ideals" and have become simply the natural response of the awakened heart and mind.

One joy of our dharma practice is when we begin to experience the difference between the *ideal* of putting others before ourselves and the *actuality* of that mode of action, when it is supported by understanding and compassion. From the outside, actions based on the motivation of putting others before oneself, as a spiritual quality, can look the same as the cultural norm or ideal that women should put others, men and their family, before themselves because we women are more naturally compassionate. The experience can be quite different from the inside. I know for myself that when I am acting, consciously or unconsciously, from the wish to conform to an internalized cultural ideal, this same action can also be accompanied by a lot of confusion. My action may appear, both to myself and others, as thoughtful and kind. In fact, it *is* thoughtful and kind. Yet internally, I may also feel a quiet resentment, even anger. Or, perhaps more common to women, such actions can stem from an often unconscious sense of low self-worth, a self-abnegation that needs confirmation of my value from others, that seeks to confirm myself through others' approval of my compassionate action. There is dis-ease and suffering involved in my inner experience, together with, hopefully, the joy of generosity and genuine caring; *and* the action can still be kind and compassionate.

Here is where I see we enter the paradox. The spiritual quality of putting others before myself arises spontaneously from the wisdom of selflessness, which manifests as compassion and generosity. When one puts others first, it is a spontaneous wish to fulfill a need. There is no reference to an idea of how I *should* act in this circumstance. The obvious response simply occurs. My inner experience is one of balance, ease, and even strength. Nothing is looked for or needed in return. It is a happiness-inducing experience, not colored by habits of neediness and feelings of inadequacy and self-doubt. It feels so much purer and freer, not so sticky. That is one way I can tell the difference for myself between actions colored by fears and needs, and actions arising from compassionate understanding.

One other very important difference between the ideal of putting others first and the spontaneous, wisdom-imbued response is that the wisdom of selflessness shows us that we are all equally worthy of compassion and love. That includes ourselves, no more or less than any other. This knowing lends a quiet strength and balance to our actions. I may be able to spontaneously respond to anger with kindness instead of vindictiveness, for example, but not at the expense of damage to myself. This is very important. To use Chögyam Trungpa's fantastic, if politically incorrect, phrase: It is the difference between the compassion of wisdom and "idiot compassion." When we recognize that responding kindly (or passively) to a chronic abuser only encourages the abuse, the clarity and strength of a wise heart sees that this is not compassion. It is enabling the abuse. What looks like kindness is actually increasing my own suffering as well as the suffering of the other. A deeper compassion entails doing what one can to end the abuse, addictive behavior, etc. Maybe the best one can do is to remove oneself from the situation. Or maybe the situation requires a confrontational, challenging, or seemingly angry response—certainly one that denies the person the opportunity to continue to cause pain to others. The wise heart does not deny the value of either oneself or the other. This understanding gives a great strength to the qualities of compassion, kindness, and nonviolence. Actions springing from such wisdom are vastly different from subservience. There is no need for outer approval and no fear of disapproval. This gives the mind space to perceive a situation in a clear way, uncomplicated by needing to be liked or right. A quiet courage underlies the way that one responds to others in this world. And sometimes, without quite realizing what has been happening, we begin to discover in ourselves that these spiritual qualities

don't feel like such distant ideals anymore. They become rather mat-
ter-of-fact. We are no longer "trying" so hard to match some ideal
(which actually can feed our sense of low self-worth and increase our
neediness); to our surprise, we notice compassion for others and ourselves arising spontaneously. Even if we experience this once, we can
begin to understand that this seeming dilemma is really not a dilemma
at all.

*3. In different ways, each of you has had some kind of experience with ordina-
tion, whether temporary, as a bhikṣuṇī, or as a Zen priest. What do you see as
the advantages and disadvantages of ordination for you as a woman? How
might the constraints be freeing?*

TC: For me, ordination has had only advantages. Monastic life isn't for
everyone, but in my case it is the single best thing I have done in my
life. Everything I've been able to accomplish in terms of dharma study,
practice, and teaching, and everything rewarding I've done in life has
been based on having received and lived in monastic ordination.

Our teacher, the Buddha, was a monastic. He lived a life of simplicity, humility, and dedication to the welfare of others; the Buddha
expressed the dharma through his choice of lifestyle. In my experience,
monastic precepts and lifestyle support the development of these qualities. Precepts are not restrictions imposed on us from outside but are
reflections of our meditation. In meditation, we observe through our
own experience the cause and effect relationship between various emotions and behaviors and their short- and long-term results. Thus we
choose not to engage in certain actions and to engage in others. Taking
precepts follows naturally from this.

As I alluded to above, ordained life makes us very mindful of our
thoughts, feelings, words, and actions in public and private. Additionally, it provides the time and circumstances to apply dharma antidotes.
We aren't distracted from doing so by having to pay attention to a partner, child, mortgage, social life, career, or obligations to extended fam-

ily. Those of us who live in a monastery must learn to give up the independence of "doing our own trip" and learn to open our hearts to people whom we normally wouldn't associate with in lay life. Monastics who do long retreats have the opportunity to delve deeply into practice for however long they wish, without a family waiting for them to reemerge and join them at the end of retreat. In short, monastic precepts establish a firm foundation for deeper practice and living in them joyfully is a reflection of having worked with our mind.

PEO: It's all about product placement! Simply living an ordained life in this society forces me to make myself available to others wherever I am. I think the formal functions are the least important. It is more about allowing my spiritual "slip" to show in public. In my bald head and priest clothing I become a reminder that spiritual dedication and attention can be the focus of one's life. Moreover, it seems that the presence of an ordained woman—whether walking down the street, in the airport, buying vegetables in the market—gives encouragement to other women, encouragement to follow their aspiration.

And, I suppose, I am also a reminder of fanaticism, of separation, and possibly of spiritual hierarchy. That this can also be true, challenges me on a daily basis to struggle to scrutinize my words and actions, to examine my relations with others—at the zendō, on the street, in the subway.

Of course, there are many ways to offer oneself. And I genuinely acknowledge and revere the highest level of Zen attainment when there are no outward signs, and the adept disappears into the marketplace, living an ordinary life among all the people.

Y: The bhikṣuṇī ordination is still maintained as a living tradition in Chinese Buddhism. Nuns at Fo Guang Shan can receive full ordination without any hindrance or difficulty. In 1980, I was sent by the temple to receive ordination along with fifty nuns. During the one-month ordination period, both monks and nuns are usually gathered for the training in one place at the same time. The former line up on one side and the latter on the other. Monks and nuns were separated only during the time when precepts were explained, during the ceremony when the precepts were transmitted and, of course, for sleeping. But women still comprise the majority of ordinands at Fo Guang Shan.

According to the Vinaya, women can receive the precepts from both monks and nuns, whereas men can only receive the precepts from other monks. The Vinaya also states that the laity are not supposed to be instructed in the monastic precepts. So when novices are sent for ordination, they do not yet know the differences between the rules for monks and nuns. I myself had not yet studied the Vinaya in depth at that time, so I did not know that we had different procedures from the monks. The only thing I remember was when the ten preceptors asked if we, the precept candidates, would vow to take only one meal a day, to take shelter under trees, to wear a ragged robe, and to use urine as medicine, I kept silent when the other candidates answered "yes" aloud. These rules were simply not practicable.

No matter how the ceremony of ordination is conducted and how much the candidate is expected to know, ordination as a bhikṣuṇī fully legitimizes a woman as a monastic. The bhikṣuṇī ordination should not be bargained down, as some monks in Sri Lanka do by arguing that women should only take ten precepts so that society won't put undue expectations on them. Nuns should be publicly held to the same expectations as monks, and society should be educated to know that women have the right to pursue their spiritual path in full without being asked to compromise.

Fo Guang Shan has been very supportive of the bhikṣuṇī ordination. Master Hsing Yun promotes reinstating the lost bhikṣuṇī traditions in other Buddhist orders. He encourages women from non-Chinese traditions to go back to their own tradition to reestablish the bhikṣuṇī lineage. In 1988 an ordination held at Hsi Lai Temple, Fo Guang Shan's main temple in the U.S., brought together many women from the Tibetan and Theravāda traditions seeking full ordination. By holding an international ordination in Bodhgaya, India, in 1998, Fo Guang Shan sought to help reestablish the bhikṣuṇī sangha in other traditions, such as those in India, Sri Lanka, Thailand, Burma, Cambodia, and Tibet. Before the ordinations, several nuns from Fo Guang Shan under Master Hsing Yun's instruction worked to win the support and endorsement of senior monks in the Tibetan and Theravāda traditions. They succeeded in bringing not only women novices but also male and female preceptors from non-Chinese traditions to be witnesses. After the ceremony, nuns from Fo Guang Shan were asked to continue to support these non-Chinese bhikṣuṇis by sponsoring nunneries in Sri Lanka or by offering their teaching in Thailand. I am always very grateful for being a bhikṣuṇī in the Chinese Buddhist tradition and especially Fo Guang Shan, and I remind myself that many women outside of my own tradition need help in pursuing their spiritual path in the way I believe the Buddha intended them to.

In the Fo Guang Shan system, nuns are encouraged to build and administrate the temples, give sermons, teach in the universities, publish books, and conduct rituals and ceremonies. Ninety-five percent of temples in the Fo Guang Shan system are founded and headed by nuns. These nuns carry out most of the duties that are traditionally considered the province of monks. They perform precept-giving rituals, funerals, and weddings—things that wouldn't be possible for nuns in other Buddhist traditions. However, there are still certain rituals that nuns in Fo Guang Shan are not encouraged to preside over, such as the *Yankou* (Flaming-mouth) and Water-land dharma ceremonies. Although nuns perform the supporting roles in these rituals, historically they have never played the role of the main officiant.

Overall I think that there are more biases in the public mind than in the monastic system. Lay supporters prefer male leadership, even within the Fo Guang Shan community. Monks tend to receive greater offerings than nuns who have the same status. The laity, most of whom are women, still prefer ceremonies presided over by monks. When I was appointed as the abbess in the temple of San Diego, a female devotee commented that many of the devotees would drive the distance to Los Angeles just to attend the same ceremony presided over by monks. I then reminded these devotees that they had a Ph.D. nun as their abbess. I want them to know that I am qualified to conduct the same ceremony. Many times I've lamented the fact that often it's the women, rather than the men, who need to be educated about women's rights.

CW: I spent about a year as a Theravāda nun in the monasteries of Thailand. This is a short period of time to experience the richness that is available in living a renunciate life in a community of dharma practitioners. Even so, I must say that the positive effect of that year for me was enormous. It did take some time to adjust, both to the renunciate lifestyle as well as to the Thai culture. The latter, in fact, was the more difficult adjustment. I would say that it took several months before I began to feel comfortable within the Thai system of monastic life. It was only after this initial adjustment that I really began to appreciate the beauty and happiness of a life of such simplicity.

I lived within the monastery grounds, ate once a day—only food that was offered, for the most part. My activities consisted of simple daily tasks and meditation. There was the option of some social contact, mostly with other nuns, occasionally with some Western monks, or I could (and did) spend the majority of the day in silence. Surrounded at all times by the palpable support of the other monks (and nuns, though much fewer than the monks) and our joint dedication to Buddhadharma, living in the forest, close to the natural environment, I grew to love the simplicity of this life and its focus on the dharma. The benefits? It is so much easier to remember the focus and commitment toward dharma when one's life is so extremely simple. The rules of monastic life serve to support this commitment, and mostly I could relate to them in that way. I would never, I believe, know so deeply the joy of simplicity without having spent this time in robes. Although this was over twenty years ago, the effects of that time are deeply alive in my experience. I would not know so surely that there can be a way to live that does not need to be driven by the speed and distractions and acquisitiveness that mark our culture so strongly these days. I know for a personal fact that a deeper and more reliable happiness is available to me than the happiness that is held out as enticement to acquire, achieve, be busy, become well known, and so on. Being a nun changed my relation to my life.

And yes, in Thailand, in the Theravāda tradition, nuns and monks are not seen as equals. Monks are much more revered and respected than are nuns. This imbalance shows up in all aspects of the monastic system. Most of the *achans* (teachers) are monks, although these days in Thailand women are finding a stronger voice, and there are more female achans. There are many more monks than nuns (or *maechees*) because the layfolk give more generously and frequently to support monks than nuns. There are also echoes of Thai social norms in the monastic system. For example, in one forest monastery where I stayed, monks were allotted small private cottages in the forest. Each cottage was out of sight of the others. Women, on the other hand, were required to stay in a room in any of the various houses that were grouped together, outside of the forest. The idea was that it was unsafe for women to live alone in the forest. So strong was this conditioning that I was often cautioned, quite kindly, not even to walk alone in the forest.

I must say, though, that within the cultural and traditional limitations, I was treated with respect, generosity, and kindness. Since I was obviously not Thai, I was allowed leniency in regard to the more strictly cultural conventions. (As an example, I was always given a room to myself, whereas Thai nuns tend to stay several to a room. Also, despite the obvious discomfort on the part of the Thai people, I continued to walk in the forest, and no one ever attempted to stop me.) I also feel that I was blessed to have already developed a profound faith in the universal nature of awakening and the teachings of the Buddha. So while at times I chafed under what I perceived as sexist biases and restrictions, somehow in my mind I naturally separated cultural traditions and habits from the dharma teachings, and I really don't feel that the distinctions and discriminations got in my way. On the other hand, I did only stay a year. I never intended to ordain in that system for life. Partly, I did not wish to live in a Thai culture, but also I was not at all attracted to a life under that discriminatory system. So I must acknowledge that the disparate treatment of the genders in the Thai Theravāda system was, ultimately, an obstacle that I chose not to work with in my life. There is sadness in this: I did love the life of a renunciate, and it is not at all clear to me whether such a life is possible in this culture. I am also very aware of my good fortune, in that I knew, and know, that the Buddhadharma itself has no gender discrimination. I knew that in leaving the robes, I was not leaving my life of commitment to dharma, and I had the previous ten years of experience of practice and service on which to ground this confidence.

4. How does being a woman inform the way you teach?

TC: I don't think it has a huge impact. Of course I understand women's general viewpoints, and I often use examples from the woman's perspective. For example, when teaching the meditation to counteract sexual attachment, I'll talk about the ugliness of the insides of a man's body first and then generalize it to all bodies that are produced by afflictions and karma. And when the dharma hall is hot, I'll joke about having compassion for middle-aged women.

For some people, having a woman teacher may make a difference. For example, men and women often feel more comfortable discussing personal difficulties with a woman. Interestingly, because both men and women share their feelings with me, I've learned that many societal stereotypes—such as those that portray women as "emotional" and men as stoic—are incorrect. Many men break down and sob when their partner leaves them, just as many women do. I've also seen that the stereotype that "women are jealous and can't live together" is false. Although men and women may tend to handle conflict differently, wherever there are sentient beings, conflicts occur, regardless of gender.

In establishing Sravasti Abbey, I aim to ensure that all aspects of training and living together will be gender equal, or more importantly, gender irrelevant. (The only difference is that the men will lift heavy objects!) Some people advised me to make the abbey only for women, but I don't see the point in dividing by gender a Western sangha that already faces numerous challenges. Furthermore, I have created enough "exclusion karma"—karma that has ripened in my facing the discrimination and exclusion mentioned above. I don't want to create further karma in order to experience that result by excluding the men who rely on me for spiritual guidance, nor does it seem very compassionate to limit those whom I teach to a certain gender. Thus women and men will live separately—in accordance with the Vinaya—but will train and offer service together to the community at Sravasti Abbey.

I want to create an atmosphere at the abbey where people can communicate compassionately and openly without the sexualized posturing that often accompanies male-female interactions. For example, when the mind is filled with attachment, let's be open about it with others in the community. That way we can receive support from other celibate dharma practitioners who have undergone the same difficulty and have resolved it. There's no sense in feeling guilty, blaming the person we're attracted to, or rationalizing that it's a deep dharma connection when it's actually attachment. Let's discover the value of being transparent and compassionate toward ourselves and others and at the same time keep our vows purely and joyfully.

I believe that we have to learn to deal with our sexuality and sexual attraction in a healthy way. Our society is highly sexualized—the media promotes the idea that sexual relationship is the highest of all happiness. That is clearly false. If it were true, we all would have reached ultimate bliss by now! We confuse love, attachment, emotional intimacy, and sexual attraction; separating these in our minds allows for healthier and more genuine relationships with others.

When our desire is very strong, it's best to avoid the object of attachment. Doing so gives us the mental space to examine the mind of attachment and to develop and strengthen our dharma antidotes to it. As we do so, we find other methods to work with physical sexual energy and the emotional needs for companionship and closeness. In order to work for the benefit of all sentient beings, it is essential to learn how to be intimate and caring without confusing these sentiments with sexual attraction. In this regard, seeing people as karmic bubbles—appearances arising from past karma—enables us to see beyond their current conventional appearance. For example, there may be a good-looking man with many of the intellectual and emotional qualities I am attracted to, but he's just a karmic bubble: nothing real, nothing lasting. He's a suffering sentient being trapped in cyclic existence by the force of afflictions and karma, and thus he's actually an object of compassion—not an object of desire.

As monastics, our job is to see reality and to develop the altruistic intention *(bodhicitta)* toward all beings. Before we can see ultimate reality—the emptiness of inherent existence of all persons and phenomena—we have to see through the propaganda of attachment that keeps us drowning in cyclic existence and to discern the causes of happiness and the causes of *duḥkha* (unsatisfactory conditions or suffering). We recognize that seeking happiness from external sources—people, relationships, status and reputation, praise and approval, and sense pleasure in general—may bring some temporary pleasure but ultimately leaves us dissatisfied. We see that gender identities are constructed and not our ultimate nature, and we learn to train our minds not to obsess over these distinctions.

PEO: The question itself compels me to first respond from the perspective of the nondual, of emptiness. As the *Vimalakīrti Sūtra* says, there is neither male nor female. And, as the *Heart Sūtra* teaches us, "emptiness is form, form is emptiness." Seen from the perspective of form, however, in this time and place, my karmic conditions have created a woman with certain identifiable values such as openness, flexible authority, and a relational, interactive approach to teaching.

As a young mother, I was influenced by the innovative educator, A.S. Neill, who developed the Summerhill program in England. At the heart of his approach is the idea that humans are fundamentally good, and that given freedom and love, they will teach themselves. This seemed to me to be another way of expressing buddha nature and a nurturing technique for teaching. Later, when I was teaching creative and expressive arts at New York University, I found much inspiration from Shunryu Suzuki's recommendation that the way to teach a cow is to give her a large field to wander in and to watch her. These ways of teaching by not-teaching further developed as I began to "teach" Zen. What has come to be more and more apparent to me, is that the moment of teaching itself is the golden opportunity to make visible the reality of the preciousness of this moment's interaction of self and other. If the teacher is just giving out what she has learned, she fails the student and the dharma. If she is willing, in the moment of interaction with the student, to drop it all and to allow the field of inquiry to be interrelational, to be mutual, and alive, then the true dharma will emerge. Even in classic kōan study, this is true. Instead of judging the student's response as pass or fail, a teacher can work actively to reciprocally uncover the relevant meaning for this unique situation.

Another element is this very willingness to experiment with new forms of teaching. As a woman who is aware of many of the biases of traditional practice, I am no doubt more willing to acknowledge the flaws of many older forms and thus to be willing to experiment with newer ones. In our dharma center we try various modalities, including inquiry exercises, regular council, writing and journal work, and creative expression such as art, mask making, and playful skits.

And then there is the question of governance. Again, it seems to me that the experimentation with more participatory and horizontal forms of leadership has been a gift of women teachers. My dharma sister, Rōshi Egyoku Nakao, has developed a Shared Leadership Program for Zen Center of Los Angeles that is a model of a responsible, collective effort toward more progressive power relationships.

Y: The older I grow, the more I appreciate the qualities of women. Many women in Chinese society raise their children alone after their husbands have left them. It is women who are most devoted to the well-being of their family. Women's love and devotion is the manifestation of compassion, warmth, and commitment. It is typically nuns who open Fo Guang Shan temples in foreign countries; most of them start a center alone. The nuns' will and persistence are like the penetrating force of water, soft but powerful.

Personally I have never felt that I have had any difficulty in teaching. I have taught at Boston University and University of the West in the U.S., McGill University in Canada, and Sun Yat-sen University in Taiwan. My approach is to emphasize education that's meaningful in life over the transmission of intellectual knowledge. I've become lifelong friends with some of my students. Since 2002, I've been conducting a monastic life program in Taiwan at Fo Guang Shan every summer. I bring about fifty college students, mostly Westerners, to Taiwan each year to experience life in the monastery. At the end of the program, many students comment that their relationship with me is like that of a child to a mother.

As chair of the Department of Religious Studies at the University of the West, I initiated a Buddhist sūtra research and translation institute in San Diego in the fall of 2005. The first two students were men. When a monk colleague asked me why I always have male students, I replied that it must be due to either the power of my karma or my vow. I feel that I work easily with men. I like to work in a systematic, organized, and focused fashion. Discipline and concentration are the guidelines for my work. I am rigorous and demanding in the work that I do, but I also like to see my students and staff enjoy their favorite things, such as food and travel. I like to bring the greatest benefit to them that I can, and I feel that I need to be like a mother to them. In Chinese culture the ideal parents combine "a strict father and a compassionate mother." I believe that discipline and love are the necessary qualities for a good teacher. It is completely possible for a female teacher to internalize and manifest these qualities. I vow to become a woman in my next life to continue this work.

CW: I don't have much to say to this question. I cannot separate being a woman from any other aspect of myself, and all of who I am informs the way I teach.

5. What particular qualities and sensibilities do women teachers offer as a counterbalance to the possible patriarchal biases in the tradition?

TC: At a certain point in our practice, we realize that our mind/heart is neither male nor female. We see that whatever gender we are, it is just a conventional label based on the arrangement of molecules in our body. We understand that we are not our body and that, in fact, there isn't a findable "I" that is male or female.

I'm somewhat puzzled when people tell me that they like studying with me because I am a woman. It's valuable for both men and women to have women role models of teachers and practitioners. Some people may feel more comfortable opening up to a woman teacher when seeking spiritual counseling, and some women may be less afraid of sexual abuse if their teacher is female. However, from my side I'm not aware of adding any special qualities to the dharma or to its presentation because of being a woman.

At the beginning of practice, externals such as gender are more important to us. Some people may be drawn to the seeming power of a male teacher; others may seek out the ostensible compassion of a female teacher. As time goes on, however, we can look beyond the gender stereotypes that we project onto dharma teachers and turn our attention to their internal qualities, regardless of the external "package" they come in.

His Holiness the Dalai Lama speaks of women having equal ability and equal responsibility. He has encouraged us to develop our good qualities and talents and to use them for the benefit of sentient beings. If we do this, others can't help but notice. Thus, while it is necessary to acknowledge patriarchal biases, I want to put my energy into going forward with joy and living a life that is beneficial for all sentient beings.

PEO: Every time I try to make a generalization, I remember a moment with one of my male teachers that exemplified the very "feminine energy" that I am talking about: openness, sensitivity to power relationships, and a more "horizontal" view of spiritual authority. That said, it is undeniable that the Buddhist tradition is permeated with patriarchal bias in terms of power relations, distribution of assets, and recognition of authority.

For women teachers, the first challenge is to free ourselves of our internalized oppression, to face our own denial of our difference and of how that difference has operated to place us in inferior positions in terms of power and authority. Such an awareness can free us and our students, male and female, from a blind and unthinking continuation of abusing the other, whether it be in terms of gender, sexuality, race, or class.

For example, in the Zen tradition, we chant the names of the lineage of teachers from Shakyamuni Buddha right down to the present teacher. Not surprisingly, the list of names has some verity and some fiction. For me, the lineage was a powerful reminder of the wonder that so many different kinds of people from different lands have partici-pated in the lineage. The recitation always gave me hope that I, too, could attain the Way. What I did not notice was that the names were all male. Immersed in a sense of the "neither male nor female," I was miss-ing an important aspect of the reality for women. Then, in Zen circles in this country, women began to put together a women's lineage. Sal-lie Jiko Tisdale was a leader in this movement and supplied us all with a rudimentary lineage of women teachers. During a retreat, I added this lineage to our daily recitation, and I was surprised to see the pow-erful effect it had on women practitioners. I was officiating, and when I looked around the room at some point, there were tears in so many women's eyes, an expression of their deepest longing to be affirmed as possible buddhas. The men in our group were also deeply affected by the women's response, seeing in them a reflection of their own feelings of disempowerment. This was an important teaching for me, as I had not recognized how I had elided the reality of this lineage chant to mean a "possible woman" rather than asking the question of where the actual women who participated in the transmission of the dharma are. Inclusion, then, is a value that many women dharma teachers hold, through our own lived experience of exclusion.

There is a Zen saying, "a duck's legs are short, a crane's legs are long." What it implies is that each creature is perfect just as it is. A duck with a crane's long legs would not function, nor would a crane with short legs and webbed feet. Embracing our difference, we can enter our mutuality. A woman teacher, a man teacher, short legs, long legs, perfect and complete.

Y: Speaking on the ultimate level, I see no difference in men and women, only differences in individual personality and karma. Some men can be very gentle, soft, or timid, whereas some women can be determined and strong-willed. In the teachings of Mahāyāna Buddhism, there is no fixed nature that can be identified as "woman-ness" or "man-ness," because everything is empty of any inherent nature. Furthermore, when we are reincarnated, we can be born as a man or woman or even an animal or heavenly being. Where can we find a fixed woman in our many lives or even in this life? Our own particular karma is accumulated through our learning and conditioning. We also internalize our society's judgments about good and bad. According to Buddhism, it is through conceptualization that we create the mind that discriminates between male and female. Bias against women can be found in Buddhist and Confucian literature, and Chinese society is not unique in discouraging women from pursuing higher education.

Education is a powerful tool for discovering and gaining confidence in our potentiality as human beings. Women deserve equal access to education. Since education can also reinforce bias against women, we need to keep examining these values critically but not cynically. We Buddhists also need to change the idea that being born as a woman is the result of bad karma. A woman's misfortune is mostly due to society, which deprives her of basic rights and condones practices of female infanticide, discouragement of education for women, and so on. We need to educate both men and women about these gender issues, and as a female teacher I need to continue to educate myself in order to teach others. Being a woman does not give me an excuse to be uneducated. Being a woman, I must not be afraid that society will not hear my voice. As long as the truth and the reality are spoken, a woman's voice will be heard. Women should embody the qualities of compassion and love, balanced by wisdom acquired through learning.

CW: I find it difficult to make a generalization that I can feel confident standing behind. I could say that women can bring a quality of emotional empathy that many men do not bring, but then I do know some male teachers with wonderful emotional empathy, much stronger than I have.

Note

This panel was not recorded, due to a problem with the recording equipment. A series of questions covering the main issues discussed in the panel was thus put together and sent to the panelists for their written response. This occasion afforded a welcome opportunity to add Yifa to the forum.

Acknowledgments

T HE IDEA FOR THE CONFERENCE had its genesis in the spring
of 2002, when Karma Lekshe Tsomo first visited the Smith
campus as part of a lecture series on Buddhism in America.
Although we had agreed that Smith would provide a perfect venue for
a conference on women and Buddhism, serious planning did not get
under way until April 2004, when Tsomo returned to Smith. A planning committee—consisting of Peter Gregory (Smith College), Susanne
Mrozik (Mount Holyoke College), Maria Heim (Amherst College),
Catherine Anraku Hondorp (Zen Center on Main Street), Marguerite
Gregory (Zen Peacemaker Circles), and Mario D'Amato (Hampshire
College)—was subsequently formed, with Tsomo always available to
share her wise counsel and to offer encouragement. It was this group
that was responsible for developing the vision for the conference as
well as for assembling the panels, organizing the workshops, and coor-
dinating the scheduling of the various events, not to mention taking
care of countless logistical tasks as the deadline approached.

The conference offered a panoply of events over a span of four days.
Thursday, Friday, and Saturday evenings showcased the creative work
of three illustrious women artists and intellectuals, whose work has
been informed by their practice of Buddhism: a poetry reading by Jane
Hirshfield, a public lecture by bell hooks, and a concert performance
by Meredith Monk. The conference began on Friday morning with

addresses by two prominent spokeswomen for Buddhism that presented different perspectives for understanding the variegated experiences of Buddhist women in North America. Karma Lekshe Tsomo, who, as cofounder and president of Sakyadhita: International Association of Buddhist Women, has for many years been a leader in the international Buddhist women's movement, discussed the international context, and Helen Tworkov, who, as founding editor for *Tricycle,* has long been an astute observer of the American scene, discussed the American context. Beginning on Friday afternoon and continuing through Saturday and Sunday morning and afternoon, the conference presented five panels with various women Buddhist teachers, artists, leaders, activists, and scholars from around the country: "Buddhism and Creativity" (with Jane Hirshfield, Meredith Monk, and Pat Enkyō O'Hara), "Women Changing Buddhism: Feminist Perspectives" (with bell hooks, Sharon Suh, Karma Lekshe Tsomo, and Susanne Mrozik), "Engaged Buddhism" (with Virginia Straus Benson, Diana Lion, Eve Marko, and Hilda Ryūmon Gutiérrez Baldoquín), "Race, Ethnicity, and Class" (with Hilda Ryūmon Gutiérrez Baldoquín, Sharon Suh, Arinna Weisman, and Carolyn Jacobs), and "Women Dharma Teachers" (with Thubten Chodron, Pat Enkyō O'Hara, Carol Wilson, and Helen Tworkov). The conference also included thirty-four workshops that featured the many creative activities in which local Buddhist women are engaged; a ritual celebration of the Buddha's birthday on April 8th; a sacred dance performance led by Tara Dhatu; a sculptural installation by Rosalyn Driscoll; and open meditation sessions in the Bodman Lounge of the Helen Hills Hills Chapel each morning. Except for the Meredith Monk concert, to which tickets were sold, all events were free and open to the public.

We would like to acknowledge the tremendous contributions of the other members of the planning committee (Maria Heim, Catherine Hondorp, Marguerite Gregory, and Mario D'Amato). There was a wonderful synergy within the committee. Each member brought different concerns and skills to the process, and the shape of the conference evolved out of the interaction of the members rather than from the idea of any one individual. Everyone played an active role in all stages of its planning, from the early brainstorming to finalizing last-minute arrangements, and each member unstintingly devoted whatever time was necessary to make the conference a success. Without their energy, resourcefulness, cooperation, and hard work the conference would never have been the success that it was.

We would also like to thank Maia Duerr (Buddhist Peace Fellowship) and Susan Burggraf (Mount Holyoke College/Naropa University). Duerr offered much helpful advice in our initial stages of discussion, although her move to Berkeley in the fall of 2004 (to take over as executive director of BPF) prevented her from playing an active role on the committee. Burggraf contributed to the initial visioning of the conference in the spring of 2004 but could not take part in the planning that began in the fall as she was preparing to move to Boulder to take up a faculty position at Naropa University.

Although held at Smith College and largely funded by the Ada Howe Kent Program, the conference was a Five-College event (Amherst, Hampshire, Mount Holyoke, and Smith Colleges; the University of Massachusetts) and could not have taken place without the generous supplemental support it received from Mount Holyoke, Amherst, and Hampshire Colleges. The conference was co-sponsored by Sakyadhita: International Association of Buddhist Women.

The conference also received strong support from broad segments across the campus at Smith. Jane Hirshfield's participation was made possible through the generous support and enthusiastic collaboration of the Poetry Center. The support of the Office of College Relations proved indispensable for such vital publicity-related areas as designing posters and flyers for national advertising and mailings, creating and maintaining a splendid conference website, placing press releases, preparing an article for *NewsSmith,* and assistance with contracts. The huge attendance at the conference would not have been possible without the effort and know-how of people like Peg Pitzer, John Eue (who created and maintained our website), and Mike Byrne (who designed our posters, flyers, and ads). We would also like to acknowledge the sensitive and patient work of Kara Noble in so successfully producing the Meredith Monk concert. Without the underlying backing of President Carol Christ and Provost Susan Bourque such a broad level of support across campus would not have been possible.

We would like to pay a special tribute to Donna Gunn for all of her administrative support over the course of more than a year. She willingly shouldered the extra burden entailed by the conference over and above her already heavy workload. She was the person who took care of the myriad details necessary for the smooth running of an event of this scale and complexity; she booked space, arranged transportation, made hotel reservations, coordinated with other offices on campus, hired and supervised student helpers, handled mailings and postering, managed the budget, fielded inquiries, and dealt with unanticipated problems as they arose. She was utterly reliable throughout, and we always knew that we could count on her to make things happen.

There are far more people deserving of thanks than we could possibly acknowledge here, but we would like to single out Kathy Gauger for transcribing the tapes, Gabriele Chase for her help with conference registration, logistics, and manuscript preparation, and Lesley Jo Weaver for her work on Alice Unno's contribution to the volume. We would also like to thank Jennifer Walters and Charlene Moran for their support in making the facilities of the Helen Hills Hills Chapel work for the conference.

Finally, as a way of acknowledging the contributions of all the women who presented workshops, we list them here.

❖ Conference Workshops

Friday afternoon, April 8th: Lama Palmo, "Meditation through the Vajra Songs of Female Masters"; Alice Unno, "Tea Ceremony"; Elana Rosenbaum, "Mindfulness-Based Stress Reduction: Living Fully in the Midst of Difficulty"; Kim Gutschow, "How to Beat Men at Their Own Game: Buddhist Women Create New Forms of Authority and Identity"; Andrea Ayvazian, "Interfaith Identities"; and Carolyn Jacobs, "Contemplative Practices and Women of Color."

Saturday morning, April 9th: Catherine Anraku Hondorp, "The Dharma Gate of Peace and Repose: The Practice of Zazen"; Kathleen Perez Dewey, "Earthly Desires Are Enlightenment: Manifesting Buddhahood in Daily Life"; Bobi Jentis, "Revitalizing Energy with the Mudras of Jin Shin Jyutsu"; Susan Burggraf, "Devotion in Buddhist Practice"; Prema Dasara and Anahata Iradah, "Dance in Praise of Tara: Embodying Wisdom and Compassion"; Cheryl Conner, "Bringing Dharma to the Law"; Kunsang Kelden, Dawa Lokyitsang, and Dechen Gonnot, "Students for a Free Tibet: Social Activism, Youth, and the Tibet Movement"; and Maia Duerr, "Workin' It Out: Creating a Buddhist, Feminist Workplace."

Saturday afternoon, April 9th: Daeja Napier, "Insight Meditation: Patience"; Catherine Anraku Hondorp, "Sexuality and Buddhist Practice"; Active Eye (Jyana Gregory, Rika Iino, and Kristine Kuroiwa), "Manifesting the Spirit in Body and Sound"; Madeline Liebling and Mary Lang, "Space, Form and Energy: An Introduction to the Dharma Art Teachings of the Vidyadhara, Chögyam Trungpa Rinpoche"; Sera Bonds, "Off the Cushion: Women and Socially Engaged Buddhism"; Marilu Gamboa and Elizabeth Tonti, "Student Volunteers in a Buddhist Nunnery in Spiti, India"; Dr. Lindsay Rockwell, "Death and Dying: Writing from Emptiness"; and Sandra Boston, "Right Speech: Being an Engaged Buddhist in a Culture of Power and Control."

Sunday morning, April 10th: Anne Marie DiGiacomo, "Tonglen: A Practice of Exchanging Self for Other"; Prema Dasara and Anahata Iradah, "Tara Tames the Eight Fears: For Children and the Young at Heart"; Arinna Weisman, "Exploring Our Spiritual Practice as a Lesbian, Gay, Bisexual, and Transgendered Community"; Adin Thayer, "Buddhism as a Basis for Peacebuilding"; Hilda Ryūmon Gutiérrez Baldoquín, "Living a Life of Vow"; and Marguerite Gregory, "Circle Practice for Personal and Social Transformation."

Sunday afternoon, April 10th: Paola Zamperini, "Perfect Just the Way You Are: A Practitioner's View of Women and Dzogchen, the Tibetan Lineage of the Great Perfection"; Watkiryvongsa Bopahrnam Sangha (Cambodian Monks, Nuns, and Laity of the Theravāda Forest Tradition), "Buddha, Dhamma, Sangha: Chanting, Dhamma Talk, and Meditation"; Dr. Phuntsog Wangmo, "Traditional Tibetan Medicine"; Sumi Loundon, "Buddhism for Young Adults"; Marguerite Gregory, Katherine Hart, Jean Roberts, and Eileen Weston-Latshang, "Practicing within a Family: Challenges and Possibilities"; and Diane Carter, "Victory Over Violence."

Contributors

Rev. Hilda Ryūmon Gutiérrez Baldoquín is a Zen Buddhist priest in the Sōtō lineage of Shunryu Suzuki Rōshi. She received ordination from San Francisco Zen Center's former abbess Zenkei Blanche Hartman Rōshi, served as *shuso* (head monk) at Green Dragon Temple/Green Gulch Farm Zen Center with Abbess Jiko Linda Cutts, and studies with the Venerable Pema Chödrön. She was born in Cuba, and her life journey has taken her from working-class, immigrant, monolingual Spanish-language origins to intellectual middle-class privileges, all due to many years of formal schooling at the Florida State University in Tallahassee, the State University College at Buffalo, New York, and at Stanford University in California. Ryūmon is invited to work with contemplative communities across the United States, leading meditation retreats for people of color, working with established white convert Buddhist sanghas in addressing issues of race, power, and privilege, and supporting emerging Buddhist communities committed to multiculturalism. Ryūmon is a member of the planning team and faculty for the program in the Contemplative Clinical Practice Advanced Certificate Program at the Smith College School for Social Work. She is also a mentor to emerging leaders, social change activists, and organizers within the Social Justice Program at the Center for Contemplative Mind in Society. The founder of Dragon Gate

Zen, Ryūmon has coauthored and/or served as advisor to publications such as *Cultural Considerations in Domestic Violence Cases: A National Judges' Benchbook; Face to Face: Solving Conflicts Without Giving In;* and *Taking the First Step: A Guide for Cultural Programming.* She has been published in *Buddhadharma: The Practitioner's Quarterly* and *Turning Wheel: The Journal of Socially Engaged Buddhism.* She is also the editor of *Dharma, Color, and Culture: New Voices in Western Buddhism.*

Virginia Straus Benson has worked for many years in the public policy sphere. She is executive director of the Boston Research Center for the 21st Century (BRC), a peace and justice institute founded by Buddhist teacher Daisaku Ikeda, president of the Soka Gakkai International. Benson has directed the center since its founding in September 1993. The center is committed to social change through dialogue and education aimed at cultivating an inclusive sense of community, locally and globally. Its current programs focus on women's leadership for peace, global citizenship education, and the philosophy and practice of community building. Before joining the center, Benson codirected Pioneer Institute, a Boston-based public policy think tank, which she helped to establish in 1987. During the 1970s she worked in government in Washington, D.C., where she served as a legislative researcher and publisher in the House of Representatives, a financial analyst in the Treasury Department, and an urban policy aide in the Carter White House.

Carolyn Chen is an assistant professor of Sociology and Asian American Studies at Northwestern University. She received her doctorate in sociology from the University of California, Berkeley in 2002. A former fellow at the Center for the Study of Religion at Princeton University, she is currently a visiting faculty fellow at the American Bar Foundation and the author of *Getting Saved in America: Taiwanese Immigrants Converting to Evangelical Christianity and Buddhism,* to be published by Princeton University Press.

Ven. Thubten Chodron was ordained as a Buddhist nun in 1977. She studied and practiced Tibetan Buddhism under the guidance of His Holiness the Dalai Lama, Tsenzhap Serkong Rinpoche, Lama Zopa Rinpoche, and other Tibetan masters for many years in India and Nepal. She has been resident teacher at Amitabha Buddhist Centre in Singapore and at Dharma Friendship Foundation in Seattle and was coorganizer of "Life as a Western Buddhist Nun," an educational program in Bodhgaya in 1996. In 2003, she founded Sravasti Abbey, one of the few Tibetan Buddhist monasteries in the United States, near Newport, Washington. She is involved in interfaith dialogue, conferences between scientists and Buddhists, meetings of Western Buddhist teachers, and gatherings of Western Buddhist monastics. She teaches Buddhist philosophy, psychology, and meditation worldwide, including in Israel, Latin America, and former communist countries, and she is active in prison work. Her many books include: *Open Heart, Clear Mind* (1990); *Blossoms of the Dharma: Living as a Buddhist Nun* (2000), *Buddhism for Beginners* (2001); *Working with Anger* (2001); *Taming the Mind* (2004); *How To Free Your Mind: Tara the Liberator* (2005), and *Cultivating a Compassionate Heart: The Yoga Method of Chenrezig* (2006).

Peter N. Gregory joined the faculty at Smith College as Jill Ker Conway Professor of Religion and East Asian Studies in 1999. After receiving his doctorate in East Asian Languages and Civilizations from Harvard University in 1981, he taught in the Program for the Study of Religion at the University of Illinois for fifteen years. He has also served as the president and executive director of the Kuroda Institute for the Study of Buddhism and Human Values since 1984, and in that capacity he has directed two publication series with the University of Hawaii Press: "Studies in East Asian Buddhism" and "Classics in East Asian Buddhism." His research has focused on medieval Chinese Buddhism, especially the Chan and Huayan traditions during the Tang and Song dynasties, on which he has written or edited seven books, including *Tsung-mi and the Sinification of Buddhism* (1991). He is currently completing a translation of a ninth-century Chinese Buddhist text on the historical and doctrinal origins of the Chan tradition. Since coming to Smith, his research and teaching have increasingly focused on Buddhism in America.

Jane Hirshfield is a poet, essayist, and translator. Her poetry has been called "passionate and radiant" by the *New York Times Book Review* and her collection of essays, *Nine Gates: Entering the Mind of Poetry* (1997), was found by the *Japan Times* to be "indispensable." A practitioner of Sōtō Zen for over thirty years, she is the author of six books of poems, most recently *After* (HarperCollins, 2006). Her previous collection, *Given Sugar, Given Salt* (2001), was a finalist for the National Book Critics Circle Award and winner of the Bay Area Book Reviewers Award. She has also edited and cotranslated three now-classic collections documenting the spiritual and emotional lives of women poets from the past. Her honors include fellowships from the Academy of American Poets, the Guggenheim and Rockefeller foundations, and the National Endowment for the Arts. Among other awards are multiple selections in the *Best American Poetry* and *Pushcart Prize* anthologies, the Poetry Center Book Award, and the California Book Award. A former visiting professor at the University of California in Berkeley, Elliston Poet in Residence at the University of Cincinnati, and member of the writing faculty of Bennington College's MFA program, Hirshfield has been featured numerous times on Garrison Keillor's *Writer's Almanac* NPR program, as well as in two Bill Moyers PBS specials.

bell hooks, a visionary feminist thinker, cultural critic, and writer, is Distinguished Professor in Residence at Berea College in Berea, Kentucky and among the leading intellectuals of her generation. Her writings address a range of topics, including gender, race, teaching, and media in contemporary culture. Her critically acclaimed love trilogy—*All About Love* (2001), *Salvation: Black People and Love* (2001), and *Communion: The Female Search for Love* (2003)—boldly and eloquently outlines her assertions and questions about a topic that has occupied and inspired human philosophy and art for centuries. Her most recent publications include: *The Will to Change: Men, Masculinity, and Love* (2004), *We Real Cool: Black Men and Masculinity* (2003), and *Teaching Community: A Pedagogy of Hope* (2003), a companion to *Teaching to Transgress: Education as the Practice of Freedom* (1994). She is also increasingly becoming known as a writer of children's books. Since her first book, *Ain't I a Woman: Black Women and Feminism*, published in 1981—which was named one of the "twenty most influential women's books of the last twenty years" by *Publishers Weekly*—hooks has written twenty-two books.

Carolyn Jacobs is the Elizabeth Marting Treuhaft Professor and Dean of the School for Social Work at Smith College. Her areas of professional interest include religion and spirituality in social work practice, social work research, and statistics. She has written and presented extensively on the topic of spirituality in social work, including presentations within the school's network of field agencies; she is the coeditor of *Ethnicity and Race: Critical Concepts in Social Work*. Jacobs received her B.A. from Sacramento State University, her M.S.W. from San Diego State University, and her doctorate from the Heller School of Brandeis University. A spiritual director trained at the Shalem Institute for Spiritual Formation, in 2001 she was also elected as Distinguished Practitioner in the National Academies of Practice in Social Work.

Diana Lion is the founding director of the national Buddhist Peace Fellowship Prison Project. A Canadian dharma practitioner, she is a long-time activist and has been doing prison dharma work at BPF since 1998. She is a graduate of Spirit Rock Meditation Center's Community Dharma Leaders Program, a certified trainer in Nonviolent Communication, and on the teaching team of the first Bay Area Buddhist chaplaincy program. She is passionately involved in dharma and diversity issues and has worked in many other activist arenas (peace, women, LGBT, farm workers, and human rights) over the last thirty years.

Eve Myōnen Marko teaches Zen meditation at the Montague Farm Zendo, the Motherhouse Zendo of the Zen Peacemakers. She cofounded

Peacemaker Circle International with Bernie Glassman and is a founding teacher of the Zen Peacemaker Order. During the 1980s and 1990s she worked with the Greyston Mandala, a Buddhist-inspired network of for-profits and not-for-profits working together to provide jobs, housing, and community services in Yonkers, New York. She is also the author of several books for young people.

Meredith Monk is a composer, singer, director/choreographer, and creator of new opera, musical theater works, films, and installations. A pioneer in what are now called "extended vocal technique" and "interdisciplinary performance," Monk creates works that thrive at the intersection of music and movement, image and object, light and sound in an effort to discover and weave together new modes of perception. Her groundbreaking exploration of the voice as an instrument, as an eloquent language in and of itself, expands the boundaries of musical composition, creating landscapes of sound that unearth feelings, energies, and memories for which we have no words. During a career that spans forty years she has been acclaimed by audiences and critics as a major creative force in the performing arts. Monk has received numerous awards throughout her career, including the prestigious MacArthur Fellowship in 1995, two Guggenheim Fellowships, three Obies (including an award for Sustained Achievement), and the 1986 National Music Theatre Award. She is a fellow of the American Academy of Arts and Sciences and holds honorary doctor of arts degrees from Bard College, the University of the Arts, The Juilliard School, the San Francisco Art Institute, and the Boston Conservatory. She has been a Shambhala Buddhist practitioner since 1985, and she has taught "Voice as Practice" at Naropa University, Zen Mountain Monastery, Omega Institute, and other international venues. In October 1999 Monk was honored to perform a vocal offering for His Holiness the Dalai Lama as part of the World Festival of Sacred Music in Los Angeles.

Susanne Mrozik is an assistant professor in the Religion Department of Mount Holyoke College, where she teaches courses on Buddhism and comparative religion. Mrozik was one of the organizers of the conference that inspired this book. She earned her M.T.S. from Harvard Divinity School and her Ph.D. from the Committee on the Study of Religion at Harvard University. A specialist in Buddhist ethics, Mrozik has written extensively on the ethical significance of gender, bodies, and emotions and is the author of *Virtuous Bodies: The Physical Dimensions of Morality in Buddhist Ethics* (Oxford University Press, 2007). Her newest research project concerns the reestablishment of the Theravāda Buddhist nun's lineage in Sri Lanka.

Rōshi Pat Enkyō O'Hara is the abbot of the Village Zendo in Manhattan. She received priest ordination from Maezumi Rōshi and dharma transmission and *inka* from Rōshi Bernie Glassman. The example of her teachers encourages her work in the ordinary running of an urban temple and in peacemaking activities. Much of O'Hara's activism is in the world of HIV/AIDS. An ongoing exploration for her is articulating a Zen Buddhist approach to issues of difference around race, class, sexuality, and health. Working with Bernie Glassman, O'Hara is involved in the design of the Maezumi Institute, a study center for Zen and peacemaking. O'Hara was associate professor at NYU's Tisch School of the Arts, where she taught video and interactive arts for twenty years.

Sharon A. Suh is the director of the Asian Studies Program and associate professor of World Religions at Seattle University. She received her Ph.D. in Buddhist Studies from Harvard University in 2000 and is the author of *Being Buddhist in a Christian World: Gender and Community in a Korean American Temple*, published by the University of Washington Press in 2004. She is currently working on a project entitled Sacred Seattle that looks at the role of Buddhism in Seattle's Asian American communities. She is particularly interested in the transmission of the dharma to younger generations. Prior to moving to Seattle in 2000, she worked as the executive director of the Korean American Museum in Los Angeles and as a researcher for the Center for Religion and Civic Culture at the University of Southern California.

Ven. Karma Lekshe Tsomo holds a Ph.D. in Comparative Asian Philosophy from the University of Hawaii and is currently an associate professor at the University of San Diego. As the author and editor of numerous books on women and Buddhism, a fully-ordained Buddhist nun, and a relentless activist for the rights of Buddhist women around the world, she is a leading scholar of and spokesperson for women in Buddhism. She helped found Sakyadhita: International Association of Buddhist Women in 1987 and as its president has coordinated a series of nine international conferences on issues pertaining to women in Buddhism. Her primary academic interests include women in Buddhism, Buddhism and bioethics, religion and cultural change, and Buddhism in the United States. To date she has published eight books on women in Buddhism: *Out of the Shadows: Socially Engaged Buddhist Women* (Sat Sriguru, 2006), *Buddhist Women and Social Justice* (SUNY, 2004), *Innovative Women in Buddhism: Swimming Against the Stream* (Curzon, 2000), *Buddhist Women Across Cultures* (SUNY, 1999), *Living and Dying in Buddhist Cultures* (Asian and Pacific Studies, University of Hawaii, 1997), *Sisters in Solitude: Two Traditions of Buddhist Monastic Ethics for Women: A Comparative Analysis of the Chinese Dharmagupta and Tibetan Mūlasarvāstivāda Bhikṣuṇī Prātimokṣa Sūtras* (SUNY, 1996), *Buddhism Through American Women's Eyes* (Snow Lion, 1994), and *Sakyadhita: Daughters of the Buddha* (Snow Lion, 1989). In addition to her academic work, she is actively involved in interfaith dialogue and in grassroots initiatives for the empowerment of women. She is also director of Jamyang Foundation, an initiative to provide educational opportunities for women in the Indian Himalayas.

Helen Tworkov grew up in New York City and studied anthropology at Hunter College and the City University of New York. From 1964 to 1966 she traveled extensively in Asia and taught English for six months in both Kyoto and Kathmandu; she also worked in a Tibetan refugee camp in Nepal. Her Buddhist studies have been primarily with teachers of the Nyingma School of Tibetan Buddhism and with Maezumi Rōshi and teachers within his Sōtō Zen lineage. She is the author of *Zen* *in America: Five Profiles of American Zen Teachers* (published by North Point Press in 1989; reprinted by Kodansha in 1994); in 1990 she founded *Tricycle: The Buddhist Review,* an independent quarterly, which she edited until 2001. Currently she works as a consultant to *Tricycle* and divides her time between upstate New York and Cape Breton, Nova Scotia.

Alice Unno is cofounder, with her husband Taitetsu Unno, of the Shin Buddhist Sangha and Dharma School for Children in Northampton, MA. She holds a B.A. and Ed.M. from Smith College and a Certificate of Advanced Graduate Studies in School Psychology from the University of Massachusetts, Amherst. She studied Zen under Yasutani Rōshi while living in Japan, as well as Shin Buddhism under leading Japanese teachers between 1962 and 1968. Unno also holds a Master's Certificate from both Urasenke Tea Ceremony and Ohara Flower Arranging schools. She served for many years as a special education teacher in Northampton Public Elementary Schools.

Rabbi Sheila Peltz Weinberg has served in multiple capacities in the Jewish community—including Hillel director, day-school teacher, and community-relations professional. She is a 1986 graduate of the Reconstructionist Rabbinical College and has served as a congregational rabbi for seventeen years. In the last sixteen years she has studied mindfulness and introduced meditation into the Jewish world as a form that can enliven and illuminate Jewish practice, ideas, and community. She teaches mindfulness meditation in a Jewish idiom to laypeople, rabbis, cantors, and other Jewish professionals and is a senior teacher and director of community outreach of the Institute for Jewish Spirituality, a retreat-based program for Jewish leaders. Her extensive writings cover a variety of subjects, including Jewish spirituality, social justice, feminism, and parenting; she is also a major contributor to the Kol Haneshamah prayer-book series. Her CD, *Preparing the Heart: Meditation for Jewish Spiritual Practice*, integrates Jewish sacred texts and meditation.

Arinna Weisman has studied insight meditation since 1979 and has been teaching since 1988. Her root teacher is Ruth Denison, who was empowered by the great Burmese master U Ba Khin. She has also studied with Thich Nhat Hanh in the Zen tradition, Punjaji in the Advaita tradition, and Tsokney Rinpoche in the Dzogchen tradition. She teaches insight meditation throughout the United States and is the founding teacher of the Insight Meditation Center of Pioneer Valley in Easthampton, MA. She is coauthor of *A Beginner's Guide to Insight Meditation*. She is particularly interested in how to manifest wisdom and compassion in the practice of building healthy communities, and so her dharma practice and teaching have been infused with political, anti-racist, and multicultural perspectives. She was the first Theravāda teacher, with Eric Kolvig, to lead insight meditation retreats for the gay, lesbian, bisexual, and transgendered community.

Carol Wilson has been involved in practicing and studying Theravāda Buddhism since 1971, including a year-long ordination as a nun in Thailand in the early 1980s. She began leading intensive meditation retreats at the Insight Meditation Society in Barre, Massachusetts in 1986. Currently she leads insight meditation *(vipassanā)* and loving-kindness *(metta)* retreats at IMS and around the world. Wilson is particularly interested in bridging ancient and more structured forms of transmitting Buddhadharma with forms appropriate for modern Western practitioners. She presently serves as a guiding teacher of the Insight Meditation Society, as well as on the board of directors for the Barre Center for Buddhist Studies and the Dharma Seed Archival Center. In the past three years, she has been inspired to be a part of the Metta Dana Project, which assists the people of the Sagaing Hills in Burma through education, health care, and the support of their monasteries and nunneries.

Ven. Yifa was born in Taiwan and was ordained as a Buddhist nun at Fo Guang Shan in 1979. After finishing a B.A. in law from National Taiwan University, she went on to receive an M.A. in Comparative Philosophy from the University of Hawaii and a Ph.D. in Chinese Buddhism from Yale University. In 2002 she published a historical study and annotated translation of the *Chanyuan Qinggui, The Origins of Buddhist Monastic Codes in China* and a book dealing with current social issues, *Safeguarding the Heart—a Buddhist Response to Suffering and September 11.* She has taught at Boston University, McGill University, and Sun Yat-sen University, served as abbess of the Greater Boston Buddhist Cultural Center, and currently serves as provost of the University of the West (formerly Hsi Lai University) in Rosemead, California, where she also chairs the Department of Religious Studies. Recently Yifa has been directing the Humanistic Buddhist Monastic Life Program, which provides youth with firsthand spiritual experience. She is involved in various interfaith dialogues such as Gethsemane Encounter and Nuns in the West. Yifa is the recipient of numerous awards, including the Outstanding Buddhist Women Award and the Juliet Hollister Award, for her contribution to peace and interfaith education.

About Wisdom Publications

WISDOM PUBLICATIONS, a nonprofit publisher, is dedicated to making available authentic works relating to Buddhism for the benefit of all. We publish books by ancient and modern masters in all traditions of Buddhism, translations of important texts, and original scholarship. Additionally, we offer books that explore East-West themes unfolding as traditional Buddhism encounters our modern culture in all its aspects. Our titles are published with the appreciation of Buddhism as a living philosophy, and with the special commitment to preserve and transmit important works from Buddhism's many traditions.

To learn more about Wisdom, or to browse books online, visit our website at www.wisdompubs.org.

You may request a copy of our catalog online or by writing to this address:

Wisdom Publications
199 Elm Street
Somerville, Massachusetts 02144 USA
Telephone: 617-776-7416
Fax: 617-776-7841
Email: info@wisdompubs.org
www.wisdompubs.org

The Wisdom Trust

As a nonprofit publisher, Wisdom is dedicated to the publication of Dharma books for the benefit of all sentient beings and dependent upon the kindness and generosity of sponsors in order to do so. If you would like to make a donation to Wisdom, you may do so through our website or our Somerville office. If you would like to help sponsor the publication of a book, please write or email us at the address above.

Thank you.

Wisdom is a nonprofit, charitable 501(c)(3) organization affiliated with the Foundation for the Preservation of the Mahayana Tradition (FPMT).

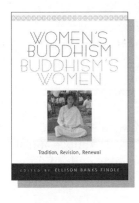

Women's Buddhism, Buddhism's Women
Tradition, Revision, Renewal
Edited by Ellison Banks Findly
512 pages, ISBN 0-86171-165-3, $24.95

"Martine Batchelor, Kate Wheeler, Helena Norberg-Hodge and many others contribute to this moving and erudite anthology that spans traditions and continents as it describes women's influence on the dharma, and the contributions dharma has made to women's lives."—*Tricycle: the Buddhist Review*

"Highly recommended."—*Library Journal*

Pure Heart, Enlightened Mind
The Life and Letters of an Irish Zen Saint
Maura O'Halloran
352 pages, ISBN 0-86171-283-8, $17.95

"Some of the most important lessons I've learned have come from Maura O'Halloran. *Pure Heart, Enlightened Mind* brought the Buddhist experience into my mind and psyche in a way that no dharma book or doctrine ever had. For me, it's a gift, offering guidance and inspiration."—Sumi Loundon, editor of *Blue Jean Buddha*, writing in the Dharma Classics section of *Buddhadharma: The Practitioner's Journal*

"A fascinating portrait of an apprentice sage. The book unfolds as a grand adventure."—*New York Times Book Review*

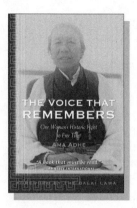

The Voice that Remembers
One Woman's Historic Fight to Free Tibet
Ama Adhe
Foreword by the Dalai Lama
272 pages, ISBN 0-86171-149-1, $16.95

"The story of a woman who sustained her human dignity, integrity, and compassion in the face of immense degradation and suffering. Compelling and inspiring."—*Feminist Book-store News*

"I have never read a book as terrifying and inspiring in my life. Ama Adhe describes— with unutterable calm—acts of unthinkable evil, and the unwavering spirit of the woman who withstood them."—*Psychology Today*